MW01168921

Let Your Voice Be Heard

Conversations on the Margins of the Church

JOAN HEBERT REISINGER

PICKWICK *Publications* · Eugene, Oregon

LET YOUR VOICE BE HEARD
Conversations on the Margins of the Church

Pickwick Publications
An Imprint of Wipf and Stock Publishers
199 W. 8th Ave., Suite 3
Eugene, OR 97401

www.wipfandstock.com

ISBN 13: 978-1-61097-678-7

Cataloging-in-Publication data:

Reisinger, Joan Hebert.

    Let your voice be heard : conversations on the margins of the church / Joan Hebert Reisinger.

    xx + 208 p. ; 23 cm. —Includes bibliographical references.

    ISBN 13: 978-1-61097-678-7

    1. Theology. Practical. 2. Catholic Church—History—1965–. I. Title.

BX1390 .R45 2012

Manufactured in the U.S.A.

To my mother, Marie Pruss Hebert,
my grandmother Anna Tresnak Pruss,
and my mother-in-law, Naomi Cheek Reisinger,
in loving memory
of all you taught me
about love, laughter, and dialogue

Contents

Tables

Preface

"Not going to Mass today, whereas I used to go. Can you tell me more about your project?"

(LANCE, DIALOGUE)

Something you said struck me: "Let your voice be heard."

(JAMES, DIALOGUE)

WHAT EXPERIENCES MOVE PEOPLE to answer an e-mail invitation, a Craigslist advertisement, or an ad in the newspaper asking for dialogue partners?[1] Lance, a young man in his twenties, is one of my dialogue partners for this practical theology research study. James, in his sixties, dialogues about his experiences as a Catholic in the Charismatic movement in the Church.[2] Conversations with those on the margins of the Roman Catholic Church ground my effort to understand the margins of the Church.[3] Those on the

---

1. The advertisement posted on Craigslist read, "Are you on the margins of the Catholic Church? Were you once active and involved and now find yourself attending Mass less frequently or not at all? Ph.D. candidate dialoguing with those on the margins." An alternative text read, "Are you on the margins of the Roman Catholic Church? Were you once active and involved and now find yourself attending Mass less frequently or not at all? Ph.D. candidate studying lived experiences of those on the margins and needs interviews."

2. The Charismatic Renewal Movement in the Catholic Church began in the 1960s and was typified by an emphasis on the Holy Spirit and the Spirit's work in each person's life and the life of the Church. James spoke about a vibrant prayer life, the Life in the Spirit seminars, moving music, and engaging parish activity that involved his whole family. These are no longer available in his area and he misses them.

3. Often, *Church* is used to refer to the hierarchical magisterium and *church* to

margins of the Church are among the faithful people of God. Often well educated and aware of the meaning of their faith in their lives, they speak as part of the community of faith.[4] They are my dialogue partners in this work, and their words appear throughout as block quotes.[5]

This volume seeks to explore and to understand the reasons why Catholics over the age of twenty-one, who were once active and involved in the Catholic Church but presently no longer attend Mass, find themselves on the margins of the Church and how they understand their own marginality. Secondly, rooted in the experience of those on the margins, it delves into the implications of the experiences of my dialogue partners. By bringing forth the voices of my dialogue partners, this study explores the dynamics of marginality and integrates these dynamics into the lived experience of church. It not only observes the consequences of a process of dialogue that does not seek agreement and uniformity, but builds on this non-consensus dialogue to privilege outside voices and a cross-disciplinary approach as important contributors to practical theology in twenty-first century.

Traveling to nine states in the United States, I dialogued with people in all four main census regions of the United States: Northeast, South, West, and Northwest.[6] I visited two cities in each region, conversing with at least nine dialogue partners in each region between June and November 2009. I dialogued with fifty-one Catholics between the ages of twenty-two and eighty-eight who stopped attending Mass since 2001. Most of

---

the broader Catholic community. The institution and the People of God as church are hard to disentangle. In this volume, I use *church* to indicate the People of God and *Church* to indicate the institution of the Roman Catholic Church. I will also be using the language that my dialogue partners used in talking about the Church. This means that official terms such as extraordinary minister of the Eucharist will be referred to as eucharistic minister, in the more common vernacular.

4. Since the earliest Church times, the Catholic Church acknowledged the Spirit's work in the People of God through its stress on the importance of the *sensus fidelium* [sense of the faithful] as one of the norms for knowledge and theological truth in the Church. The *sensus fidelium* "refers to the ongoing process by which the community of faith acknowledges that a teaching or a practice enjoined by church authority is a genuine expression of the church's faith and therefore true and binding, and makes that teaching or practice its own" (Phan, "'Reception' or 'Subversion' of Vatican II by the Asian Churches?").

5. Dialogue will be quoted as utterances. An utterance is more than a sentence. An utterance comprises a complete thought, saying something, responding to something, and anticipating a response. See Appendix A for more information about my dialogue partners, their pseudonyms, and their ages.

6. These are the four regions identified by the U.S. Census Bureau.

our conversations lasted forty-five minutes to an hour. My conversations include people living at the margins of the Church, all of whom identify themselves as Catholic. Some are Catholics in full communion with the Church but not attending Mass yet maintaining corporate spirituality. These Catholics connect with Catholic worship in a number of ways through small Christian communities, Intentional Eucharistic Communities, and other forms of regular group-based spiritual practices or worship. Some in this group feel marginalized, while others, though labeled and described by other people as on the margins, would not describe themselves as marginalized from the larger Catholic Church. They would describe themselves as marginalized from the institutional, hierarchical Catholic Church. Other Catholics identify themselves as Catholic, do not attend Mass, but maintain spirituality and individual spiritual practices. Another group interviewed connects with corporate worship and identify themselves as Catholic. A new pastor asked this group of interviewees, regular Sunday Mass attendees, to leave their Catholic Church after worshiping as a community in a parish in the same fashion led by three different priests over the course of forty years. They now worship in an Intentional Eucharistic Community.[7] There are several other groups of people on the margins who are not part of this study: those who, though they are on the margins, worshiping at their Catholic parish Church, those who no longer identify as Catholic and now belong to another denomination and identify with that denomination, and those who no longer identify themselves as a person of faith. For the purpose of this study's interest, these people will not be involved in conversation.

7. Intentional Eucharistic Communities (IECs), small faith communities rooted in the Catholic tradition and mutuality and inclusiveness, join together to celebrate the sacred texts and rituals of their tradition and to sustain each other as a transformative public presence in culture and society (Veling, *Practical Theology*, 3). "Born in the enthusiasm flowing from Vatican II for a church of the people, some IECs were instituted in parishes, some were created as alternatives to the parish, some retain close ties with the institutional church, and some function independently. All are characterized by shared responsibility for the governance and life of the community" (Intentional Eucharistic Communities, "Embracing and Shaping Our Future"). These groups share liturgical life and mutually support each other with the purpose of living Gospel-centered lives, growing spiritually, and working for peace and justice commitments.

NUANCING THE MARGINS OF THE CHURCH

> I always looked at this period in my life as a kind of, I still do to some extent, as a temporary lapse from the Church. I expect at some point that I'll come back into the Church and be involved again. I don't know if that's an honest thing for me to think of myself, but for some reason that's in my head, and so—and again, I don't know the term; *lapsed* maybe, or something—that doesn't necessarily mean that I'm permanently disengaged from the Catholic Church because I don't feel that way even though some of my thoughts and beliefs are fairly disconnected from the current teachings maybe. I still don't think of myself as someone who would consider being inactive in the Church. (Terry, dialogue)

Some of my dialogue partners, like Terry, indicate a willingness to return to active participation in the Catholic Church at some point in the future. I wonder about their current attitudes of Church and what might lead them back to the Catholic Church in the future. I ask myself what this process of being on the margins and the issues they face there means to their faith journey, and question how they currently see their faith journey in light of their experiences on the margins. These are all topics for discussion in my dialogues.

"What's in Your Bones?"—Towards Understanding

> *Would you still define yourself as Catholic?*[8]
>
> Yes, but it's like it's in my bones. It's like, I can't not be Catholic. I have no desire to go to an Episcopal Church, or a Lutheran Church, or another Church.
>
> *So, what would you describe that's in your bones?*
>
> Roman Catholicism. Oh, that's a good question. What is in my bones? (pause) That I'm attached to that Church somehow. But, I keep saying that Church is us, as people. (Judy, dialogue)

Dialogues are opportunities for the individual's story to be in conversation with the stories of others on the margins of the Church becoming

---

8. Throughout this volume, I use italics to distinguish my words from those of my dialogue partners.

a communal story. This yields new creative insights into the experience of marginality for practical theology, and for my dialogue partners as well.[9] I received e-mails after dialogues stating, as Lily did, "I enjoyed meeting you and responding to your questions. My time with you has helped me clarify my feelings and frustration with the Church." These dialogues also raise questions that were difficult at times for some to answer. Judy, my second dialogue partner on the margins, describes herself as being Catholic because it is "in her bones." The question, "What is in your bones?" became a question asked of all dialogue partners, framed in their own language, to probe what they identify within themselves that *is* Catholic. This question sparked thoughtful reflection, and some protests that the question is difficult. Andrew commented by e-mail.

> Thanks for a great cup of coffee and for being a captive audience. While having lunch with friends today "religion" came up—one of the guests is in training as a Methodist minister and mentioned a communion monthly/quarterly—which helped me develop an answer to your "Catholic" question. It is the centrality of the Eucharist and the meal to which all are invited that makes it Catholic for me—that the liturgy revolves around the meal rather than the homily is what makes it Catholic for me—or my tradition. So the focus on the table/meal sets the Catholic liturgy apart of all others for me. (Andrew, dialogue)

Dialogues help develop a frame for my dialogue partners' lived experiences of the margins of the Catholic Church and answer the question, "What is it to feel that one belongs to the margins, to claim an identity as one on the margins, to experience marginality?" Dialogues are integral components to the practical theology research detailed in this book.

9. Dialogue educates each partner about him or herself and about the person with whom he or she is in dialogue, discovering potential and creating potential for new creative understandings about the self and the situation being discussed. This knowing of oneself and the world through dialogue with the other in all the other's diversity is a key action of human existence (Morson and Emerson, *Mikhail Bakhtin*, 209–10). Relationship is primary as a person's self-definition and self-perception, as well as knowledge and meaning, are formed through dialogic relationships with others (Bakhtin, *Art and Answerability*, 32).

INVITING THE VOICES OF THE PEOPLE TO
PRACTICAL THEOLOGY

Practical theology emerges from the experiences of life.[10] It is contextual, oriented toward framing, situating, and identifying particular patterns of a contemporary situation and describing theologically the way the Christian faith occurs in this contemporary situation.[11] The task of practical theology is to promote authentic discipleship in its concrete and contemporary situations.[12] In this discipleship, practical theology goes beyond church-centered ministry to engage the postmodern, pluralistic world and culture, seeking a genuine and strategic commitment toward action for the common good.[13]

In this study ethnography is employed to flesh out the insights into dialogue. Both dialogic praxis rising in everyday experiences and theory formed through multi-voiced dialogue provide the foundation for the praxis/theory relationship in my practical theology methodology. Practical theology utilizes this empirical theological methodology in a cross-disciplinary dialogue with other disciplines in the social and human sciences, and with theological disciplines, Scripture, and tradition. This dialogue does not seek agreement, but rather pays attention to the differences and similarities in each person's narrative in a reciprocal give and take. It reciprocally invites my dialogue partners into the practical theology conversation by sharing and building practical theology knowledge based on the dialogue and shared, examined, and reexamined knowledge.[14] An under-

---

10. Practical theology is no longer situated only in the church, but rather engages the interactions of Christianity and religious and non-religious phenomena both in the church and outside the church (Van der Ven, *Practical Theology*, 38).

11. Fulkerson, *Places of Redemption*, 7–9. Practical theologian Mary McClintock Fulkerson examines the concept of postmodern place through practical theology and ethnographic research exploring the practices of an interracial church that includes people with disabilities. She contextualizes and situates that conversation in a theory of practices and place that create a space for all to appear (ibid., 231). See Fulkerson's book *Places of Redemption* for an in-depth discussion.

12. Cahalan and Neiman, "Mapping the Field of Practical Theology," 67, 70.

13. O'Brien, "Reconciling Identity," 233; O'Brien. "Practical Theology and Postmodern Religious Education," 316. Practical theologian and religious educator Maureen O'Brien suggests that practical theology can be important in revealing patterns of practice, as well as implicit assumptions that contextualize and affect our interpretation of prominent events in our lives (O'Brien, "Reconciling Identity," 237). This suggests the need for dialogue that will allow theological reflection about marginalization and those on the margins.

14. My practical theology model can be broadly placed within a feminist model,

standing of practical theology as public theology suggests that practical theology not only asks what the experience, beliefs, or practices mean to the local community but also what they mean to all those affected by the decisions and commitments of these communities.[15]

> The thing is, the Church is causing pain. Now as a Catholic . . . I hope the Church would stop this pain and also understand the discontent of its people and the whole issue of Catholics being different in the United States because we are a democracy. To have a Church that is so hierarchical just goes against the grain. (Steve, dialogue)

> We were told we had three weeks to shape up. Um, I don't remember having any great dilemma, and I wasn't facing any great dilemma. I knew that my place was not going to be at St. _____ anymore. It was like someone took a knife, opened my chest, took my heart out, and . . . [crying] How they can destroy something that was so real? I don't even see what it gains them; just power. (Harry, dialogue)[16]

Steve and Harry poignantly express the hurt that so many of my dialogue partners on the margins of the Church feel as they cope with

---

informed by a doctrine of God as Trinity and grounded in a participative emancipatory paradigm (Tashakkori and Teddlie, *Handbook of Mixed Methods in Social and Behavioral Research*; Denzin and Lincoln, eds., *Collecting and Interpreting Qualitative Materials*). This methodology seeks the empowerment of those on the margins and a change in the power imbalance for all the marginalized.

15. Davaney, *Historicism*, 167.

16. The parishioners at this parish were asked to suspend their liturgical prayer style that had developed over four decades but, in 2008, did not conform to the 2002 General Instruction of the Roman Missal (GIRM). In one member's words, "We the community of the church of ___, are standing at a painful crossroads. For forty years we have been a cohesive, intentional, conscience-driven community committed to justice. We cherish the Church of our baptism where we are fed by the Gospel, Vatican II, and the Church's social teaching. We struggle to live the challenge of Christ by being present to the people of our neighborhood, even though inadequately, to serve their needs through the various programs of the parish. Our work is fueled by a wonderful, inclusive communal prayer that evolved through prayerful discernment over four decades. For thirty-eight of these forty years, we have had priests walk with us on our journey of praying with integrity and listening to the voice of the Spirit alive among us. Now we have been told that there is no room for us to pray and worship as we have for so long . . . We are committed to the future of the Catholic Church that builds loving, inclusive, prayerful, justice-service communities of faith. We must move away from a culture of clerical power, control, privilege, and secrecy. We are not against authority. We are against patriarchy, which disrespects people. Unity is not uniformity. Unity can be attained by respecting diversity" (Dan, dialogue).

loving a Church tradition and no longer feeling that they can be a part of it. Practical theology attends to the structure of this experience in all its details and depictions of life. It mandates a commitment to transformation for the common good.[17] Transformation cannot be predetermined. Dialogue with multiple diverse partners including biblical and tradition elements and allied disciplines enables practical theology reflection to foster a creative space, a place of newness.[18] New understandings flow from this creative space and lead to new actions and further reflection in a continuing theological spiral.

This volume begins by seeking to understand current theory about the margins of the Church through an examination of empirical research that informs the suppositions and perceptions of the margins of the Church. Chapter 1 then details my own phenomenological practical theology research. Developing a theology of marginality, chapter 2 makes marginality central to imagining the creative potential available from the diversity and difference that moves people to the margins. Drawing on the work of Korean-American theologian Jung Young Lee, this chapter provides the basis for the refusal to let the implications of dissent be construed in terms of being either "inside" or "outside" of the church. It rather suggests that margins are both/and places where one can be both in the margins and in the center simultaneously. Drawing from this theology of marginality and ongoing engagement with my dialogue partners, I continue by linking Trinitarian theology and the communication theory of Mikhail Bakhtin to propose an anthropology that is relational and dialogic (chapter 3). A Trinitarian ecclesiology informed by pneumatology suggests in turn a transformative vision of catholicity, communion, and dialogic communication. I add to this a conversation on models of Church (chapter 4). Building on these dialogues on marginality, anthropology, and ecclesiology, I offer a discussion of practical theology and a cross-disciplinary methodology that emphasizes praxis and multiple voices (chapter 5). Next I explore the implications of a hermeneutical understanding of dialogue that does not seek agreement or consensus to practical theology (chapter 6). Appreciating the fact that my dialogue partners on the margins of the Catholic Church are defining a space for themselves in a Church whose leaders do not define a space for them, a final discussion with my dialogue partners' concerns the implications of this dialogue to our understanding

17. O'Brien, "Reconciling Identity," 316.

18. When diversity is accepted and valued, the margins provide an opportunity for insight. The margin is the crucial point, a new and creative core where the two worlds of the center and the margin can coexist together (J. Y. Lee, *Marginality*, 98).

of the margins of the Catholic Church (chapter 7). I conclude with suggestions for the future (chapter 8).

Acknowledgments

THERE ARE MANY PEOPLE I would like to thank as this book comes to fruition. I am indebted to Bryan Froehle, Mary McClintock Fulkerson, Maureen O'Brien, and Sue Gallagher, all early readers of my work. I am grateful for their critical reading, their affirmations, their suggestions, and their generous support. I wish to thank the women and men whose critical conversations helped me in articulating my understanding of the margins: Angelique Montgomery-Goodnough, Nathaniel Holmes, Mary Moran, Toni Muirhead, Joan Nigen, Diane Shoaf, Pierre Petit-Frere, Beth Ann and Ray Rufo, and Lidia Vazquez. I am grateful for their support and all the dialogue we shared that did not seek consensus or agreement! I wish to acknowledge my dialogue partners from around the country for their gracious conversation, their vulnerability, and their honesty. Thanks to my enthusiastic editor, Jacob Martin. My husband, Ed, and my sons, Edward and Dan, provided encouragement, dialogue, and wonderful questions along the way. I thank them for the communion of family.

1

The Faithful People of God on the Margins of the Catholic Church

AN HOUR OF COFFEE AND DIALOGUE

"I don't really know why. But if you buy me coffee next week, I guess we can talk."

(RAY, DIALOGUE)

I DRIVE TO THE coffee shop, nervous but excited to be finally having conversations with people who identify themselves on the margin of the Catholic Church. In my own Church community I listen to these stories and watch as marginality increases. Progressive, feminist, and marginalized myself, I witness the pain of people I meet who express the feeling of being isolated or the pain of being without a Church community. I wonder at this phenomenon that seems to be growing in my local Catholic parish community. Now, I am sitting in a coffee shop, in a strange city, miles from my home, testing my tape recorder in the noisy environment, and scanning the room for a woman in a pink shirt.

God Called Me in Here, Why Didn't God Call Me Out?

The odd thing is I felt so called into the Catholic Church. It was a strong call and it felt like coming home. I don't feel called out yet, and I don't understand that. I wrestle with it. God called me in here, and I'm not active. Why didn't He call me out? But I feel like I have to stay where I am and I don't know what that means. (Jane, dialogue)

I'm eighty, born Catholic, high school, college, family, Peace Corps. A few years ago my husband was diagnosed with cancer, multiple myeloma. So, I'd be upset about something personal at Church and he would say, that's not one of the essentials, forget it. After my husband died the Church started pushing the rules and I started backing up. It was very troublesome. I actually agonized a long time about "what are the essentials?" I hang on to the Gospel values and peace and justice. I was a eucharistic minister. Wouldn't you know that last year the priest came out and decided we'll be the traffic managers at the back. So, we were standing there and he was saying, "'Don't go out this door; go out that door. The Body of Christ, Body of Christ, don't go out this way, Body of Christ." He then, at one point, pulled my sweater to block the door better. That priest broke the straw. And then there was the lying, the cheating, and the scapegoating. The knowledge that the priests were abusing people and it had been covered up was horrific. That's part of it but part of it was the hypocrisy. Hypocrisy was huge. (Bea, dialogue)

Jane and Bea, two dialogue partners, both struggle to understand their feelings of marginality. They feel a part of the people of God, and both belong to small local communities engaged in corporate prayer and worship. Bea and Jane's marginality develops within their life experiences. Jane feels she needs to remain a part of the Catholic Church yet finds it difficult to attend Mass. Bea is active in progressive Catholic movements, but no longer wants to be a part of the institutional Catholic Church. Practical theology invites attention to the ways in which Bea's and Jane's lived decisions are incorporated into their future dialogue and action. It invites attention to the context and particular circumstances in which the tradition of the Church, as a communicative process and practice, may be being reconstructed, revised, and reinterpreted as circumstances change.[1] My dialogue partners initiate a depiction of the context and circumstances of

---

1. Tilley, *Inventing Catholic Tradition*, 9, 29.

their life on the margins of the Church. Their voices are important voices in enunciating an understanding of the Church in the twenty-first century.

> I would be willing to be interviewed for your research. Not sure if I am the person you're looking for as I have been a Catholic all my life, attended Catholic schools from grades 1–12 and have worked as a Catholic school teacher for the last nineteen years. I'll probably never leave the Catholic Church, but I am embarrassed at the image they have created for themselves: pedophilia, resistance/hostility to change, and a reputation for being hierarchical, rigid, and dogmatic. I'm leaving my teaching job in a Catholic school this year to work in a public school. I don't know if I'm on the margins or just not a good Catholic, but I would be willing to be a part of your research. (Rita, dialogue)

> One of the things about having the education like I did involves your conscience, and one of the things I always prayed for was the gift of discernment, because I think it's so important to understand what God asks us, or requires of us. Growing up in the Catholic Church is sort of a hard thing if you're gay, not from the standpoint of shame which is really what the Catholic Church in traditional terms is often about—shame. There's a difference between guilt and shame. Guilt is when you do something bad and you should feel bad 'cause you did something bad. Shame is feeling bad because of who you are or what you are and it's not healthy and it's not real. The Church shames gay people. I have people who say, "Oh this is a tolerant community." There is nothing to tolerate in my relationship with (Name). It's something to celebrate. I have someone who loves me and I love and we had a great underpinning of belief in each other and we're partners in life. This is not something to be ashamed of; this is something my parents hope for their kids. So one of the things that's hard about growing up in the Church is that when you find out that something the Church is teaching is wrong suddenly. (Harry, dialogue)

What are the reasons that people are marginalized? What does it mean for people to be defining a place in a Church that does not define a space for them? Rita and Harry have dissimilar experiences of marginality. They describe their own marginality differently and even question their own and the institutional Church's understanding of marginality. Dialogue aims to understand the dialogue partners' process of ceasing attendance, and the dynamics of their marginality now.

In this chapter, I begin by examining the available empirical research that theoretically informs a perspective of the margins of the Church. I do this to understand the state of what is currently known about the margins of the Church. Exploring this data provides a basis for an appreciation of where the understanding of marginality has come from and where it has grown. With the experience of postmodernity,[2] religion in the United States changed. Such changes can be found in groups such as the Emergent Church movement,[3] which seeks new ways of being Church in our emerging culture, and within the Catholic Church as well. Past research on the margins of the Church varies. Some research tracks overall actual trends, while other research is more in-depth. Historically, there has not been as much research engaged directly with the voices of the people. Proceeding from the more traditional quantitative research, this chapter reviews this research as well as phenomenological research[4] that hears more of the voices of the people within different religions in the United States, particularly that research with a Catholic focus. Building on the tradition of research in the United States, I finish this chapter with details of my own phenomenological practical theology research.

2. Modernity's effects included differentiations in the functions of society, a changing emphasis on policies rather than personal loyalty, individualism, and a leveling of social authority (Jodock, ed., *Catholicism Contending with Modernity*, 338). Postmodernity may be seen as a reaction to modernity. This generation is living in a pluralistic, diverse age. The advent of the computer and of the Internet brings with it the availability of global knowledge never before imagined. Rapidly changing technology, a global economy, and accessible movement across the globe have provided a context of increasing pluralism, difference, and diversity. The meaning of postmodernity varies in the literature, but there is agreement that it is a moment in time in which cultural, social, and theoretical shifts are located historically and systemically (Fergusen and Wicke, *Feminism and Postmodernism*, 2).

3. The emergent church movement is an ecumenical group of evangelical Protestants, mainstream Protestants, and Catholics. Brian McLaren and Richard Rohr are several of the writers and speakers in this movement. More information can be found at http://www.emergentvillage.com/.

4. Phenomenological research seeks to allow the participants to describe the essence of human experiences studied through procedures that involve a smaller number of subjects. The development of patterns and relationships of meaning allows the researcher to better understand the lived experiences of those involved in the research (Creswell *Research Design*, 15).

TRACING THE MARGINS OF THE CHURCH: EMPIRICAL RESEARCH

> Let's talk about who we are, what we do, and where we're going in our Intentional Eucharistic Community. Yes, I wanted to be connected with the Church. In the canon law there is room for what we were doing. There is room for particular communities to be not regulated, to be not as strict in their liturgy, as well as in their mission. Well, we called ourselves Catholics and my question is: What does that mean? (Dan, dialogue)

> Well, a quote of the psychologist Jung . . . he said, and I can butcher it, but, "What's truth in the morning of our lives doesn't work at noon and is a lie by evening." So, is that just this? Does that happen with God? With spirituality and religion, as well as other things in our lives? I don't know. (Judy, dialogue)

Dan understands Church as inclusive and wants to probe the bigger question of what Catholic means. Judy questions the changes in her own interpretations of the traditions of her life. Theologian Terrence Tilley suggests that traditions shape people and that people reshape those same traditions as they receive and enact them both individually and corporately.[5] Empirically, quantitatively oriented research is useful for understanding broad shifts in the importance of religion in a person's life. Exploring this data gives a picture of the margins of the Church and provides a basis for a beginning awareness of marginality within the Church.

Church Attendance Steady?

The Center for Applied Research in the Apostolate (CARA) suggests that the frequency of Mass attendance is a strong indicator of the general importance of Catholic faith in a person's life and of his or her level of commitment to living out the faith.[6] Overall, church attendance among Christians in the United States has been fairly steady since the 1950s, averaging about 42 percent.[7] Catholics formerly attended Church in greater

---

5. Tilley, *Inventing Catholic Tradition*, 122.

6. Gray and Perl, *Sacraments Today*, 2.

7. Gallup, "Churchgoing Among U.S. Catholics Slides to Tie Protestants." Gallup has studied human nature and behavior since the 1930s with a focus on empirical evidence.

numbers, but attendance dropped in the 1970s and then leveled off to about the same attendance rate as Protestants.[8]

Table 1: Church Attendance in the United States—Multidenominational Data

	Attendance at Christian Worship Weekly	Seldom/Never Attend Christian Worship	Attendance at Catholic Mass 2009	Seldom/Never Attend Catholic Mass 2009
Gallup Poll 2010	43.1%	45%	42%	
Baylor ISR Dazer 2006	32% to 45% depending on denomination	9% to 14% depending on denomination	33%	9%
Pew Forum for Religion in Public Life 2008	39%	23%	43% 30+ years of age; 34% 18–29 years of age	
Barna Group 2006			55%	

The Catholic Church: A Diminishing Influence?

The Catholic Church in the United States is both an immigrant Church, and one of the earliest established in the United States. [9] In the late nineteenth century and early twentieth century, European Catholic immigrants moved into ethnic enclaves upon arriving in the United States, and for many the religious and ethnic identities were hard to distinguish.

> The first time I met my grandmother, I remember because I was still in the crib. That's the image I am left with. I was still in the crib and I woke up in the night and my grandmother was visiting. It was pretty exciting, I was put to bed at the regular time, but I woke up during the night, and she was sitting beside my crib in a rocking chair. Of course, we all had rocking chairs and I could hear her beads. She prayed in German. She was German-Irish. (Sarah, dialogue)

As Catholics began to move from ethnic enclaves into the mainstream of society, their Church followed them. Perhaps the central event in this process was the experience of World War II. The war, and Catholics'

8. Ibid.

9. Manuel et al., *Catholic Church and the Nation-State*, 71.

participation in the war efforts, confirmed that they were an integral part of society and that fundamental American ideals were consistent with Catholicism.[10] But the 1950s gave way to the turbulent 1960s, and the ensuing decades brought changing times and with them new religious attitudes about the importance of religious faith in people's lives. By 2010, when CARA surveyed Catholics on the Catholic faith's importance to them, generational differences were evident. CARA currently uses three generations based on life experiences relevant to Catholics: Pre-Vatican II Generation (born prior to 1943), the Vatican II Generation (born between 1943–1960), and the Post-Vatican II Generation (born after 1960).[11] CARA divides the Post-Vatican II Generation into two segments: one for those older than aged thirty and one for those between the ages of eighteen and thirty. The Pre-Vatican II Generation attends Mass more frequently and in general shows greater loyalty to Church practices. Many of the Post-Vatican II Catholics of the Millennial Generation still live with family so that their religious practices may be comparable to that of their families.[12] The Pre-Vatican II Generation, aged sixty-nine and above, is twice as likely to indicate that religion is very important to them as is the Millennial Generation, aged eighteen to twenty-nine.[13] However, few indicate that their faith is of no importance.[14]

Catholics No Longer Attending Mass?

I've always had a struggle with the doctrines and structure within the Catholic Church as long as I've been going to church. I love the community, but there's just certain rules and boundaries . . . the Church is not necessarily growing and keeping up with what's going on around it and I understand the reason behind it. "Well, we don't want to make abrupt changes because society changes so quickly." But these were the rules when my mom was a kid, and life and humans are progressing so quickly now that you can't wait and see anymore. When I moved here I was going to mass at _____, I really couldn't find a home church. The parishes never felt like home to me. Being the age that I

10. Massa, *Catholics and American Culture*, 8.

11. Gray and Perl, *Sacraments Today*, 16.

12. Ibid., 20.

13. Bendyna and Perl, "Young Adult Catholics in the Context of Other Catholic Generations," 22.

14. Ibid., 22–23.

am I need some place with young people. And it's hard to find. You know you have older Catholics that are married, you have young teenagers who are going with their parents; but you rarely find that twenty-five to thirty-five, unmarried, single person. I really long for, like, "Let's do Bible study. Let's do this; let's do that." So that's when I started pulling apart because I need more. (Caroline, dialogue)

Caroline, quoted above, would attend a Catholic church if she found one with a community of young people and relevant preaching. The fact that she finds few people her age at Mass on Sunday affects her desire to participate in a community that does not meet her needs. Her position coincides with the position of other young adults in research by theologian Dean R. Hoge and his associates who found that young adults will attend Mass when it contains relevant homilies, good music, and is connected with a strong vibrant community.[15] Like Hoge et al., Angelique Montgomery Goodnough, researching Catholic identity at Catholic universities, found that young people prize community and relationship as identifying markers of what it means to be "Catholic."[16] Kevin Meme and Jeffrey Guhn, young Catholics themselves, find that no one story can summarize the increasing complex reality of young adult Catholic spirituality. Rather young Catholics are struggling to articulate their vision of the world, their place in it and the place of their Catholic faith in their life.[17]

"Few Catholics who attend Mass a few times a year or less think of themselves as practicing their Catholic faith."[18] Gray and Perl's survey asked respondents to determine from a given list what reasons explained their lack of Mass attendance. The list included: "a busy schedule or lack of time, family responsibilities, health problems or a disability, I don't believe that missing Mass is a sin, conflict with work, inconvenient Mass schedule, and I am not a very religious person."[19] The most common reasons cited by those who attend Mass a few times a year were that they don't believe "missing Mass is a sin" (64 percent) and that they are "not a very religious

15. Hoge et al., *Young Adult Catholics*, 161. Dean Hogue (1937–2008) was a sociologist at The Catholic University of America.

16. Goodnough, "Treasure Buried," 4. Practical theologian Angelique Montgomery Goodnough lives and works in Austin, Texas. She is an adjunct professor in the School of Humanities teaching Religious Studies at St. Edward's University.

17. Meme and Guhin, *Young and Catholic in America*, xiii–xiv

18. Gray and Perl, *Sacraments Today*, 98.

19. Ibid., 49.

person" (50 percent)."[20] Interestingly, these reasons were not given by my dialogue partners. Rather, they reported experiences of marginalization due to structural or systemic problems in the Church, personal issues in particular church communities or particular, personal experiences that made it difficult for them to feel nourished through church attendance and participation. My dialogue partners differed from Gray and Perl's population who were self-identified adult Catholics. They self-identified themselves as on the margins of the Catholic Church and responded to an invitation to dialogue.

> I still go to Mass. I don't go every Sunday, but I do go once in awhile, like the holidays cause I think, once you're a Catholic, you're always a Catholic. (Chloe dialogue)

While religious faith may be of varying importance, other issues also are important to those on the margins of the Church. Kate and Lily are adamant about women's full participation in the Church. Jillian questions the Church's teachings on sexual ethics. The reasons for increased marginality differ with each person.

> One thing we haven't talked about is women. That's one thing that caused me to leave because women are so . . . and I never wanted to be a priest or anything, but I just felt that women just weren't valued. (Kate, dialogue)

> And being an attorney, there are issues of justice, especially the women's stuff, the women's issues in the Church. To me that goes to just plain ole justice. (Lily, dialogue)

> I have concerns about birth control and actually, I think with my love of anthropology and studying developing cultures, that was when I really got upset with the Catholic Church. There were a lot of women who had a million kids because they weren't supposed to use birth control. They couldn't care for them, didn't take care of them, and they didn't want a million kids. They were exhausted. They didn't know how to take care of them all, but they had to because that was what the Church told them they had to do. I really think, "Do they really want us to have more kids to take care of?" You know, women have to go through all of this, a lot of work and lots of stress on their bodies. And I heard these women say you can't use birth control 'cause you'll go to hell. They were scared of the Church. I really never thought about it much until I started travelling and saw the impact of

20. Ibid.

the Church's teaching on poor women particularly. (Jillian, dialogue)

The Numbers Are Confusing, but Pain and Rejection Remain

In the words of the U.S. Conference of Catholic Bishops (USCCB), "For a variety of reasons, people leave the Church. They may seek out or be re-cruited into non-denominational, evangelical, or fundamentalist churches, or into New Age or other religious movements. Far too often they simply abandon the Christian faith altogether."[21] Yet, despite those leaving the Catholic Church, the number of Catholics in the United States is not de-clining and even increasing.[22] The primary growth in the Church is due to population increase in the largely Catholic Hispanic/Latino community.[23]

> I feel pain now for a Church that's lagging behind. Theology always moves faster than the Church. Like the ship that you can't turn in the ocean right away. They are resisting and putting barriers up and telling people, forbidding them from discussing or doing their work and they're fighting it tooth and nail but it cannot be stopped. It can't be stopped. The people hopefully will begin to understand that there's more to the Church than what they are getting at Church on Sundays; that we have an obliga-tion to ourselves to begin to become aware of those things. And it may take a hundred years but eventually, eventually I think there has to be, there has to be a change. (Maria, dialogue)

Maria and James cease involvement in their Church communities despite years of faithful and deeply committed ministry in their Church communities yet they still long for a Church community. Maria contin-ues to search. James below is devastated by a breach of trust in the sexual abuse scandal and cover-up and states that he gets up on Sunday morning and feels he should go to Church, but he does not go. Jillian is raising a

21. USCCB, *Our Hearts Were Burning within Us*, 36.

22. Recent estimates of the population of Catholics in the United States are 65.6 million, or 21 percent of the population (CARA, *Frequently Requested Catholic Church Statistics*). In 1965, Catholics numbered forty-five million, or 24 percent of the popula-tion (ibid.). Mass attendance in 1965 was at approximately 72 percent. Today, just 22 percent of Catholics report that they attend Mass once a week or more (ibid.). These numbers suggest a move to non-Mass attendance from previous years. The question is, why?

23. USCCB, "Catholic Church in America: Meeting Real Needs in Your Neighborhood."

family and longs for a Church in which she can raise her child, but is not presently a part of such a Church.

> This is part of my problem now, the (priest's name) a pedophile. Oh, I tell you if anybody would tell me that early on, I would tell them, "No way." This would be absolutely unbelievable. The man was so sensitive, cry all the time, that type of thing. When I heard that, I was beside myself. My kids, they were not abused . . . but, I think things were close, let's put it that way. It could have happened. You know, I trusted my children to this man. This is still in our midst today. I went to see a priest, Fr. (name). I told him that I haven't been to Church in quite awhile now and I told him, "This is why." He knew Fr. (name), and he tried to tell me that it's happening all over. I didn't want to hear that. You people, I'm sorry, are put upon a pedestal. You're entrusted, you know. More than the school teacher, I would trust a priest. This type of thing, and he kind of blew me off. I didn't want to hear that. I didn't know what I wanted to hear at that time, but I didn't want to hear that. No, it wasn't ok because my way of thinking, (name) should be in jail, 'cause a few of them should be in jail. But instead they transfer them to Rome. You know, if that were me, I would be away for good. (James, dialogue)

> My Catholic Church was very liberal too. I learned a lot about social justice and environmental issues that really led into my main views in college, very little on the law and the aspect of Catholicism I don't like. But the more I thought about when I am in a Church and I'm going to give my money to a Church I'm going to support, I really don't want to support a Church where woman aren't allowed to be leaders at the highest level. So, to me, I don't want to bring my daughter up in a Church where she's not viewed as equal. (Jillian, dialogue)

Catholics around the United States generously volunteered for conversation about the Catholic Church and their own marginality. My dialogue partners expressed pleasure in joining with others and contributing to a work of practical theology on the margins of the Catholic Church. Where were these generous conversation partners located?

Dialoguing Where Catholics Are

Catholics are more evenly distributed around the United States than other denominations. "The rectangle that connects Milwaukee and St.

Louis in the Midwest to Boston and Baltimore in the East defines the Catholic heartland initially settled by European immigrants."[24] Religion by Region, a project of the Leonard E. Greenberg Center for the Study of Religion in Public Life at Trinity College at Hartford, identifies eight regions in the United States and attempts to show how religion shapes and is being shaped by the culture.[25] In these regions, Religion by Region explores the way politics, public policies, and civil society relate to religion.[26] Some states have denser Catholic culture than others. A dense Catholic culture is typified by a denser network of Catholic Churches, schools and universities, and organizations as well as the impact on public culture. States in the Northeast generally have the densest Catholic culture due to nineteenth and twentieth century successive waves of immigration.[27] My dialogue partners reside in six of eight of the *Religion and Public Life* regions of the United States.

For the purpose of discussing my dialogue partners' locations, I divide the United States into four regions of the U.S. Census: the Northeast, West, South, and Midwest regions. My dialogue partners reside in all four of these regions.

Table 2: Catholics and Dialogue Partners by Four Geographic Regions[28]

Regions	States[A]	Percentage of Catholics[B]	Attendance at Mass[C]	Percentage of Dialogue Partners	Number of Dialogue Partners
Northeast	CT, ME, MA, NH, NJ, NY, PA, RI, and VT	29%	19%	24%	12
Midwest	IL, IN, IA, KS, MI, MN, MO, NE, ND, OH, SD, and WI	22%	23%	30%	16
Regions	States[A]	Percentage of Catholics[B]	Attendance at Mass[C]	Percentage of Dialogue Partners	Number of Dialogue Partners

24. Froehle and Gautier, *Catholicism USA*, 6.

25. Walsh and Silk, eds., *Religion and Public Life in New England*, 7.

26. Ibid., 8.

27. Ibid., 42. Froehle and Gautier, *Catholicism USA*, 207

28. U.S. Census Bureau 2008.

South	AL, AR, DE, FL, GA, KY, LA, MD, MI, NC, OK, SC, TN, TX, VA, Washington, DC, and WV	25%	32%	24%	12
West	AK, AZ, CA, CO, HI, ID, MT, NE, NM, OR, UT, WA, and WY	24%	20%	22%	11

A. CARA, *Frequently Requested Catholic Church Statistics*, 16.
B. Ibid., 16.
C. Ibid., 17.

My dialogue partners come from all four regions of the United States in generally similar percentages to the percentage of Catholics in the region. Most of my dialogue partners in the Midwest (87 percent) came from an Intentional Eucharistic Community that formerly worshipped together for forty years with a Catholic parish in the region. This is interesting because this region, according to Barlow and Silk, is more open to adaptation and experimentation within the Catholic Church, notably in the area of liturgy.[29]

Summary of Research in Actual Trends

Numerous studies indicate declining numbers in Catholic Church attendance, as well as an overall lack of identification with denominational religion. There is some fluidity in attitudes and beliefs among Catholics. All religions inherently are responsive to cultural and social environmental changes. Because of this, changes in attitudes and beliefs can be expected. While Catholicism may be responsive to changes, the numbers cannot reveal further information about these changes.[30] What is needed is dialogue that asks questions about these changes in beliefs and attitudes.

LIMITATIONS OF QUANTITATIVE RESEARCH

In or Out of the Church . . . Where Are the Voices?

One of the main limitations of the less phenomenological methods used in the above studies is that they do not provide any in-depth detail as to

29. Barlow and Silk, *Religion and Public Life in the Midwest*, 110.
30. Walsh and Silk, *Religion and Public Life in New England*, 79.

the lived experiences of the people. While studies such as these are useful, they do not allow us to hear the voices of the people, or understand what the experiences look like from their point of view. It is difficult to determine why people stop attending Mass because survey questions do not allow room for complex answers. Gray and Perl's survey asked questions to identify why people attend Mass less frequently, but they were close-ended responses forcing respondents to choose those most appropriate for them. Research that actively interacts with the participants, builds rapport, and involves the participants directly in the process yields a greater level of detail, a thicker description and a more holistic, interactive encompassing narrative.[31]

Clifford Geertz famously used the term "thick description" in ethnography to describe the type of description necessary to yield the meaning of a cultural sign.[32] In order to identify the changes and relational understandings happening of the margins of the Church a thick description is critical. This thick description assists in determining the social significance of marginality, and the value of issues of marginality in the Catholic Church through a multilayered, rich description that finds personal experiences and converses with people about those experiences.[33]

Allowing the Margins to Define the Margins?

In addition to the limitations of this less phenomenological research, present research proceeds from a traditional understanding of marginality perceived from the perspective of centrality. It defines the margin from the center and views the margin with *either/or* thinking. One is *either* in the center *or* on the margin. This allows the perspectives of the center to draw the peripheries, conceiving and defining the margins from the center. The participants' rating of behaviors and feelings in predetermined ways, the lack of emphasis on dialogue, labels such as lapsed, disconnected, and de-churched emphasize this centralist view of the margins by allowing the center to define the margins. The resulting meaning yields a view of the margins that is limited and incomplete. In order to allow the margins to define the margins, the voices of those on the margins are necessary. A shift to dialogue and narrative to engage the voices of people on the margins promises to shift the focus from

31. Creswell, *Research Design*, 179–83.
32. Geertz, *Interpretation of Cultures*, 13.
33. Ibid.

centrality to marginality. Research from the perspective of the margins rather than in the center, allows for the discernment of the dynamics at work in marginality in the Catholic Church.

Yet few phenomenological studies focus on the dynamics that underlie engagement and affiliation patterns, facilitating an understanding of the lives of those on the margins.

> You know Karl Rahner once was asked the question if he had it to do all over again and if he didn't know Jesus, and if he hadn't learned about the Catholic Church, how he would feel about religion. And he scratched his head and he said, "I can't possibly answer that question because who I am has been informed by my entire life, and all my life I have known nothing but that." I feel the same way. I have known nothing but the Catholic Church as my family. I've also branched out. I've explored different spiritual traditions. I meditate, and Yogananda is one of my very wonderful authors that I look to. I see connections with spirituality with Buddhism, the spirituality of the East. The Dalai Lama is a living saint as far as I'm concerned. You don't have to be Catholic to go to God. I just happened to be born Catholic and feel most comfortable in that tradition. I also feel comfortable in a synagogue, and I also feel comfortable in a temple. That's where I am. I'm a spiritual being and I'm aware, so there's something inside of me that always says, "Don't judge. Let people evolve the way they evolve and look to the Scriptures, where God said, 'There are many rooms in my mansion.'" (Miriam, dialogue)

Miriam's dialogue reveals the dynamics present in her understanding of the margins, an ecumenism that undergirds her statement, "Don't judge!" Further phenomenological studies reveal other dynamics.

PHENOMENOLOGICAL RESEARCH: A THICKER DESCRIPTION OF THE MARGINS OF THE CHURCH

Some People Are Seeking a Relevant and Authentic Way of Being Church

There is much discussion about the emerging church movement, sometimes also called the Emergent church movement.[34] For the last twenty to twenty-five years this movement understands themselves as a part of

---

34. See also http://www.emergentvillage.com for more information.

the larger church, providing middle, relevant, and authentic ways of being church that bridge both conservative and liberal churches. Emergent church spokespersons, among them Richard Rohr, Phyllis Tickle, and Brian McLaren, encourage Roman Catholic, Mainline Protestant, Evangelical, and other Christians to explore together the emergence and convergence of new ways of being church. Important topics in the emerging church literature include discussion of a fresh understanding of Jesus, a spirituality that links contemplation and action, social justice and holistic mission, and an authentic community. Research into the Emerging Church movement continues with researchers exploring methods of Church leadership, Church ritual, images of God and Jesus, salvation and justification and its importance to a lived spirituality.[35]

DYNAMICS IN THE MARGINS

Losing a Faith Once Valued

The works of Hammond, Dillon, and Hoge et al. explore the dynamics on the margins of the Church. Hammond discusses what it means to experience a loss of religious community and reasons why this may happen.[36] Dillon examines a group of Catholics who find themselves in a dynamic process of marginality, but working with their identity as Catholics.[37] Hoge and his colleagues contribute a perspective on young adults in the Catholic Church who exhibit generational differences from their parents and grandparents.[38]

Hammond describes the "dechurched" as those "who have lost a faith that they once valued or have left a body of believers with whom they were once deeply engaged."[39] Hammond explores the reasons for dechurching through interviews with people who are or have been dechurched. She finds "small issues sometimes trigger or mask much larger issues that are harder to name and address."[40] Hammond's five reasons people may leave the Church and become dechurched are:

35. McLaren, *Everything Must Change*; Simcox, "Performing Postmodern Christian."

36. Hammond, *Church and the Dechurched*, 36–46.

37. Dillon, *Catholic Identity*, 13.

38. Hoge et al., *Young Adult Catholics*, 36–69.

39. Hammond, *Church and the Dechurched*, 1.

40. Ibid., 37.

- An inability to be honest in church about personal life issues.

- Structural abuse, prejudices, and personal abuse. "All abuse—whether sexual, physical, emotional, or intellectual (such as mind control)—has consequences of a profound spiritual nature . . . When the abuser claims to follow Christ, the abused receives destructive messages about God, the church, and the life of faith."[41]

- The experience of the four rules of a dysfunctional family, "Don't think, don't feel, don't talk, and don't trust." [42]

- Disenfranchisement in the failure to acknowledge experiences of trauma or disabilities by our church leaders and communities.

- A personal perception of the irrelevancy of the church's mission and/ or disillusionment with church policies.[43]

Hammond's work explores the dynamics present in religious marginality. The reasons she details for this marginality are similar to many expressed by my dialogue partners, though her population was not specifically Catholic. Disenfranchisement, the clergy sex abuse scandal and more importantly the cover-up, disillusionment with Church policies, and issues of trust are all issues for my own dialogue partners. But these issues do not define my dialogue partners. They continue to wish for and act towards inclusive ways of expressing their faith and spirituality.

> People want to get back to Church but they don't. They, we, want a reason to go back, that's what we're looking for. We want a reason, give us something, and give us something not new and exciting, but interactive, get us back there. Show us that you want us still, that we can trust you. We have lost the trust completely, between all the history and the denials and the scandals, how are we supposed to trust you? We have faith in God, we don't have faith in the Catholic Church anymore and that's the

41. Ibid., 36.

42. Ibid., 46.

43. Researchers in the United Kingdom exploring the margins of the church include British sociologist Grace Davie, who states that the percentage of Christians attending church there is about 10 percent (*Religion in Britain since 1945*, 1). She believes that people in Europe and the United Kingdom treat the Church as a public utility to which one turns passively when it is needed—"believing while not belonging." Questions that plumb this notion of "believing while not belonging" yield more authentic data (ibid., 3). Voas and Crockett contest these findings, arguing that the belief systems of people who leave the church change over time to include vague beliefs that have little social or personal significance ("Religion in Britain," 11–18).

difference. Yeah, I'm still Catholic. It's a big part of my life. It always will be. (Kim, dialogue)

Mass Is Not a Priority, but Alienation and Boredom Matter Too

Several qualitative research studies find that other Sunday obligations take priority over Mass for many Catholics in the United States. Camille and Schorn examined reasons that Catholics in the United States separate from the Church, finding that often specific Catholic teachings, the feeling of being ignored, and a sense of boredom during Mass affected their decision.[44] Hoge and his colleagues found that young adult Catholics between the ages of twenty and forty became inactive for a variety of reasons after Confirmation. These reasons included alienation, lack of agreement with or disbelief in Church teachings, boredom, and the irrelevance of Church teachings.[45] Hoge and his colleagues suggest that the next generation of Catholics will not remain Catholic in the old way, or simply return to the Church keeping with life cycle patterns, in part because we live in a culture of choice where compliance behavior cannot be forced.[46] He and his colleagues call for Catholicism to "present itself as distinct, vital, relevant and worthwhile as a living tradition of discipleship, community, and sacramental consciousness."[47] Janet's story shares her perspective of her marginality, beginning in her teen years. Her feelings of marginality continue today, even though she works for a Catholic school.

> Religion was a requirement in our house, a very strong Catholic culture. In high school everything changed because my Dad was an alcoholic and he lost his job and we had no money to give to the Church. So my brother was up for Confirmation and they told my family they would confirm my brother but that was it—we could no longer come to the Church because we did not have the money. They just made us go. My family just all walked away en masse. I used to go to the Cathedral downtown as a teenager to High Mass and sit and cry through it all. (Janet, dialogue)

44. Camille and Schorn, *Faith Interrupted*, 25.
45. Hogue et al., *Young Adult Catholics*, 36–69.
46. Ibid., 238.
47. Ibid.

Disagreeing and Engaging with the Church Clarifies Catholic Identity

Dillon examines why people choose to remain Catholic despite being institutionally marginalized, focusing on how these Catholics negotiate their identity. She engaged pro-change Roman Catholic activists and professional Catholic theologians as response partners to show how people remain Catholics and maintain their commitment to building an inclusive Church.[48] Her study shows that the institutional context informs and empowers pro change Catholics' identity.[49] This happens because these Catholics must engage with official Roman Catholic Church pronouncements and institutional practices with which they disagree. This engagement enables them to further clarify their own identity. Her findings "illustrate the complex and multifaceted nature of individual experiences, the importance of shared group membership in both anchoring and mobilizing individuals, and the differentiated nature of the Catholic Church as both a doctrinal tradition and an institutional environment."[50]

My dialogue partners, while still considering themselves Catholic, also wrestle with Church pronouncements with which they disagree. Among other things, this informs their identity.[51] Practical theology examines the reality in which people live. Matt's reality, given his life experiences, leads him to disagree with his understanding of the Church teaching.

> You know, I'll tell you what, the first thing that really, when I began to question something was when my older sister got married to this nice guy. I was about four or five years old when she got married, so he was always around. He was like a big brother. He wasn't Catholic. I'm not sure what religion he was, but we learned as kids, like, oh my God, if you're not a Catholic then something is wrong. So, that's not fair. This guy is nice. He's a nice guy, he doesn't go to church like we do, but he's around and he's a nice guy. And then I started wondering, that was the first big question I had so, like, why should he be punished? (Matt, dialogue)

48. Dillon, *Catholic Identity*, 113.

49. Ibid., 13.

50. Ibid., 242.

51. Chapter 3 suggests that human identity and anthropology begins with the person as a relational being.

Miriam is a Catholic woman who describes herself as traditional and who sought ordination in the Catholic Womanpriest movement. Her experiences too have shaped her faith response and lead her to continue to worship in a Catholic community as well as to lead her own community.

> I'm a traditional Catholic. I'm not someone who would necessarily rally for inclusive language, although I know inclusive language works and I use it. I wouldn't have said, "Oh, we mustn't say this mass unless we cut out all the lords, and ladies and all the men and men language." I'm also not someone who would go out there and change the liturgy so that people don't understand it so that people don't recognize it. I am someone who feels that we take out tradition seriously and there's a capital T and a small t and both of them need to be honored in their own way. Both of them also need to have adjustments with every age. (Miriam, dialogue)

These phenomenological studies begin to give detail of the reasons for marginality. Yet, the dynamics of life on the margins are still difficult to discern. How do people sustain their faith? Are people continuing corporate worship? How do they define and live their own marginality? How do they understand their lives on the margins of the Catholic Church?

Catholics Once Active, but Now Gone

One study, the earliest model of directing its attention to people who were once active in the Catholic Church and who left, is an in-depth phenomenological study utilizing interviews by Robert Dixon. His work, commissioned by the Australian Catholic Bishops, seeks to address the gap in current research to learn the reasons why Catholics' attendance at Mass is decreasing, whether Catholics still describe themselves as belonging to the Catholic Church, and to discover if there are any factors that could attract these Catholics to begin attending Mass again.[52] His research team interviewed forty-one Catholics, aged twenty five and above, once active and engaged in their Church. The interviewed people, identified by their parish council, no longer attended weekly Catholic Mass. Participants' participation was obtained with the help of the parish councils in their former parishes. His research includes the participants' voices, his own voice, and that of fellow researchers in comments in the summary narrative. Dixon's data, which reflects the social context

52. Dixon et al., *Research Project on Catholics Who Have Stopped Attending Mass.*

of Australia, reveals a variety of factors that lead to a gradual decline in Church attendance. Participants often voice disagreement with the Church's teaching or policies, the irrelevance of the Church to a person's life, or disappointment with various aspects of the Church's performance including issues of misuse of power. While these are major reasons for a cessation of attendance at Mass, often smaller issues also lead to the final decision to stop Church attendance.[53]

Grounding Understanding in the Lived Experiences of the Margins

There is relatively little phenomenological research in the margins of the Catholic Church to help us understand the life-worlds on the margins of the Church. The research to date indicates shifts in church attendance and participation, marked by decreasing Catholic involvement. Such studies however give little information about the context of the margins, the meaning and relevance of marginality. This gap in research, reflecting a lack of dialogue with those on the margin, beckons practical theology.[54] Practical theology research attends to the shifts in the contemporary situation in a fluid, situational, continuous process, allowing the past and present to meet in new ways.[55] It guides its action toward individual and social transformation.[56] One of the transformations of a theology of marginality is that marginal persons move to an understanding of themselves as *in-beyond* people who can hold both being in the margins and the center together without merging these identities into one. Living *in-beyond* does not mean a person on the margins is free of the different worlds in which people exist, but rather lives in both of them without being bound by either of them.[57] A hermeneutics of transformation "articulates a new vision for a new humanity, a new global ecology, and a new religious community, in which relations of domination inscribed in texts, traditions, and everyday

53. Ibid.

54. Fulkerson notes that feminist theology has an orientation toward transformation (1994). She cites Fiorenza in her insistence that a sense of knowing is a positioned and value judgment, but also an issue of praxis that insists on an action orientation. She also notes Russell's treatment of feminist theology as praxis, "action that is concurrent with reflection or analysis and leads to new questions, actions, and reflections; it is a change in society" (Fulkerson, *Changing the Subject*, 39).

55. Fulkerson, *Places of Redemption*, 234.

56. Browning, *Fundamental Practical Theology*, 36.

57. Lee, *Marginality*, 63.

life are transformed by God's power at work in a community of believers into relationships of equality, dignity, and mutuality."[58]

A Perspective of Understanding and Living Faith

Dialogue with those on the margins of the Catholic Church grounds practical theology research in the lived experiences of those on the margins. It provides a perspective of the contribution of those on the margins to the ways we understand and live religion in the Catholic Church in the United States, as our traditions are being shaped in the context and circumstances of the world today. "The task is to fund, to provide the pieces, the materials and resources out of which a new world can be imagined. Our responsibility then, is not a grand scheme or coherent system, but the voicing of a lot of little pieces out of which people can put life together in fresh configurations."[59] Ted's comments point the way for the dialogue that is necessary.

> I think it's important that there be room for listening and that there is some action done. If there is a call, there needs to be a response, a couple of things here. I would like to see what they did in South America, South Africa about truth and reconciliation. That needs to happen, even in the St. ____ community, they say, "You guys that are upset about this, you need to get over it." Well, we didn't get over it when we had a racist priest and the whole parish marched down to the Archdiocese in the late sixties, and we're still talking about that. This disconnection or feeling of being alienated is just as powerful and it's very painful. So I think that's one thing that could happen, just to name that there is this disconnection. We need to seek to understand and we need to understand it together. Well that's just one thing, if the Church would do that, that would at least start the process of reconnecting and even if for the reason for clearing in the communities the negativity and the pain, even if just for that, even if people don't come back it's creating a space to clear this negative stuff that just hangs on us so that we all can move on. (Ted, dialogue)

---

58. Reid, *Taking Up the Cross*, 6. Biblical theologian Barbara Reid utilizes seven steps in biblical interpretation for exploration of all hermeneutic steps, including the hermeneutics of transformation from feminist, liberation perspectives.

59. Brueggemann, *Texts Under Negotiation*, 20.

My practical theology research tries to do just this—to seek to understand the margins of the Church together with those on the margins of the Church.

DIALOGUING ON THE MARGINS: PRACTICAL THEOLOGY RECIPROCAL ETHNOGRAPHY

Trinitarian Reciprocal Practical Theology Method

The practical theology method used in this research is cross-disciplinary in its methodological foundation and dialogic and reciprocal in its method. The doctrine of God as Trinity provides a theological foundation for the relational nature. I understand my practical theology method as praxis-centered, active dialogue that does not seek consensus, privileging multiple voices. Each stage progresses in dialogue with my dialogue partners, and in dialogue with four sources for practical theology: experience, tradition, reason, and the social sciences.[60] As a practical theologian I began each dialogue with my dialogue partners and with the multiple disciplines with which I am working with prayer, a dialogue with God. I sought to be open to the engagement of the Holy Spirit in the great mystery that the experiences of our daily lives reveal and prayed with hope that transformation, however that might look, will be possible out of this experience.

My practical theology research seeks the empowerment of those on the margins of the Church. It pays attention to the differences of each person's narrative as a means for identifying where the narrative threads reveal a new creative core developing. Its design is a feminist, reciprocal ethnography.[61] The knowledge shared and built in this method is based on dialogue in a collaborative, multi-voiced model. Ethnography asks questions about the lived experiences, daily lives and social context of groups of people, attempting to understand the 'life-world' of the margins of the Church, using the self to do so. In reciprocal ethnography the participants, as dialogue partners, ask and answer these questions as well. Reciprocal ethnography deepens the hermeneutical epistemology and furthers knowledge construction rather than affirming what I think I know. Both

---

60. Osmer, *Teaching Ministry of Congregations*, 307.

61. Lawless, *Holy Women, Wholly Women*. Elaine Lawless first used the term "reciprocal ethnography" to indicate research that involved the participants she was observing.

interviews and focus group experiences provide phenomenological research data.

My dialogue with dialogue partners consisted of semi-structured dialogues, audio-recorded, lasting approximately one hour. I exercised my own judgment and sought the participant's judgment about what is significant in both the interviews and the transcripts.[62] Many dialogue partners came to the conversation having reflected on the question themes that I had previously sent them, with points they wanted to emphasize to me. I received e-mail after the interviews with additional thoughts about the questions from several dialogue partners. Our conversations included discussion of the dialogue partners' involvement in their Church, and the process of ceasing attendance and their current attitudes about Church. Dialogue included my dialogue partners' discussion of their faith journey, any names they might call themselves indicating their space on the margins of the Church, and factors that might lead them to a Church in the future.[63]

Are You on the Margins of the Institutional Catholic Church?
I Want Your Voice to Be Heard!

Dialogue partners answered advertisements in Craigslist and local newspapers, or e-mails sent by progressive Catholic organizations such as Call To Action. None of the Craigslist or local newspaper advertisements generated dialogue partners who expressed their marginality as stemming from a wish for a more conservative Church. In the Northeast the advertisements placed in Craigslist and local newspapers initially produced only a couple of people volunteering to be dialogue partners. I changed the advertisement. Two changes motivated people to call according to their report. I added the statement "Let your voice be heard." I specified understanding the space on the margins as on the margins from the mainstream, *institutionalized* Catholic Church. A snowball strategy with dialogue partners recruiting other dialogue partners then generated sixteen e-mails within thirty-six hours and eleven dialogue partners.

62. Seidman, *Interviewing as Qualitative Research*, 100.

63. See Appendix B for the semi-structured interview guide I use. These questions were similar to those used by Robert Dixon in his study in Australia. Although my research questions are similar to Dixon's and there are similarities in our methods, my study also differs methodologically from Dixon's, giving more attention to phenomenological and theological considerations.

Making Knowledge Together

I facilitated two in-depth communal dialogues in focus groups in addition to individual dialogues. "The hallmark of focus groups is the explicit use of group interaction to produce data and insights that would be less accessible without the interaction found in the group."[64] Focus groups are beneficial in drawing out opinions on marginality as well as useful in addressing limitations of analysis. The two focus groups consisted of dialogue partners who are on the margins of the Church who, once interviewed, expressed an interest in conversation in these groups. After interview dialogue was coded for main themes and sub-themes, focus groups allowed for the theological reflection and social analysis of data generated from the dialogic interviews. Focus groups gathered twice, once in the South and once in the Midwest. All dialogue partners in driving distance to the focus group were invited to participate. Participants dialogued together, looking at themes and sub-themes from the dialogues and linking them relationally in a way that expresses their understanding of the experience of marginality in the Catholic Church. This process allows for theological reflection and social analysis of data generated from the dialogic interviews. It ensures that my dialogue partners are involved in making practical theology knowledge.

Awareness of the Effects of Context and Environment

I recorded reflections after each dialogue, and kept a journal in an attempt to identify biases and assumptions and to practice "holistic reflexivity."[65] I also explored how my own theoretical position and biography has affected my choice of dialogue partners and topics. I am attentive to my own structural, political, and cultural context and that of my participants throughout the dialogue process with my dialogue partners. My environment and context affects the research process and product. For that reason, I have worked to be fully transparent regarding my environment and context and to treat that as part of the data.[66]

64. Hesse-Biber and Leavy, *Feminist Research Practice*, 277.

65. Hesse-Biber, ed., *Handbook of Feminist Research*, 496.

66. Ibid.

WHO'S WHO IN DIALOGUE

Then I Started Doing Some Reading, which Is a Dangerous Thing

As young parents do, we had our children baptized. My faith life started to grow again as I started to be involved in their education. I started out teaching CCD at First Communion prep. I did Youth Group, as my kids grew. I was involved in liturgy, I was a, you know, a communion and a cup server, and I was on the liturgy committee. I was on the faith development committee. I was on all of the commissions except for Parish Council because I didn't want to be involved in the politics. And at some point my pastor said, "You know, you can do this for a living. Why don't you go back to school and get your MDiv and do this? You obviously have a bent for it." And so I did. (Jane, dialogue)

I went back for theology and philosophy credits and then decided to put it into a PhD and ended up doing up the Masters in Counseling. Before I applied for the PhD, I went for a second Masters in Divinity. But the Pope came over here and shook his finger at Sister Theresa Kane, that famous time, because she said in Abigail Adams' words, "Remember the women."[67] It was mild, totally mild, and he shook his finger at her. We were all watching this and I thought, "Oh, my God, I can't use this Masters of Divinity in the Church. I went on a retreat and I said, what the heck am I going to do? (Jackie, dialogue)

67. In 1979, Sister Theresa Kane addressed the Pope in his visit to the United States. "As women we have heard the powerful message of our church addressing the dignity and reverence of all persons. As women we have pondered these words. Our contemplation leads us to state that the church in its struggle to be faithful to its call for reverence and dignity for all persons must respond by providing the possibility of women as persons being included in all ministries of the church." The Pope was visibly annoyed (Jones, "Her 1979 Plea Unanswered").

Table 3: Dialogue Partners' Education

Generation (Age Range)	Percentage of Dialogue Partners	Total by Generation	Percentage with College Degrees	Total with College Degrees	Degrees in Theology/MDiv	Total Degrees in Theology/MDiv
Pre-Vatican II (70+)	30%	15	80%	12	40%	6
Vatican II(50–69)	32%	16	87.5%	14	25%	4
Post-Vatican II (30–49)	22%	11	54.5%	6	0	0
Post-Vatican II Millennial Generation (18–29)	16%	8	87.5%	7	14%	1
Total	50	50	78%	39	22%	11

Like Jane and Jackie, my dialogue partners as a group are very well educated.

Along with the eleven who have degrees in theology or divinity, many were active in Church ministries and participated in the conventions and training that often comes with such involvement. Many dialogue partners, like Bill, mentioned education, its importance, and its effect on opening them to new ideas.

> Listening to other people's stories and some people welcoming us to share our story, where we were and where we thought we were going; and asking for their guidance, their wisdom. It was an incredibly enriching experience. It was one of the turning points to experience that. I think it began to raise questions in my mind and then I started doing some reading, which is a dangerous thing, you know, you start looking at stuff. Suddenly, the Scripture classes that I'd been taking, New Testament and primarily the Gospels, the whole contemporary Scripture scholarship—you can't really say, "Well, it's in the Bible, this is what really happened." I went to hear a couple of lectures by Ray Brown a couple of years ago, and then I had a Gospel of Luke class and things just started clicking. So, between that and then my own life experience, reading a little bit of the history of the church. When you start reading, and whether it's the whole notion of celibacy, the history of ministry in the church, you start

studying about the early church, the life of the early church and what those early church communities looked like and sounded like, who was doing what, you start questioning and you start saying, "Why?" Somehow, I guess my understanding is that the hierarchy would like us to remain in the first century Palestinian mindset and culture and I don't think that's what Jesus really intended. I think Jesus intended that we live in today, and we're now in the twenty-first century. (Bill dialogue)

Education does not cause marginality. Rather, "Christian thinking arises in an organic way out of Christian life in order to address problems."[68] Education affects our practices and evokes responses. My dialogue partners address the experiences of their lives with creative thinking that is formed by a combination of their theological, cultural, political and autobiographical convictions. The high education level of my dialogue partners is reflected in their knowledge of Church structure and theological issues.

Living Faithfully

Most of my dialogue partners were active and involved Catholics in their parishes rather than "Sunday only" Catholics. My dialogue partners are lay, ordained, and religious. Their ministries ranged from spiritual direction, religious education, and prayer ministries to serving as liturgical and Eucharistic ministers, retreat work, and leading a number of Church programs. A number served on their parish councils. Peace and justice work, particularly work with the homeless and hungry, is extremely important to the majority of my dialogue partners. Their social justice ministries continue as my dialogue partners live on the margins of the Church. One participant is a retired priest in good standing, two are religious sisters, and three were priests who had sought and were granted laicization in order to marry.

A Window into the Reality of the Margins of the Catholic Church

This brief sketch of the available literature about people on the margins of the Church life, my own practical theology research, and my dialogue partners provides a small window into the reality of marginality today. In

---

68. Fulkerson, *Places of Redemption*, 233.

connection with my dialogue partners, a picture emerges of people who are well educated, active at one time in their Church, still active in peace and justice work, and claiming their catholicity by entering into a conversation with a practical theologian whom they had never met.

The next chapter builds from this chapter's empirical grounding to a more theoretical look at marginality.

> I don't know where the margin starts. You know, we're a minority, but minorities are not always marginalized. Sometimes they are the essence. The margins are where the change, the potential lies. It's all evolving. I might be marginalized and someone else might be way ahead of me. You have to catch up. Hey, wait for me, I'm your leader! So margins change. (Colleen, dialogue)[69]

69. It is remarkable that Colleen's comment emphasizing that margins are the places of change and potential coincides with Pope Benedict's own suggestions of the importance of creative minorities in this pluralistic postmodern moment. English historian Arnold Toynbee (1889–1975) suggested that creative minorities are able to generate the ideas and methods for meeting the challenges of today's world. These ideas and methods are then adopted by the majorities. See http://www.myriobiblos.gr/texts/english/toynbee.html.

2

Exploring the *Both-And*
of the Margins

I think my spirituality and my practice is (pause). I think where I am is more the center of the true Church than where the current institutional Church is. (Kellie, dialogue)

I guess I should say I was aware that we were outside the box but not how far. I was not aware of how much an exception we were, but I was aware that we were exceptional. Maybe more than I thought about previously. Yeah, I'm not outside the box and I am outside the box. It is the same. But now doing what feels right, and what feels like a life in the Gospel, and feels like what I was raised to think was important doesn't happen to match up with the box. (Anne, dialogue)

When you said margin, I saw myself there but you're out there, you're on the edge, you are barely a part of this big thing, so that's how I would translate it. (Sarah, dialogue)

KELLIE, ANNE, AND SARAH describe the margins of the Church differently. Kellie and Sarah understand the margins in relation to the center. Anne sees the margins as a *both-and* place that is both in the center and in the margin.[1] These different perspectives affect the meaning of margins for

---

1. I am choosing to write *both-and* with a hyphen rather than both/and, acknowledging the liminal space that is present on the margins with the understanding of being in both the margins and the center simultaneously.

those in them. The particular perspective of the margins taken by those on the margins and by the readers, whether oriented from the center or the margin, determines the meaning drawn from their narratives.

While chapter 1 and the dialogue of my conversation partners presents information about the lived experiences on the margins, this chapter's primary focus is a deeper understanding of the margins through the work of theologians and other theorists. They add to the dialogue by helping to critically advance our thinking about the context of the margins. Following a consideration of the concept of 'margin' as contextually formed embodied practices and an exploration of definitions of the margins, I consider the theology of marginality of Jung Young Lee, an Asian-American theologian. Lee's theology is rooted in the contextual, the autobiographical, and narrative. Exploration of a theology of marginality provides an understanding of the margins as *both-and* places that have the potential to move to an *in-beyond* creative space by bringing about inclusive relationship and an honoring of difference. Grounding the perspectives of the margins with this theology develops the narrative and allows further meaning and relationships to be discerned.

Naming the Context

> I would be interested in meeting with you. I'm a very appreciative graduate of Catholic schools where I learned values that have sustained me all these years. Also, I'm grateful for my wonderful childhood in a Catholic home. Like many of my friends, I feel betrayed by the institutional Church. "Power corrupts" is an apt adage for the leaders of my Church . . . (Potential dialogue partner, e-mail)[2]

I sit at the computer in a strange city clicking on an empty e-mail box, again. In three weeks I will arrive in another state for more dialogues with those on the margins. With airline tickets and car reserved, I have exactly two interviews scheduled. Are there people on the margins of the Church in this area willing to dialogue? Today, a dialogue partner described the context of her city: "People here are very, very closed in terms of who they are. Don't get me wrong, they are very warm and welcoming to people who are visiting, but when it comes to baring their laundry and talking

---

2. This dialogue partner continues to attend Mass and so is not among the fifty dialogue partners with whom I conversed.

about things, you almost have to be inside the circle in order for you to be acceptable for them to give you an opinion." I wonder, "Is this happening in ___?" I consider my own context as a woman, my journey learning to speak up when necessary and gaining my voice. I rewrite my Craigslist invitation to dialogue. I add, "Let your voice be heard." Another dialogue partner explains his context to me. He is on the margins of the institutional Church, but not on the margins of the Church understood as People of God. Do I need to spell out the context more explicitly in my invitation for this area of the country? I tweak my Craigslist invitation specifying understanding the space on the margins as on the margins from the mainstream *institutionalized* Catholic Church. Context matters. I receive sixteen e-mails in thirty-six hours. Eleven become dialogue partners.

CONTEXT: SPACE AND TIME

I lived in a Catholic community and the Church played an important social role in the community as well as a religious role in society. The social activity in the town revolved around the Church and some of the organizations of the Church like the Knights of Columbus and the Altar Society. My dad was very active. The whole psyche and psychology of everyone in this country was different. You helped your fellow man. My folks would get together with others and fill a box with food and canned goods and leave it out on the porch, knock and run off so they would not be beholden. We were raised with the Church and the belief of "Love your neighbor as yourself," and "Be your brother's keeper." Church was the center of your life. (Max, dialogue)

Interestingly, there are so many different perspectives out there, and so many different religions for that matter. It is tough to believe that I was just fortunate to be born and brought up in the right one. I really have a hard time with the line between these people who are going to be saved and these people who aren't. It doesn't necessarily determine whether you are a good person or not. To me, that's the ultimate question. Salvation or after life, if that exists, would be based on the quality of your life and how good a person you are and how you have treated others, not necessarily if you were taught XYZ and if you followed them. (Terry dialogue)

Born in the 1920s, Max grew up in a small town where the Church was the center of society. Terry was raised in the 1980s and 1990s when life and the world were in many ways more complex. In both cases one can understand the margins in terms of specific questions of culture, social relationships, and politics. Context matters when examining the perspectives of those on the margins.

Postmodernity: Influencing Our Language and Historicizing Our Imagination

For people on the margins and for practical theologians as well, conversations about the margins reflect a sense of belonging to the traditions in the past and the present, a critique of these traditions, and the ability to hold both in tension. Larger socio-cultural movements influence language and historicize our imagination.[3] Rapidly changing technology, a global economy, and accessible movement across the globe provide a context of increasing pluralism, difference, and diversity. These suggest a postmodern milieu.

Postmodernity can be defined in part as a reaction to the modern age of Western culture. The endorsement of universal reason, its assertion of an unchanging and absolute truth, and its ignorance of power relations inherent in relationships typify the modern age.[4] The theological understanding that humans "live within multiple historical trajectories, organizing and interpreting [their] lives out of plural sets of influences, not singular points to which all other values, commitments, and convictions are subordinated" confronts modernity's understandings.[5] The meaning of postmodernity varies, but the literature agrees that it is a moment in

3. Theologian Sheila Greeve Davaney proposes a pragmatic historicism that understands experiences in their broader social, political, and intellectual contexts. This movement rejects permanence and absoluteness, insists on self-criticism and continuing revision of its claims and conclusions. It is situated in the wider understanding of the contexts of embodiment and language. Language and ideas reflect the embodied selves in the physical universe. Power affects both (Davaney, *Pragmatic Historicism*; Dean, "Humanistic Historicism").

4. Davaney, *Historicism*, 141.

5. Ibid., 141. Modernity counters any monopolizing view of the self with logical, explicable principles. Modernity is basically about order, about rationality and rationalization bringing order from chaos. "The assumption is that creating more rationality is conducive to creating more order, and that the more ordered a society is, the better it will function (the more rationally it will function)" (Klages, "Postmodernity"). "In postmodernity, we are left with the task to utilize the relative and 'multi-relational' nature of knowledge to unite the disjointed fragments of legacies from relevant academic canons so that we can confront the issue of self-understanding squarely" (Lui, "Rethinking Cultural Marginality in a Postmodern Age," 13.)

time in which historical and systematic shifts in social arena, culture, and theory react to the modern age of Western civilization.[6] Today's postmodern society challenges a monochromatic view of the world. The margins in this postmodern view are not a single place or even a single lived experience; rather, margins consist of multiple experiences and multiple dialogues which exist side by side rather than merging into each other.[7] The margins reflect a place of shared dialogue, a postmodern place.

Framing the Margins: A Gathering of Embodied Practices

Can the margin of the Church exist as postmodern place? Rather than being a geographical location, postmodern place denotes a territory of meaning—an embodied gathering that frames a contemporary situation.[8] The margin of the Church as postmodern place consists of people who are making meaning out of their lived experiences. It cannot be defined narrowly as an *either* "in the church" *or* "out of the church" place. This defines the margins in traditional ways, from the institutional center. A theological reflection on the postmodern place of the margins insists on close attention to the bodily continuum of the experience and emphasizes the essential need for attending to the marginalizing differences.[9] This, plus the complexity of place compels the understanding of margins away

---

6. Ferguson and Wicke, eds., *Feminism and Postmodernism*, 2.

7. Bakhtin, *Problem's of Dostoevsky's Poetics*, 289. Mikhail Bakhtin (1895–1975) was a Russian communication theorist, philosopher, and literary critic. He lived through extraordinary times in Russia. Born in 1895, he survived the 1917 Russian Revolution, the Civil War afterwards, the Stalinist repression, the German invasion of the Soviet Union, the Cold War, the years of Khrushchev and Brezhnev (Dentith, *Bakhtinian Thought*, 1–21; Emerson, *First Hundred Years of Mikhail Bakhtin*, 3–23; Green, *Mikhail Bakhtin and Biblical Scholarship*, 11–23). He led a scholarly life despite his exile to Kazakhstan and his poor health, which was due to a debilitating bone disease, ostomyelitis (Clark and Holquist, *Mikhail Bakhtin*, 254; Emerson, *First Hundred Years of Mikhail Bakhtin*, 3, 70, 123).

8. Fulkerson, *Places of Redemption*, 28. Practical theologian Mary McClintock Fulkerson's work on postmodern place frames this conversation about the margins, allowing these margins to be seen as contextualized, fluid, grace-filled places where the Spirit of God is at work in the reality of people's experiences. Her book *Places of Redemption: Theology for a Worldly Church* provides a full discussion of postmodern place theory and its benefits for practical theology in conjunction with her exploration of practices in an interracial church.

9. Ibid., 232–52.

from common indicators of normal ecclesial boundaries such as institutions, set beliefs, or fixed practices.[10]

The margins of the Church are produced by their practices.[11] Feelings and narratives provide a unity of place that holds diversity and division, as well as complementarities with both those on the margins of the Church and those in the institutionalized or hierarchical Church. Both centrifugal and centripetal forces emerge in this embodied place bringing fluidity and characterizing it by constant process. Practices in the church through the culturally marked bodies of participants bring people face to face in communication with each other.

> I'm not under the umbrella of the teeny-tiny Catholic Church, but I consider myself under the umbrella of the broader universal Church; certainly not under the smaller umbrella of the hierarchical Church. On the other hand, I think Christ called us to live a certain kind of life. I think that lots of different people, lots of different groups who are doing that. (Cindy, dialogue)

In the multiplicity of narratives of those on the margins, the use of language reflects hermeneutic understanding of social locations and traditions. An awareness of marginalizing differences takes into account diverse interpretations in theological thought, the diverse voices, the assortment of feelings, and the multiplicity of narratives of those who are on the margins of the Church. Historical context influences these hermeneutic interpretations making them both changeable and fragile.[12] Conceptions of the past interconnect with interpretations that include our present understandings, our values, and commitments.[13] The time in which we are

10. Ibid., 254.

11. Sociologist, anthropologist, and philosopher Pierre Bourdieu (1930–2002) brings an understanding of practices as habitus that is embodied, socially, culturally, and politically shaped (ibid., 36–38).

12. This is reflective of the theological reflection of pragmatic historicism. It "grounds itself in the assumption that human beings, as biological and cultural creatures, reside within the complex fabric of interwoven realities, realities that depend upon both each other and the fabric as a whole to exist, survive and flourish" (Hopkins and Davaney, *Changing Conversations*, 35). This approach to theology determines responses and actions in the larger religious, cultural, and intellectual world of today.

13. "Languages are philosophies not abstract but concrete, social philosophies, penetrated by a system of values inseparable from living practice and class struggle" (Bakhtin, *Problems of Dostoevsky's Poetics*, 471). Philosopher John Macmurray (1891–1976), understanding the self as always in relationship, points to the power of communication as the capability to understand. Our power to communicate is "the capacity to enter into reciprocal communication with others" (MacMurray, *Persons*

living cannot be understood as totally different and disconnected from the past. It can be understood instead as constituted by that past and open to transformation in the present.[14] Dan gives an example.

> You and I sitting here, is essentially according to what I, anyway, think is essentially unconscious. But we acted. It forms our vision. And so then, we try to understand the context of our vision. And when we do that we get a sense of our contemporary culture and the sense of the society we live in. With that in mind, I am suggesting that, the way that I experience the hierarchy today, I am expected to deny that vision and deny the culture that I live in and the kind of society I live in, to deny the myths or the symbols of my vision. And I am supposed to leave it outside the Church as I walk in the Church door, so that I can adapt a pre-seventeenth century language. It is clearly Galileo revisited, and to me these are intelligent people. (Dan, dialogue)

Belonging and Non-Belonging: Toward a Creative In-Between?

In defining the margins, practical theologian Terry Veling proposes a hermeneutics that allows people to understand their experience of belonging and non-belonging to a tradition through a critique of their beliefs about the tradition that he terms dialogic hermeneutics.[15] This critique allows their experience of non-belonging to give rise to a hermeneutics of suspicion—exilic hermeneutics—and allows them to ponder both the belonging and non-belonging, permitting a creative in-between—marginal hermeneutics.[16] In this creativity, marginal place is the opening in which hermeneutics begins and ends—forms and reforms. One of the goals of this practical theology work is to bring forth the voices of those living on the margins of the Catholic Church and to begin to allow my dialogue partners to define their own understandings of this creative potential in

---

in Relation, 60).

14. This context begins with the assumption that we are historical people that exist in natural and cultural contexts. These historical contexts become the "product of intricate conscious and unconscious processes whereby the element of a given past and the contending dimensions of the current setting together result in distinctive configurations of historical existence" (Davaney, *Pragmatic Historicism*, 148). Thus, my dialogue partners reflect both modern and postmodern movements in their conversations.

15. Veling, *Practical Theology*, 18.

16. Ibid., 18–20.

their marginality. Jane's narrative is an example of one voice discussing both belonging and non-belonging.

> Anger is healthy and I think I feel let down by the Church. I know how systems are not . . . the Church was never nimble. But there's something about the tradition that still speaks to me and when I get back to that, there's great joy in that mystery, that unknowing, and being in touch with that. (Jane, dialogue)

In sum, a marginal hermeneutics invites belonging and non-belonging to exist side by side, holding the paradox. The embodied hermeneutic of postmodern place invites the voices of difference to participate in naming and defining the margins of the Church. I turn now to definitions of the margin, looking for the variety of definitions of margins, understanding they may be defined from the center. This undergirds the contemporary experience of margins providing clues to the past and opening the margins for transformation in the present.

DEFINING THE MARGINS: FORMED BY THE PAST AND OPEN TO TRANSFORMATION IN THE PRESENT

What's in the Word Margin?

Different words for the margins—including margin, marginal, and marginality—emerged at different times in history. The meaning of the word *margin* changed since its first use during the Middle Ages. *Margin* was first used in the fourteenth century to mean a border space. The word *marginal* was later applied to an individual or social group isolated from, or not conforming to, the dominant society or culture, and was used as an economic term in 1926, indicating of little effect or importance. Gradually, modern culture began to accept that people on the margin are marginalized in the economic, cultural, and political aspects of their lives, unable to contribute in important areas of society. Today, *marginality*, a dynamic word, has been defined spatially as "straddling two different concrete areas, sharing something of both but belonging entirely to neither."[17]

17. Meier, *Marginal Jew*, 7.

Marginality

Janice Perlman worked in the late 1960s in Brazil to understand the "myth of marginality"—the myth that those on the margins are unable to contribute in important areas of society. She discredited this idea by finding that those on the economic margins due to poverty in fact contributed to society. However, they did not benefit from the goods and services of the society and instead were manipulated, suppressed, and exploited.[18] The myth of marginality benefited the status quo by creating the perception that the poor are incapable of such contribution.

Perlman's study suggests questions about contributions of others on the margins as well, including those on the margins of the Catholic Church. It suggests a need to ask questions concerning attitudes that correlate the place on the margins of the Church with lack of contribution by people on the margins. This leads to an exploration of the dynamics of marginality and relationship on the margins of the Church. In what ways do people on the margins and the dynamics of marginality related to the dynamics of the larger Church contribute to the larger institutional Church?

Marginalizing Giving Way to Exclusion?

Perlman includes exclusion in the experience of being marginalized. Exclusion puts people outside the margins, making them nonexistent.[19] Perlman argues that "factors of power relations, agency, culture and social identities come into play [in exclusion], an environment in which individuals do not have access to public resources, [and] as a result they are able to contribute but not able to receive."[20] Perlman states that since the 1990s, the myth of marginality is the reality of marginality for the poor, particularly the poor in Brazil whom she studied. Similarly, practical theologian Norbert Mette suggests that in the twenty-first century, exclusion replaces

18. Perlman, *Myth of Marginality*. Perlman, founder and president of the Megacities Project and professor of urban and regional planning, received numerous awards for her work and for her book *Myth of Marginality*, which is considered one of the most important books on urban studies in the last forty years. Her work reiterates the necessity of understanding that too often the margin is defined by those in political, cultural, or social power (Perlman, *Myth of Marginality*).

19. Mette, "Exclusion," 93–94. Practical theologian Norbert Mette is at Dortmund University's Institute of Catholic Theology in Germany.

20. Perlman, *Myth of Marginality*, 12.

marginality with nonexistence. Because exclusion declares human beings superfluous, their ability to participate and contribute in the social life of the community is taken away.[21] Mette proposes that exclusion "does matter to Christians especially . . . This exclusion does not only refer to Christians but also to members of other religions and philosophies of life. Therefore a dialogue with these members is necessary and cooperation in solidarity. Common matter must be to put up resistance against the fact that human beings are declared excluded and unnecessary and to insist on the fundamental dignity of every human being."[22]

> It's my church, you're not going to take me out. I was born and raised in this family and who are you to tell me that I can't be. Who are you to tell me that my grandmother and my grandfather, all these people who brought me up, surrounded me with love. The church is saying to me, and I want you to put this in your thesis. The church is exactly saying to me, "I do not exist." A woman who is working on a large article on me called the archdiocese. She called the archdiocese and said she would like to have an opposite viewpoint. "She does not exist," is what they said. She said, "Oh really, I just had an interview with her." They said, "Well that might be you, but as far as we are concerned, she does not exist." (Miriam, dialogue)

> So it's some of the real teachings that's going on that exclude people. I think so and have a certain amount of shame or guilt that is tied to it and should we really feel that way? But maybe some of those things didn't bother me until all of a sudden because of my divorce I was put into a category of shame. (Sade, dialogue)

Changing Things with Your Feet or Your Money

Michel de Certeau adds to the concept of marginality by rooting it in modernity's emphasis on consumerism.[23] Marginality today is "no longer limited to minority groups, but is rather massive and pervasive, this cultural

21. Mette, "Exclusion," 96.

22. Ibid.

23. Michel de Certeau (1925–1986), French Jesuit philosopher, proposes that a representation of everyday practice is necessary to understand the way people who are marginalized superimpose their own practices on cultural systems that would use groups or individuals (Certeau, *Practice of Everyday Life*, 64). While Certeau wrote in modern times, his analysis is still an important one today in consumerist, individualistic culture.

activity of the non-producers of culture . . . Marginality is becoming universal. A marginal group has now become a silent majority."[24] This definition exposes the hidden power relations of production and its effect—marginalization. For Certeau, consumption is really production because its expression is through the many ways that the dominant economic order imposes use of products. People on the margins, from their place on the margins, reinterpret and appropriate the uses of the production in ways different than the culture would demand in their everyday life. My dialogue partners evidenced Certeau's concept of marginality in two ways. First, they superimposed their practice of withholding contributions to the church as a means of expressing discontent by challenging the cultural expectation for support of Church. Cindy and Julian provide examples.

> I really think the only true way to change things is either with your feet or with your money, and if people really left in droves and quit contributing, I think the powers that be would listen a little more. (Cindy, dialogue)

> But the more I thought about when I am in a church and I'm going to give my money to a church I'm going to support I really don't want to support a church where woman aren't allowed to be leaders at the highest level. (Julian, dialogue)

Secondly, dialogue partners use their economic resources in ways that are countercultural and important to their faith beliefs. Harry is an example of this.

> You know, it all goes back to when I was thirteen or fourteen years old when I had my first income. I took $149 and went to the bank, got a cashier's check and gave it to one of the nuns at school. I said, "Use this to teach the kids in Bogotá." They had a mission down in Bogotá. It didn't hurt very much, and so ever since then I've been doing non-profit stuff and contributing. Now I'm on four non-profit boards. (Harry, dialogue)

Sites of Resistance

Writing a decade later, in 1990, feminist English professor and social activist bell hooks describes margins differently as sites that are socially constructed for people considered to be of no account by dominant

---

24. Ibid., xvii.

groups. This concept of marginality is located in the experiences of marginalized groups. These often emotional experiences may be places for connection to other marginalized people or sites for struggle in support of important beliefs. "I make a distinction between that marginality that is imposed by oppressive structures and that marginality one chooses as a site of resistance."[25] Both Deb and Sarah, in some ways, choose their place on the margins. Deb wonders about life experiences that cause her to share differences of opinion with the Church, increasing her marginality. Sarah understands her place on the margins as a prophetic place that is a site for struggle.

> I don't know if it's that I've not found the right place, or even if as I've gotten older that my personal, political, whatever you want to call it, beliefs may not necessarily mesh in with those of the Church. The conservative values are not necessarily the ones that I want to believe in, just a personal preference in all the big issues of the Church. (Deb, dialogue)

> So, we had liturgy, of course, and I don't go to liturgies in my congregation because we neglect the inclusive language and we neglect inclusive imagery; we still are afraid, so I don't go anymore. This is what I do. My community knows that I stand in protest when we have these liturgies without inclusivity. You know, I do believe that a prophet is one who stands up and speaks when everybody else is seated and silent. And who in their right mind wants to be called a prophet? (Sarah, dialogue)

A THEOLOGY OF MARGINALITY

Moving from Either/Or to Both-And to In-Beyond

Jung Young Lee[26] proposes a theology of marginality to provide another way to understand the margins and marginality. The theology of J. Y. Lee creates a space for dialogue in both the center and the margins. It holds promise for allowing those on the margin of the Church to transform their negative experiences and pain into something positive. I find Asian and Asian-American theologies rich and relevant as I continue to learn

25. hooks, *Yearning*, 153.

26 Korean American theologian Jung Young Lee (1930–1996) developed a theology of marginality that theologically brings together the *in-between* of both cultures, understanding himself *in-both* worlds.

from the blessings of diversity. While western culture is more comfortable with a dualistic mind, Asian theology, with an Eastern mindset, contributes to the ability to hold ambiguity and paradox.[27] This enables the ability to hold both the Christian tradition of the past and the present together by respecting both for the contributions they make.[28] J. Y. Lee offers his work for others to use. "While I write this to assist my own understanding of marginality and to help determine a way to cope with my own marginal status in North America, I hope this work may become a catalyst for others to reflect on their experience . . . My study may appeal to all marginalized people."[29]

J. Y. Lee moves through his own autobiographical journey to share how this understanding impacts the Christian story[30] As an adult immigrant to the United States from Korea, J. Y. Lee was often on the margin of American society as both an Asian and an American in the United States. These experiences caused him to insist that the self-understanding of those on the margin is important for a full understanding of margin.[31] While Lee understands the margins from an Asian-American focus, I am trying to understand the margins of the Catholic Church by focusing on dialogues with people on the margins of the Catholic Church.

27. A binary way of thinking, dividing things into opposites and choosing between them, is characteristic of the Western mode of thought; the Eastern mode sees life and the opposites present not so much as in opposition or conflict, but as a part of a whole (T. Fox, *Pentacost in Asia*, 96)

28. It is with respect and humility that I draw on Asian theologians who have been influential in providing wisdom and relevant perspectives for my understanding of the margins, particularly Dr. Jung Young Lee. Choan-Seng Song's work provides the value of story (Song, *Tell Us Our Names*). Chun Hyun Kyung engages with the poignant and powerful story of struggling in suffering to claim identity as one created by God (Kyung, *Stuggle to Be the Sun Again*). Kwok Pui-lan's work imparts a feminist postcolonial theology (Pui Lan, *Postcolonial Imaginationa and Feminist Theology*). Peter Phan provides insights into an Asian American theology (Phan, *Journeys on the Margin*). Finally, Chansoon Lim offers an understanding of the work of Jung Young Lee in the context of postmodernity (Lim, "Suffering, Change, and Marginality").

29. J. Y. Lee, *Marginality*, 2.

30 Ibid., 33. Johann Baptist Metz (b. 1928) understands theology as biography rising from an understanding of Christianity as a community that remembers and tells stories with a practical intent. It is "in [such stories that] the mystical biography of religious experience, one's life history before the hidden face of God, is inscribed into the doxography of faith" (Metz, *Faith in History and Society*, 199). This impacts my own theological understanding of the margins, bringing out the importance of the voices of the people and their narratives.

31. Phan, "Jesus the Christ with an Asian Face," 414.

THE CLASSIC VIEW OF MARGINS AS EITHER/OR

J. Y. Lee understands marginality differently from the traditional perception of people on the margins as *either* in *or* out. The classic definition of 'margins' defines the margin solely from the center by focusing on an *either/or* situation or experience, *either* in the center *or* out.[32] When the margin is defined from the perspective of the center, the margin becomes secondary. This is the traditional definition of the margins. Jean draws the lines for the margins of the Church from the center as related to the institutional church. For her, the margins are *either/or*, either in the institutional Church or out, and she considers herself out. Julia also considers the margins in an *either/or* way.

> I'm a cultural Catholic, I was born Catholic, my language is Catholic, my perspective is Catholic; it sort of get's into your DNA, I'm not an institutional Catholic. (Jean, dialogue)

> From that point on I would tell people I left the Catholic Church to beat the rush. So, for awhile after that I just didn't go to church. (Julia, dialogue)

In this part of Julia's narrative, she states that she is definitely not in the Church, because she has chosen to leave. For Julia, at this time in her narrative, she is either in or out. Yet, margins are interdependent on each other for definition. Without the center there is no margin, but there is also no center without the margins.[33]

Julia, later in her narrative, expresses a different understanding of marginality.

> Somebody can be on the margins, but also in the center of things. I'll tell you that the one thing that drives me absolutely crazy is when people who are traditional, conservative Catholics say, "If you're a progressive Catholic, you're not part of the Church. They're not real Catholics." They are two different places on a continuum. What makes you get to say that you are the right one, the official one? Just because you have the backing of the bishops, that isn't a particularly convincing argument to me. So, it really bugs me when the progressive wing, and we are a wing, is somehow illegitimate and the conservative wing is legitimate. (Julia, dialogue)

32. J. Y. Lee, *Marginality*, 62, 69.
33. Ibid., 30.

This narrative suggests a perception of the margins different than the classic perspective. Julia's concept of margin moves from an initial understanding in which she is *either* in *or* out of the Church during our dialogue to an understanding of the margins that is defined on a continuum. Marginality and centrality can be seen as mutually inclusive with neither deserving stress over the other.[34] The margins, defined in the lived experiences of those on the margins, are dependent on the contexts in which this marginal status is defined.[35]

JESUS-CHRIST: THE CREATIVE CORE OF THE MARGINS

Our Story Engages with Jesus' Story

A theology of marginality begins first with a person's own story, and provides the context for the theology. Then, taking the centralist understanding of the margins as *in-between*, or *either/or,* it moves this understanding to *both-and*, in *both* the center *and* the margins. It engages the *both-and*, uniting our story with the Jesus story: Jesus' life, death, and resurrection. In his full humanity and full divinity, he is *both-and* Jesus-Christ.[36] Feminist theologian Kwok Pui-lan notes Jesus-Christ and Jesus/Christ as a hybridized concept where the space "between Jesus and Christ is unsettling and fluid, resisting easy categorization and closure."[37] The hyphen in Jesus-Christ is the liminal place—the place where a new understanding of Jesus-Christ reaches beyond the interpretations that have been made by those in the center. Jesus-Christ in his life and ministry used reception rather

34. Ibid., 31.

35. Ibid., 3. Many of my dialogue partners are on the margins of the Catholic Church, but leaders and solidly in the center in Small Christian Communities, Intentional Eucharistic Communities, social justice organizations, and in their professional lives. They may be on the margins of the Roman Catholic Church but many are in the center economically, racially, ethnically, etc. Many were also once in the center of the Roman Catholic Church and have now moved to the margins. This holds some important psychological differences among other things. It is a very different marginality from being poor, which "means not only economic, material deprivation but also being subjected to cultural rules that convey a complete lack of recognition of poor people as bearers of rights" (Perlman, *The Myth of Marginality*, 12).

36. J. Y. Lee writes Jesus-Christ with a hyphen to indicate his marginality because Jesus is the Christ and Christ is Jesus (Lee, *Marginality*, 78).

37. Pui-Lan, *Postcolonial Imagination and Feminist Theology*, 171.

than dominance to change the world.[38] Reception rather than dominance informs J. Y. Lee's theology.

The Incarnation of Jesus-Christ: Living Fully, Loving

J. Y. Lee reinterprets Jesus as divine marginality that indicates the incarnation of Jesus changes everything.[39] "Both incarnation and creation are divine marginalizations: incarnation is the subjective or inner marginalization of the divine while creation is the objective or outer marginalization of the divine."[40] God cares for God's 'marginal' creation. God's covenant (*berith* in Hebrew), so powerfully seen in God's care of the Jewish people, is now a covenant for people through the ages through God's kenosis, God becoming fully human in Jesus. It is a movement of God into humanity, into suffering, and into the margin. God is revealed in Jesus and in this revealing what it means to be human is broken open and expanded. "God comes to us disguised as our life." [41]

God, revealed in the person of Jesus as a marginal person, is very different from past expectations.[42] Jesus, marginalized by historians and politicians of his time as insignificant, by his birth to an unwed woman in a stable, and by his death on a cross as a criminal, is puzzling. His marginalization by his association with the sick and the poor, the weak and the rejected, by his teachings and healings, and the fact that he marginalized himself, becoming an itinerant preacher for those who were culturally, ethnically, socially, physically, sexually, and politically marginal is also

38. Lee, *Marginality*, 71–72.

39. Teilhard de Chardin's vision provides understanding of this. His vision was helping people see Christ in all things and all things in Christ so that people could see and feel the presence of God everywhere (King, *Christ in All Things*).

40. J. Y. Lee, *Marginality*, 173.

41. Rohr, *Things Hidden*.

42. A midrash approach, retrieving our roots in Judaism, is congruent with an understanding of Jesus in the theology of marginality. "The midrashic approach finds the division between 'the Jesus of history' and 'the Christ of faith' to be a false dichotomy, based on a misguided assumption of two stages of reality: (1) the 'real' Jesus and (2) myths created about him. The dichotomy dissolves if one approaches Mark's text [and I would add other Jesus texts] as a midrashic composition in which, from the beginning, history and faith intersect. Reading Mark as midrash raises the expectation of multiple and varying scriptural perspectives intersecting with history and arranged into a poetic whole that provides neither a biography nor a 'definition' of Jesus but rather engages its audience in reflecting on the mystery of his identity" (Sabin, *Reopening the Word*, 116–17).

puzzling. Jesus' marginality roots theology in the margins. "The usefulness of the historical Jesus to theology is that he ultimately eludes all our neat theological programs; he brings all of them into question by refusing to fit into the boxes we create for him."[43]

The whirlwind, according to Kwok Pui-lan, represents the many voices of those throughout the centuries who have been marginalized by the boxes we create and centralist understandings of Jesus. "Sometimes we need to get out of our comfort zone in order to encounter God anew and to listen to the gentle voice of God arising from the whirlwind." [44] Theological discourse, like any other, is not neutral but reproduces the shape of the world as it is experienced by dominant populations.[45] Because of this, all understandings of Jesus reflect the ideologies and social situations of the person or community interpreting them.[46] Too often "his followers wanted to be part of the central authority to rule and dominate the world. Christians became increasingly interested in his power and forgot that it is his weakness that made him powerful and his humility that raised him to be the Lord of Lords."[47]

> My relationship with Jesus changes if I get over that big story that Jesus had to die for my sins. If I can do away with that, then I can look at Jesus more personally and deeper and he came to teach and to bring love and his life was so full of love and it just changes the whole person of Jesus, the whole concept of Jesus. It's this far off person who suffered for me, that's what I grew up with. It brings God to you differently. (Lily, dialogue)

Lee's theological understanding of marginality beckons Christians to follow Jesus as new marginal people of God.[48] His foundations for this theological understanding are the doctrine of God as Trinity and Asian yin-yang thinking. Both emphasize the harmonizing of opposites, inclusivity, and relationality. Understanding an embodied humanity Lee's

---

43. Meier, *A Marginal Jew*, 199. Biblical scholar Msgr. John Meier has written multiple books on Jesus, "the marginal Jew," linking the Jesus of faith with the Jesus of history.

44. Pui-Lan, *Postcolonial Imagination and Feminist Theology*, 170.

45. Fulkerson, *Places of Redemption*, 254.

46. B. Lee, *Jesus and the Metaphors of God*. "Every interpreter comes with a history, a social situation, a social class and a vested interest" (ibid., 25).

47. J. Y. Lee, *Marginality*, 78.

48. Ibid., 101.

theology stresses movement rather than stasis and interconnectedness.[49] These lead to a focus on *both-and* thinking where unity and coexistence in relationship change both the margin and the center as relationship changes.[50]

Margins as Both-And Places—
Opening to a New Definition of Margin

Both-and thinking is a holistic and open-ended thought process that forms the margins and the center into a harmonious whole.[51] People on the margins live at multiple margins or centers, depending on the perspectives of those involved, as they both define their status as *either* in the center *or* in the margin, or as *both* in the margin *and* in the center at the same time. Margins hold both perspectives. Understanding the margins as *both-and* places restores the balance that was lost from defining the margins from a position of centrality. *Both-and* thinking affirms both worlds, even if one world denies the other's existence. A *both-and* definition uses both the positive and negative elements of the margin and views marginality as dynamic and unfixed.

A practical theological understanding of the margins as *both-and* draws on the ancient Hebrew people's way of understanding a word. This perspective uses the epistemological function of narrative structure, providing information about who God is, as "a kind of deep story that a people live out of in all its particular stories."[52] The deep story is not created by the person, but rather a person awakens to it and makes it real by living the story out in a historical moment.[53] "The Hebrew word is not a 'movement

49. Lee, *The Trinity in Asian Perspective*, 50–70.

50. Ibid., 50–60.

51. Lee, *Marginality*, 69.

52. B. Lee, *Jesus and the Metaphors of God*, 29. Practical theologian Bernard Lee understands the Hebraic tradition as always open to redevelopment, through the process of responding and interacting with new social situations and new religious experiences (ibid., 113). The implications for our construct of knowledge are enormous. The Jewish tradition is formed with more of an empirical imagination. "Knowing is for the sake of practice. It is in the service of qualitative living" (B. Lee, *Galilean Jewishness of Jesus*, 23) "One critical dimension of fidelity to Jesus is a commitment to continuing reinterpretation of the meaning of God in new historical, social and cultural institutions." Interpretation "not only projects the meaning behind the texts, but more primordially projects new possibilities out in front of our lives." (B. Lee, *Galilean Jewishness of Jesus*, 117).

53. This suggests a movement in Christian self-understanding that moves from

away' from itself towards vision and abstraction; the word leads inward into itself, not outwards towards the 'thing.'"[54] This type of thinking leaves the word margin open to multiple meanings, and interpretations which are dynamic, yet rooted in the word and the past interpretations which have taken place. It allows one on the margins to feel the tension of both belonging to and voicing one's critical analysis of the tradition, attempting to allow each its justifiable claim and living with the ambiguity of is-like and is-not-like in order to understand a fuller meaning.[55] When the paradox of belonging and non-belonging exists at the same time, it signals a move to *in-beyond*.

IN-BEYOND HARMONIZING THE DIFFERENCES

In-beyond brings together both our "roots and [our] branches," the traditions of our past with the traditions of the present, respecting both, and sitting in the paradox of their relationship.[56] A person *in-beyond* lives in both worlds by harmonizing the differences not transcending them.[57] "The essence of being *in-beyond* is not a by-product of being in-between or being in-both; rather it embodies a state of being in both of them without either being blended."[58] This means living in both worlds without being bound to either of them. [59]

> I think that's where Jesus was, he was always on the margins, there's no doubt about that, but there are a lot of people whose

our traditional Christian understanding of perfection and God as changeless to an understanding of mutuality with God and God in Jesus—God in relation and changing according to human need. Understanding God from this perspective opens the margins to new interpretation of religious norms based on God's particular work in history.

54. Veling, *Living in the Margins*, 156. This understanding brings together dualistic and non-dualistic thinking. Western thought patterns reflect the Greek philosophy path where there is a dualistic split between spirit and matter, divinity and humanity, with spirit more highly valued. This has led to a devaluing of the body and a hypervaluing of rationality. The Hebrew historical pattern uses a more non-dualistic view of creation. It sees God as loving, active, and involved in history. Spirit and matter both are perceived as important. (Johnson, *Quest for the Living God*, 108–9). The Asian thought path reflects the Hebraic pattern.

55. Veling, *Living in the Margins*, 135.

56. J. Y. Lee, *Marginality*, 49.

57. Ibid., 63

58. Ibid., 62.

59. Ibid., 64.

life experiences have kinda put them where they are. That's where they are and I think that's where I need to meet them and welcome them. (Bill, dialogue)

When the margins become *in-beyond* places, a holistic picture of the margins forms. The *in-between* and the *both-and* come together in the *in-beyond*, each having its place. As in-beyond is affirmed, the value of the center changes and the space becomes the margin of marginality. The margin is the crucial point, a new and creative core—where the two worlds of the center and the margin co-exist.[60] A theology of marginality is open to the viewpoints from the center as well as those from the margin. *In-beyond* affirms both in-between and in-both, and balances the two poles of centrality and marginality. Thus, it brings harmony.

The Federation of Asian Bishops' Conferences (FABC) suggests that in Asian theology and culture "harmony embodies 'the realities of order, well-being, justice and love as seen in human interaction' . . . Harmony is not simply the absence of strife . . . The test of true harmony lies in acceptance of diversity and richness."[61] When diversity is accepted and valued, the margins can provide an opportunity for insight. Joe holds both his feelings of marginalization and the knowledge that he is in the center as a priest together in tension.

> I can't work with them [the current hierarchy] easily so that has kind of brought me on the margins, that phrase, you know, comfortable but fortunately in my retirement . . . And so I have been retired for fifteen years and during these years I find that a good part of my ministry is to people who are alienated or disenchanted or are on the margins and looking for something that will bring them spiritual nourishment . . . What's going to happen eventually, I feel in my heart, progress will eventually be made. We have to have that faith because I believe that good never dies. Good does not die. The good that the Council proposed will prevail. We're going through a backlash; I don't really want to call it a historical thing. We're right in the midst of it. But, uh we have to be faithful in our own way and help one another where we're at. It's God's work. (Joe, dialogue)

A theology of marginality encourages the *in-beyond* through dialogue and an opportunity to voice the experiences and needs that contribute to alienation and marginalization. This action moves those on the margins to

60. Ibid., 98.

61. USCCB, *Asian and Pacific Presence*, 278.

opportunities for creative understanding of the margins. Transformation results and often produces a space *in-beyond* where "centrality becomes marginality, marginality changes to new marginality and all people become marginal."[62]

TRANSFORMING THE MARGINS IN LIMINAL SPACE

A theology of marginality shifts attention from living always seeking centrality to living with ambiguity and paradox, affirming marginality rather than denying it. The margin can never become a new center because a theology of marginality seeks inclusivity, cooperation, service to others, and non-domination of others. "Marginality is not a stage toward centrality but a radical process of shifting one's value system, itself, which is an egalitarian principle to radically reconstruct the existence of the center."[63] When the margins coexist they encourage inclusivity and also the most relational forms of thinking.[64] Margin then becomes a relational term.

IT'S DIFFICULT BUT WORTH ENCOUNTERING GOD IN THE MARGINS

While J. Y. Lee's theology of marginality is a theology formed in the margins of ethnic marginality, I appropriate it here for those on the ecclesial margins of the Catholic Church. It begins in the validation of the experience of those on the margins and their perspectives.[65] It suggests pursuing genuine participation and dialogue, valuing those on the margins as partners in theological reflection. This requires an awareness of the multidimensions of marginality and involves questions of agency. The theology of marginality seeks practical theological awareness of a theologian's own marginality or lack of it. With awareness, theologies may emerge from the

62. J. Y. Lee, *Marginality*, 169–70.

63. Lim, "Suffering, Change, and Marginality," 192.

64. J. Y. Lee, *Marginality*, 70.

65. Ibid., 172. Jung Young Lee's theology of marginality deepens understanding of practical theology in line with other practical theologians, including Schleiermacher, Van der Ven, and Immink. Schleiermacher's (1768–1834) theology understood experience as the starting point for all theology. "That he viewed praxis as the basis and organizing principle for theology as a whole . . . is clear from his understanding of theology as a positive science"(Heitink, *Practical Theology*, 25). Schleiermacher rooted the action of theology in Christianity in the context of changing society, in the praxis of the faith, and in the Church (ibid.).

margins that address the concrete social, political, cultural, and religious concerns of the people and relate the Christian tradition directly to the experiences of the people.

In sum, given an understanding of the margins as *both-and* places, the margins can be defined on a continuum including both margin and center. A theology of marginality seeks a holistic understanding of the margins.[66] Yet, it realizes that any theology of marginality will always be unfinished work.[67] Marginality is a process of movement, creativity, and change for those who risk encountering God in the margin. Fully reaching the potential of the margins described by my dialogue partners requires a relational anthropological understanding. It requires a way to hear the movement in the dialogue through the life experiences told in the narrative of dialogue.

The next chapter turns to anthropology asking, "Who are we as humans?" Fully answering these questions requires exploring the doctrine of God as Trinity, which leads to an anthropology that is relational. I put this relational anthropology into dialogue the communication theory of Mikhail Bakhtin on dialogue, outsideness, and authoring. My purpose is to further uncover relationality, contributing to an understanding of the margins from the standpoint of relationship and dialogue.

66. J. Y. Lee, *Marginality*, 67.
67. Ibid., 172.

3

Contemplating Self-Identity

> I went through some of the catacombs, you know, we stopped
> and the tour guide was jabbering away, and there was a niche
> right beside me, and I just ran my hand over the dirt, and I was
> just thinking, this is part of our family; this dirt is part of one of
> our family. (Bill, dialogue)

TODAY, IN THE LIMINALITY of the margins, intersubjective space is shared
in ways unknown before, due in part to the current advances of technology. Yet, people continue to contemplate self-identity, much as those in
the early Christian communities did, trying to understand themselves as
Jewish followers of Jesus after the destruction of the temples in 70 CE.[1]
A relational anthropology provides a frame for dialogue with people on
the margins of the Catholic Church and shapes the conversation in this
chapter as well as later chapters.

The primary focus of this chapter is to establish an understanding of
the human person as relational, in light of the doctrine of God as Trinity informed by pneumatology and communication theory. The doctrine of God
as Trinity provides the foundation for understanding human relationality.[2]
The work of Mikhail Bakhtin suggests that relational anthropology may enable the action of dialogue to form and re-form us as humans.[3] Through

1. Senior, "Matthew's Gospel and the Jewish Context of Early Christianity."

2. LaCugna, *God for Us*, 289.

3. Communication theorist Mikhail Bakhtin (1895–1975) suggests, as did many

the use of the Bakhtian concepts of dialogism (dialogue) as well as related theories of authoring and outsideness, I endeavor to surmount any binary and/or dualistic thinking and develop intersubjective thinking to help situate practical theology dialogue of those on the margins of the Church.

FORMING RELATIONSHIP

It is late afternoon in a strange city, and I head for a small apartment where I will meet my next dialogue partner. We conversed via postal service mail, as she does not "do computers." She serves as one of my contacts for the Intentional Eucharistic Community with whom I am in dialogue. She is a delightful "wisdom woman" of a certain age, extroverted to the extreme, full of vim and vigor, and passionate about social justice. We begin talking about relationships in the Church, and this leads us to images of God.

> I think that thinking brings you to new experiences and moves the concept of God. You know, it isn't just vertical. God with the beard is gone forever more. The more you get involved with people's lives, the more horizontal the God concept is and your spirituality is involved with other people. You know women happen to be made in the image and likeness of God as well as men. It just helps to know that God is mother, father, whatever. I don't see God as neutral either because all we've got in life is male and female, whether its bugs or humans. The male/female process is where life comes from, so I see God as male/female. It is a he/she, my he/she God. I don't even like to see it in terms as man/woman, that's another concept. There's got to be a word that includes both, but I see it as a male and female concept, God is bigger than man/woman. The male qualities and the female qualities are what give life to something so that's how my concept of God is. (Colleen, dialogue)

The time passes swiftly. Colleen's understanding of God as relational undergirds her understanding of herself called to relationship. She is outspoken in just war issues and the need for relationship with the poor and needy, the hungry, and the homeless. She describes herself as a discovering

---

others in his time, that dialogue turns away from thinking about identities as fixed, toward the idea of persons who construct their identities through dialogue with others. This "moves toward a vision that presents identities that humans hold as multiple and variable, yet at the same time situated and specific constructions, grounded in the spatio-temporal and discursive contexts of their intersubjective articulations" (Peeren, *Intersubjectivities and Popular Culture*, 11).

Catholic. "I just keep discovering new ways of discovering community and God. It's always new and that's how I like to see myself."

GOD'S INVITATION TO RELATIONSHIP

As human beings, both female and male, this likeness to God shows itself relationally in relationship to God and relationship with all of creation.[4] Ecological theologian Sallie McFague asks, "What if we begin to realize that the community model—the model in which human individuals must fit into a just, sustainable planet—is a necessity?"[5] Her work offers a holistic anthropology that understands human persons as related to the whole cosmos as well as each other. Dan's relational understanding of our connectedness to those in our past and our future informs his actions on the margins of the Church. Catholic anthropology holds that, as human people, people are social beings in need of others in order to realize our true humanity.[6]

> In Chartes, one of the doors, there's a carving; the doorframe is actually a series of people who are ascending into heaven. The image is that each person is holding on to the heel of the person above them—probably a thirty-foot door frame, carved in stone. And it's just a reminder that we're not in this alone, we're holding onto our ancestors, and it's part of who I am. It's not Roman in exclusion of the Jerusalem church, or the Antioch church, or anything like that, but it's very much that we're in this together. (Dan, dialogue)

CREATED FOR RELATIONSHIP: A TRINITARIAN ANTHROPOLOGY

Made in the *Imago Dei*

A theological understanding of God as Trinity begins in an understanding of the person as embodied. Genesis' statement that humans are made in God's image (*imago Dei*)[7] suggests that human beings are imprinted

4. Bowe, *Biblical Foundations of Spirituality*.

5. McFague, *A New Climate for Theology*, 44.

6. Groome, *Educating for Life*, 181.

7. *Imago Dei* is Latin for "image of God," and this reference to the human being made in the image of God is found in Genesis 1:26–27.

with the divine. This not so simple statement grounds a Trinitarian understanding of the human as sacred, body and soul. Human beings are an embodied people. The configuration of the person as both body and spirit reinstates not only human agency, but also human worth. Made in the image of the divine, the body is sacred and the spirit is corporeal.[8] This understanding addresses a politics of identity and difference that renders some people more privileged that others because of the ways in which their bodies are gendered or made. It questions any dualistic understanding of the human that sees humanity separated into a mind-male/body-female duality. Malaysian feminist theologian Sharon Bong suggests that "a theology that matters is one that is embodied."[9]

Made in the Image of Trinity

An embodied theology, with its foundation of the Trinity, offers a way to begin to understand the living God as Trinity present in experience. God is imaged as one God. Yet three separate persons validate diversity and difference in this experience. The presence of Creator God, Jesus, and the Spirit deepens the statement that humans are made in the *imago Dei*, suggesting more definitively that humans are made in the *imago Trinitatis*, the image of God as Trinity, and are thus deeply relationally centered.[10] Thus, it teaches about God's life with people and people's life with each other.[11]

INSIGHTS INTO TRINITY: COMMUNITY, LOVE, DIFFERENCE, AND HARMONY

Classic Understandings of the Doctrine of the Trinity

The early Christians, themselves monotheists, understood God's saving action in their lives through God's presence in the Exodus experience, through the prophets, but above all through the life and ministry of Jesus. They greeted each other, "The grace of our Lord Jesus Christ, the love of

---

8. Bong, "Suffering Christ and the Asian Body," 190.

9. Ibid., 180.

10. LaCugna, *God With Us*, 289.

11. Ibid., 1. Catherine LaCugna was a theologian at the University of Notre Dame who is best known for her groundbreaking work on the Trinity.

God, and the fellowship of the Holy Spirit be with you all" (2 Cor 13:13).[12] This phrasing reflected their talk about the Trinitarian God.

Many in the early Church put forth considerable effort to think through their relationships with God the Father, Jesus, and the Holy Spirit.[13] In the fourth century, the Council of Nicaea composed the Nicene Creed, affirming God as one in being with the Father, in large part as a response to a question of the divinity of Jesus in Christian circles at that time. Fifty years later, at the Council of Constantinople, the church expanded the statement of faith to include a reference to the Holy Spirit as the power by which Jesus came into the world.[14]

Perichoresis: God Active and Relational

The early church used the term *perichoresis* to explain the concept of Trinity by emphasizing the dynamic and vital character of the Triune God.[15] The notion of *perichoresis* stems from its root words: *peri*, meaning "around," and *choresis*, meaning "dance." This introduces the metaphor or analogy for Trinity as a divine dance by imaging a cyclical movement in which each of the persons of the Trinity is present to and permeated by the others.[16] While *perichoresis* advances a relational understanding of Godself, it also allows an understanding of God as active in human history, bringing people together in the divine circling spiral of love.[17] Harry reflects this understanding in talking about how people and communities act on this understanding of God in relationship and the way God works through each person.

> In the gay community the norm is why do you go to a place of oppression? I say, "The church is an instrument of oppression, but my community isn't. We're trying to show a way to be Catholic that is not oppressive." At St. _____ we were the place that if you were divorced and feeling unwelcome, or you were gay, or you were radical or something, you would come to St.____ because it was the place where you were accepted, you were nurtured, you were welcomed and cherished. I never felt

12. Johnson, *Quest for the Living God*, 203–5.

13. Groody, *Globalization, Spirituality, and Justice*, 61.

14. Kärkkäinen, *Pneumatology*, 45.

15. Groody, *Globalization, Spirituality, and Justice*, 62; LaCugna, *God With Us*, 171.

16. Groody, *Globalization, Spirituality, and Justice*, 62.

17. Johnson, *Quest for the Living God*, 210–12.

that people tolerated me at St. _____'s, I felt that people just loved
the fact that I was there. You know, you can't continue to oppress groups of people and expect people who demand justice to
acquiesce. That's a perfect word for it. The people at [Intentional
Eucharistic Community] demand justice because they believe
God does. There's a wonderful song and it goes: "What does our
God require of you? What does our God require of you? Justice,
kindness, walk completely with God." (Harry, dialogue)

Perichoresis reveals God's invitation to humanity to realize the interconnectedness and the relational core of the human being. This invitation
calls for joining the Trinity with actions of love in the world as God works
God's love in the cosmos.[18]

A Western Trinitarian Orientation: One True God, Three Persons

During the fourth century, Augustine (354–430) laid the foundation for
a Western Trinitarian orientation. He insisted on one, true God existing
simultaneously as three persons, Father, Son, and Spirit, with the Spirit
proceeding through the Father and the Son. He also contributed to the
understanding of the Spirit in pneumatology by grounding the Holy Spirit
in the three most traditional names for the Spirit's nature: Holy Spirit,
Love, and Gift.[19] Augustine suggests that rather than uniting all people in
knowledge that the Spirit unites all people *in communio* with the Father
and Son in love.[20]

A Medieval Emphasis on Pneumatology

Medieval mystics advanced a rich spirituality of the doctrine of God in the
Trinity that is informed by pneumatology. Their themes of love, community, and unity in the Trinity are today being developed in contemporary
understandings of the Trinity. For example, medieval monastic Bernard
of Clairvaux speaks of the mutual love of the Father and the Son with the
Spirit as he links human sinfulness and God's grace with liveliness and

18. Groody, *Globalization, Spirituality, and Justice*, 63.

19. Kärkkäinen, *Pneumatology*, 46.

20. Ibid. The ontological assertion that "God is love" is an intrinsic concept of
relationality in Christian faith (1 John 4:16; Tracy, "Approaching the Christian Understanding of God," 146).

growth in the Spirit.[21] According to Bernard, the Spirit makes knowing revelation possible. Even more, the Spirit represents the intimacy of love within the Trinity and between God and believers.[22] Writing in the early Franciscan tradition, Bonaventure understands the Spirit as holding the community together. He sees this action of the Holy Spirit as central to the narrative of Pentecost and successive forms of Christian life. Doctor of the Church, Catherine of Siena moves toward a more unifying understanding of the Trinity, combining the understanding of God, the Creator, present in creation and humanity, and God in the human experience of God's saving work. "In Catherine of Siena's holistic theology, the entire Trinity works together in both creation and redemption."[23]

An Eastern Perspective: Trinity—Harmony in Diversity

J. Y. Lee brings a balance to the understanding of Trinity. Coming from an Eastern perspective of the Trinity, he emphasizes unity rather than individuality in terms of the Trinity. Such an understanding appreciates the Trinity as an inclusive whole and essential continuum, moving from unity to the diversity present in the inner process of change in all things.[24] It relocates the Trinity to a *both-and* understanding of the oneness of three persons in God and the threeness in one God.[25] This allows for appreciating both the unity and the diversity of God. An Eastern perspective of Trinity also acknowledges the reciprocal nature of the Trinitarian persons focusing on God's creation of humans in God's image.[26]

J. Y. Lee's doctrine of God as the Trinity roots the liberation experience of God in the understanding of humans as children of God and, as such, joined with God in the family of the divine Trinity. This understanding unifies all creation by God the Father with the redemptive work of Jesus, understanding Jesus as the agent of creation.[27] J. Y. Lee suggests that the fact that humans are created to be different by a Trinitarian God indicates that humans have inherited God's plurality.[28] This plurality exists

21. Kärkkäinen, *Pneumatology*, 52.

22. Ibid.

23. Ibid., 54.

24. J. Y. Lee, *Theology of Change*, 115–17.

25. J. Y. Lee, *Trinity in Asian Perspective*, 115.

26. Kärkkäinen, *Trinity*, 45.

27. J. Y. Lee, *Trinity in Asian Perspective*, 102.

28. Ibid., 105.

harmoniously. "Thus unity in difference is possible through harmony, and harmony is possible because of individual plurality."[29] This understanding rejects centralist notions of sameness and singularity that criticize and marginalize the different. It holds instead a belief that human identity is relational and coexists in universal kinship with all people.

ENGAGING THE MARGINS

The doctrine of God as Trinity theologizes the margins concretizing Christ's preferential option for the poor, where compassion and interconnectedness with those on the margins stretches to imagine and act together toward a better tomorrow.[30] It does this by in solidarity and relationship and allowing the plural voices of the marginalized to speak with dignity. The experience of Jesus from a theology that begins in the margins in the everyday suffering and healing of human life realizes equitable and just relationship. The experience of God's Spirit working in this experience heralds the experience of action, the Spirit of freedom, speech, and community.[31] Thus, the margins become sites of creativity where God the Creator, in Jesus, and through the Spirit is present making all things new.

THE TRINITY—TWO PERSPECTIVES

Feminist theologians Elizabeth Johnson and Catherine LaCugna bring two different perspectives of the Trinity to the understanding of the nature and significance of personhood through the Trinity. Yet each theologian points to the relational nature of Trinity and the impact of this on an understanding of the human as relational.

Johnson rejects an undue emphasis on personhood in the Trinity in favor of the mystery of the transcendent God. God is not a person as humans understand person, but rather is interpersonal and transpersonal, always richly beyond what can be known.[32] Likewise Johnson suggests that the intent of speaking of the Trinity with the numbers one and three is subtle. Talking of one God in three "is intended to negate division, thus affirming the unity of the divine being. To say that the persons are three

---

29. Ibid., 102.

30. Pui-lan, *Hope Abundant*, 188.

31. Kärkkäinen, *Trinity*, 155–56.

32. Johnson, *She Who Is*, 203.

is intended to relate singleness, thus affirming a communion in God."[33] Johnson suggests that God as Trinity affirms the one God "who is not a solitary God, but a communion in love marked by overflowing life."[34]

The image of God as Trinity, an inclusive whole yet plural, enables an understanding of God as *communio*, "making it possible to speak of how the mystery of God is capable of relating to what is creaturely and laced with history."[35] Johnson emphasizes that the Spirit of God that unites the world in its unity and diversity is also the Spirit of God that is utterly transcendent with a difference that is necessary to our humanity and to the understanding of God.[36] This suggests a freedom of Spirit that understands relationality intrinsic to God's being in the world.[37] "The relation is mutual while differences remain and are respected . . . the universe, both matter and spirit, is encompassed by the matrix of the living God in an encircling which generates uniqueness, futurity, and self-transcendence in the context of the interconnected whole."[38] This Trinitarian theological perspective of diversity within wholeness puts forward patterns of differentiation that are non-hierarchical and forms of relationship that do not include dominance.[39] This suggests patterns of relationship that include the margins as part of the whole, in all their uniqueness, a relationship that values them equally and respects their diversity.

LaCugna places a greater emphasis on God as social and the communal aspects of the Trinity than Johnson providing another lens in which to understand the Trinity and human relationality. She emphasizes the human capacity to know God as well as God's intimate relation to the world through the divine persons. In offering a clear definition of the key elements of personhood, she emphasizes a relational anthropology. To be human is always to be in relationship with God and with each other. "The doctrine of the Trinity, ultimately, must measure its reflections on personhood by the revelation of divine personhood in the face of Christ and the activity of the Holy Spirit."[40] This indicates that the mystery of God coming to us through Christ and the mystery of Spirit "has far-

33. Ibid., 204.
34. Ibid., 222.
35. Johnson , "To Let the Symbol Sing Again," 228.
36. Johnson, *She Who Is*, 147.
37. Ibid., 247.
38. Johnson, "To Let the Symbol Sing Again," 231–32.
39. Johnson, *She Who Is*, 219.
40. LaCugna, *God for Us*, 292–93.

reaching social implications . . . for it promotes mutuality and undermines all hierarchical structures among humans."[41] Both Johnson and LaCugna point to the doctrine of God as Trinity revealing the essence of the person as relational.[42] The symbol of the Trinity suggests a "mutual relationship of different equals as the mutual paradigm of personal and social life."[43] LaCugna further informs an understanding of interconnectedness, insisting that a person's own particularity, which cannot be fully comprehended by another, is shaped in relations with others.[44]

To summarize, the doctrine of God as Trinity lays the foundation for new understandings of the human as a relational being, made for relationship in the *imago Trinitatis*. God's unity and diversity ground our embodied being in particularity and universality suggesting that the human develops in relationship with God and others. Interestingly, contemporary scientific studies in neuroscience that make this relationality visually apparent through the neuroscience of mirror neurons. Today, scientific studies in neuroscience offer a means for exploring the significance and the processes of our human interconnectedness in ways that provide an embodied corroboration for an understanding of a relational anthropology.

THE WONDER OF CREATION: NEUROSCIENCE AND MIRROR NEURONS

Our Human Connectedness Seen through Science

The discovery of mirror neurons gives rise to speculation about the ways in which they ground our social cognition in our body in the world, the ways in which we engage in cooperative, communal actions and how we understand them. Mirror neurons expand our insight into knowledge, language, and understanding of the self as embodied, and increase our appreciation for the way in which we are so wonderfully made that our interconnection with others is a part of who we are.

---

41. Metzler, "Trinity in Contemporary Theology," 281.

42. Johnson, "To Let the Symbol Sing Again," 219; LaCugna, *God for Us*, 192–93.

43. Johnson, "To Let the Symbol Sing Again," 222.

44. LaCugna, *God for Us*, 289.

An Interpersonal Link with Other Acting Individuals

Mirror neurons were first discovered by Rizzolatti as he was experimenting with macaque monkeys.[45] He noticed that the neurons activated when the monkey performed a purposeful object-oriented action were also activated when the monkey was an observer of that same action performed by another. [46]Such neurons are not just triggered by visual input. Audio-visual mirror neurons are triggered by and discriminate between the sound of different actions. They do this whether the action is just heard as well as when the action is being performed. All mirror neurons contribute to an internal storage of motor knowledge that activates when a goal-driven action is seen or heard, giving a mental representation of that action. The monkey watching the action actually experiences the firing of the motor neurons in a space of the brain just as the monkey doing the action. This space where the motor neurons are fired is dynamic and may vary according to the change of the object's spatial location in time.[47] "This suggests that a set of mirror neurons encodes the observed motor acts not only for action understanding, but also to analyze such acts in terms of features that are relevant to generating appropriate behaviors."[48]

Brain imaging studies in humans show that mirror neurons are also present in the parietal and premotor areas and activated when we observe and perform actions.[49] Speech actions activate premotor regions of Broca's area, a portion of the brain known for its connection to communication and language. Mirror neurons receive input from other parts of the brain, enabling their functioning to integrate this process of mirror neuron

45. Rizzolatti and Craighero, "Mirror Neuron System."

46. Tummolini et al., "From Mirror Neurons to Joint Actions."

47. Fogassi and Ferrari, "Mirror Neurons and the Evolution of Embodied Language."

48. Caggiano et al., "Mirror Neurons Differentially Encode the Peripersonal and Extrapersonal," 403.

49. Fogassi and Ferrari, "Mirror Neurons and the Evolution of Embodied Language," 137. It is important to note that there are both minimalist and maximalist understandings of mirror neurons. The maximalist understanding, to which this author adheres, understands that mirror systems may involve more than just mirror neurons. This is significant because it suggests that there is more to know regarding motor neuron firing, and more to brain functioning in regards to more complex operations. Many parts of the brain may be involved in more complex operations. Yet, these studies indicate the presence of actions, of motor neuron firing, that cannot take place without another. We are truly made for relationship. Gallese is a proponent of maximalist interpretations of mirror neurons (Tummolini et al., "From Mirror Neurons to Joint Actions," 103). Gallese's work can be explored at www.interdisciplines.com.

activation and encode it into the brains and body's motor system.[50] Observation of an action performed by another person causes an automatic simulated re-enactment of the same action within an observer and forms the basis for the observer's understanding of the action. The encoding, by mirror neurons, of agent-object interactions within a motor space is dynamic and affected by time. This gives information about ourselves. It facilitates social connectedness by reducing the gap between self and other by allowing a person to see the other with the other's sameness and difference.[51] Mirror neurons reveal in very real ways deep intuition and theology has been telling humanity throughout history. Humans are relational beings needing others even in the way human bodies function.

Establishing a Sense of Identity

Gallese proposes that the motor neuron circuits involved in action control and in the experience of emotions and sensations are also active when a person witnesses actions and emotions.[52] These neural circuits, as well as other mirroring neuron clusters outside of the motor domain, provide the neural foundation for a common underlying functional mechanism—embodied simulation. This can be understood as "an automatic unconscious and prereflective functional mechanism, whose functioning is the modeling of objects, agents, and events."[53]

Knowing the World Relationally

This functional mechanism in the brain plays a major role in people's epistemic approach to the world. It enables the capacity to establish a sense of identity as the person observes actions, intentions, feelings, and emotions of others by automatically establishing an interpersonal link when other individuals are observed. Mirror neurons preside over our pragmatic relation with the world of others, establishing a sense of social

50. Gallese, "Mirror Neurons, Embodied Simulation, and the Neural Basis of Social Identification," 519–36.

51. Bakhtin proposed this as an important component of dialogue in the twentieth century, unaware that future findings of neuroscience would corroborate his intuition.

52. Gallese, "Mirror Neurons, Embodied Simulation, and the Neural Basis of Social Identification," 519–36.

53. Gallese, "Intentional Attunement," 4.

identity.[54] This social identity is based on shared meaning in intersubjective space through the embodied link our mirror neurons establish. This leads to social identification, empathy, and "we-ness" which are the basic foundation of our development and being.[55] Bodies comprehend the acting 'bodies' of the others sharing their world through the embodied simulation of mirror neurons. This shareability of the matter and actions of people's brains and bodies in their intentional relations with others produces an intentional attunement.

"The advantage of such an epistemological approach is that it generates predictions about the intrinsic functional nature of our social cognitive operations . . ."[56] The exploration of mirror neurons leads to an understanding of abstract thought and imagination that suggests an intersubjective bodily way of knowing through the joint significance of intentionally meaningful sensory-motor actions. Knowing/knowledge arises from the sharing of situated experiences of action and emotion generated by the mirror neurons. Relations with others in the brain-body system, though prelinguistic and pretheoretical, are nevertheless contributing to the conceptual content of knowledge. Embodied personal knowledge is contingent on the multi-leveled connectedness that is shared with others. Thus, "we-ness and intersubjectivity ontologically ground the human condition, in which reciprocity foundationally defines human existence."[57]

In summary, a doctrine of God as Trinity suggests that humans are created in the *imago Trinitatis* as relational beings. The neurosciences as interdisciplinary dialogue partners provide a scientific window in which we see one of the ways that diverse relational beings function in and through relationship. Mirror neurons provide an epistemological basis for the embodied we-ness that ontologically grounds the person.

How do we begin to take seriously this identity of the human as relational, the particularity and universality in relationship? Dialogue that begins in the multiplicity of the voices on the margins holds epistemological promise for practical theology. It enables the person to form and be formed through dialogic relationship.

54. Gallese, "Mirror Neurons, Embodied Simulation, and the Neural Basis of Social Identification," 522.

55. Gallese, "We-ness, Embodied Simulation, and Psychoanalysis," 580–84.

56. Gallese, "Embodied Simulation," 31.

57. Gallese, "Mirror Neurons, Embodied Simulation, and the Neural Basis of Social Identification," 530.

DIALOGUE AND RELATIONSHIP: DIALOGISM, AUTHORING, AND OUTSIDENESS

A relational concept of dialogue is infused with the awareness of the dialogic that realizes the edges, surfaces, and depths of the reality of one's self are constantly entering into relationship with the reality of another.[58] The work of Bakhtin grounds itself in this awareness. The multi-leveled connectedness shared with others, and the reciprocity that foundationally defines human existence establishes anthropology as relational beings that form and are formed through the embodied action of dialogue.[59] Bakhtin bases his communication theory of dialogue called dialogism in a paradigm that includes multiple voices, emphasizing the ordinary rather than the ideal situation. It suggests practices for practical theology that spark attention to the multiple voices of the other and allow the honoring of difference, enabling the margins to contribute to theological discussion.

DIALOGUE AND RELATIONSHIP: DIALOGISM, AUTHORING, AND OUTSIDENESS

Dialogism

Relationships Adjusting to the Other

Dialogism is a set of diverse concepts unified by the insight that encountering the other is crucial for our consciousness and being, and for others as well.[60] Dialogism is the inherent orientation and adjustment of all discourse to the utterances of others.[61] It engages the entire realm of dialogic interaction itself rather than language in isolation.[62] This concept extends the concept of dialogue to include not only direct, face-to-face vocalized

---

58. Green, *Mikhail Bakhtin and Biblical Scholarship*, 34–37.

59. Bakhtin, *Toward a Philosophy of the Act*, 287.

60. Green, *Mikhail Bakhtin and Biblical Scholarship*, 25.

61. Gardiner, *Dialogics of Critique*, 37; Pechey, *Mikhail Bakhtin*, 17–18. Eschewing linguistics as telling only about the formal structure of language, but revealing little about language as a living concrete reality, Bakhtin instead used a theoretical approach he dubbed translinguistics, which later became known as dialogism (Danow, *Thought of Mikhail Bakhtin*; Gardiner, *Dialogics of Critique*, 23–31). The theory of dialogism began with Bakhtin's dialogic reading of Dostoevsky, but his insight into dialogism grew beyond the textual or even intertextual to embrace the whole social world (Gardiner, *Dialogics of Critique*, 25–31).

62. Gardiner, *Dialogics of Critique*, 37.

verbal behavior such as verbal communication but also books—verbal performance in print, as well as anything intended for active perception involving inner responsiveness, attentive reading, and reaction.[63] Dialogism is constituted through social interaction in dialogic relationships between individuals and groups. It performs social functions and has practical effects on the everyday life and the persons involved. It insists on a non-consensus seeking dialogue that privileges the multiple voices of the other. Dialogism encompasses four processes relevant to a discussion of a relational anthropology: heteroglossia, dialogue, outsideness, and authoring. Each interconnects with the other synergistically to provide the whole of dialogism.

Heteroglossia

Multiple Voices Interconnected in the Past, Present, and Future

Heteroglossia informs any discussion of dialogue that finds the welcoming of multiple voices necessary. Heteroglossia encompasses the multiple conflicting voices from multiple social locations, cultures, and geographies. Bakhtin's turn toward the narrative through dialogue acknowledges the inherent relationship of ideology and utterances. Therefore, dialogue lives in its historical and social context. Language reflects the multi-temporality of human life by emphasizing the interconnections in the past, present, and future forms of life associated with different speech genres and cultures.[64] "Though a huge concept, it [heteroglossia] can be presented succinctly as the joyful recognition that in life or in a literary work there are a number of 'social language systems' in play at the same time, rubbing shoulders with each other, often in the mouth of the same speaker."[65] Speakers and listeners hear the various languages in contention with each other, understanding that there are many meanings that can be construed from the same words. Cindy, one dialogue partner, shows an innate understanding of this listening in her comments about the listening she believes is required on the margins of the Church.

> At Pentecost it says they all spoke in different languages so that everybody understood. We need Pentecost listening for all these Pentecost voices. (Cindy dialogue)

63. Dentith, *Bakhtinian Thought*, 139–40.
64. Bell and Gardiner, *Bakhtin and the Human Sciences*, 208.
65. Green, *Mikhail Bakhtin and Biblical Scholarship*, 54.

Dialogue

Dialogue, like dialogism, is not just verbal communication. It is the umbrella under which all language stands, acknowledging the multiplicity and interconnectedness of voices, the many levels of language, and the multiple ways of hearing such languages.[66] Dialogue looks at language outside the traditional sense.[67] Language consists of utterances (rather than individual words or sentences) that involve interaction and take into account the words of another.[68] An utterance comprises what is actually articulated and what is also assumed.[69] These utterances are the basic unit of speech communication.[70] An utterance has two aspects. First, it is characterized by a referential semantic content that refers to specific meanings and specific contexts, and it has a particular aim. Second, the speaker of the utterance actively evaluates the referential semantic content of his or her utterance. "Someone must say it to someone, must respond to something and anticipate a response, must be accomplishing something by the saying of it."[71] Each word, each utterance is distinct and has subtle differences in the often contradictory "talking components."[72] Bakhtin writes, "For a word is not a material thing but rather the eternally mobile, eternally fickle medium of dialogic interactions. It never gravitates to a single consciousness or a single voice. The life of the word is contained

66. Ibid., 46.

67. The traditional understanding is that language represents concepts through an arbitrary symbol system that is socially shared and organized and governed by rules (Owens, *Language Development*, 7). Language and speech are part of a bigger process—that of communication, which involves the sending and receiving of messages about information, ideas, feelings, etc. (Hulit and Howard, *Born to Talk*, 3–11). Language has three major components: content, form, and use, which include semantics (how we code ideas and their meanings), syntax (the rules governing word order), phonology (the sound units), morphology (the appropriate words and ending and beginning sounds), and pragmatics (the rules governing language use in the communicative context) (Owens, *Language Development*, 6–29). Bakhtin challenges the study of language in linguistics and its study of the sentence and enlarges the concept of utterances beyond the idea that utterances are mechanistic units of language (words, sentences). He emphasizes that the utterance is characterized by an exchange with someone that anticipates a response, and responds (Morson and Emerson, *Mikhail Bakhtin*, 125–27).

68. Bell and Gardiner, *Bakhtin and the Human Sciences*, 54.

69. Green, *Mikhail Bakhtin and Biblical Scholarship*, 53.

70. An utterance may be as short as a nonverbal shrug or a one-word exclamation, or as long as multiple sentences (Morson and Emerson, *Mikhail Bakhtin*, 125–27).

71. Ibid., 126.

72. Emerson, *First Hundred Years of Mikhail Bakhtin*, 36.

in its transfer from one mouth to an other, from one context to another, from one social collective to another, from one generation to another. In this process the word does not forget its own path and cannot completely free itself from the power of these concrete contexts into which it has entered."[73] Thus, words include different contexts, times, and places which affect the meaning of every utterance. The speaker, listener, the writer and/ or reader differ, and meanings differ making each utterance unique. "An utterance is never just a reflection or an expression of something already existing and outside it that is given and final. It always creates something that never existed before; something absolutely new and unrepeatable."[74]

Creative Understanding—Difference Is Foundational

In dialogue, both centrifugal forces pushing towards unity and order and centripetal forces pushing towards multiplicity and diversity exist together. As a person speaks, anticipation of the responses obtained from the listeners helps form the utterances. The meaning of words is determined equally by whose word it is and for whom it is meant. Words are shaped in the dialogue. The task for the listener participating in dialogue is to understand and respond to the words spoken with agreement or disagreement, with compassion, in expansion, etc.[75] Dialogic relationships preserve alterity and are able to hold difference and distance as well as similarity neither seeking negation of the difference or assimilation.[76] Perhaps, Bakhtin's most important contribution is this awareness that dialogue is enhanced by the difference of the "other." In fact, difference is foundational.[77] Because of this, dialogue does not demand agreement, nor does it reduce the dialogue to a single denominator. Dialogue, enhanced by the difference of the other, educates each partner about itself and about the other. It discovers potential and creates potential as the self takes on the creative understandings generated in the dialogue about self and other and fashions these into provisional self-narratives. Maria's narrative of a turning point is an example.

73. Bakhtin, *Problems of Dostoevsky's Poetics*, 202.

74. Bakhtin, *Speech Genres*, 119–20.

75. Bell and Gardiner, *Bakhtin and the Human Sciences*, 24.

76. Peeren, *Intersubjectivities and Popular Culture*, 100.

77. The fact that difference is foundational contributes to my methodology, informing the methods used, my research hypotheses, and the outcome of my research. This contributes to my understanding of the margins as relational, dialogic space.

I'll never forget. St. ___'s church had a nun. Vatican II had already been established for a while. She was the head of religious
education and she wanted family Mass instead of Mass just for
the adults; family catechism instead of just the children. And
so she instituted Sunday Mass with family religious education
and conversation with each other and that was the beginning for
me, for seeing a woman who was active in the church, who was
proactive, out there. She talked about women becoming priests.
That to me was such a revolutionary idea, I never had thought of
anything like that. But here she was, on the cutting edge of doing
things that nobody else was doing. We would stand around the
altar all the families, holding hands, watching the priest, going
through the Mass and the children there participating. It was to
me the beginning of where we are today in our belief that we are
the church. I never knew that before. The church was the priest,
the Pope, the hierarchy, what we were told, that's what we did.
That to me was a turning point in my life; to have this insight
and to be a part of the Mass and to be there, not excluded, not
sitting over here watching a man who was doing something. We
were a part of it. (Maria, dialogue)

The importance of an awareness of power dynamics cannot be
stressed enough with this concept. Dialogic relationships do not demand
adherence to one point of view, or relegate another to the margins. It is
the responsibility of each partner in dialogue to take seriously the politics
of recognition and inclusion. Dialogue educates the self and the other
through recognizing and including a multiplicity of voices. Because of the
inclusive nature of dialogue, each dialogue partner experiences the particularity and the universality of self, the particularity and the universality
of the other. True dialogue understands that a person can never be where I
am, or see themselves as I see them.[78] Nor does one need to do so. "To live
answerably is to sign one's name to one's life."[79] It is to take responsibility
for where I stand, how I choose to live, for the quality of my life, how I live
my life, and the self I become. "The thing that distinguishes the dialogic
relation . . . is that every word calls for a reply, so that the more I answer,
the more I am responsible."[80]

78. Pechey, *Mikhail Bakhtin*, 157.
79. Green, *Mikhail Bakhtin and Biblical Scholarship*, 44.
80. Ibid., 45.

Outsideness

Because of creative understanding produced through dialogue, dialogue allows the self to know itself through the responses of real, imagined, historical, and generalized others. It creates dynamic intersubjective relationships among individuals, social groups and cultures. The creative processes of dialogue are present because of what Bakhtin terms "outsideness."

Relating with the Other in Dialogue—Understanding the Self

Outsideness is a major characteristic of dialogic relationship. When one meets another in dialogue, one meets in a spatial-temporal context.[81] Dialogue for Bakhtin "takes place not in the neutral space of 'communication' but in a charged and irreducibly sociopolitical space of its own making and remaking."[82] This spatial-temporal context is permeated with meaning and significance and is indicative of relationships.[83] A person is always outside the other in relationship during dialogue never duplicating their space or time. Each person in dialogue sees facets unseeable to the other. Through outsideness, a person learns to understand the self, the other, and culture in a way that helps each to reveal and actualize potential.[84]

Authoring

Self in Relationship

"What underlies the unity of an answerable consciousness is not a principle as a starting point, but the fact of an actual acknowledgement of one's own participation in unitary Being-as-event, and this cannot be adequately expressed in theoretical terms, but can only be described and participatively experienced."[85] This participative experience is authoring. Authoring is the way the dialogical self knows itself through the responses of others.[86] It is "the primary activity of all selves in the world dominated by the self/

---

81. Bakhtin, *Dialogic Imagination*, 84–85.
82. Pechey, *Mikhail Bakhtin*, 13–14.
83. Bakhtin, *Dialogic Imagination*, 84–85.
84. Morson and Emerson, *Mikhail Bakhtin*, 54–55.
85. Bakhtin, *Toward a Philosophy of the Act*, 40.
86. Bakhtin, *Problems of Dostoevsky's Poetics*, 59.

other distinction."[87] Authoring has three aspects: authoring of self, other, and art. It may be seen as God interacting with humans and creation, the self authoring of a deed, the creation of a work of art, the writing of a dissertation, or a conversation between people as in Maria's story earlier. Authoring takes place in dialogue. It is important to remember that dialogue includes the entire realm of dialogic communication not only direct face to face vocalized verbal behavior. Authoring can be imagined as a dance[88] or as a set of concentric circles.[89] What is constant and vital is difference. "Outsideness is a prerequisite for authoring."[90] The difference of the other is foundational for authoring.

The dialogical self knows itself through the responses of real, imagined, historical, and generalized others.[91] Authoring the other is always connected to authoring the self. As we author the other, the other we shape is an exploration of the self. The authoring of self has three aspects: *I-for-the-other, I-for-myself,* and *the other-for-me.*[92] The authoring of self is a process of self-formation in response to images given by others through dialogue. It allows the self to mutually create a response and actively shape itself from that response. As I see myself and the other in dialogue, I give form to myself and I also give form to the other, perceiving what I think the other is. At the same time, the other perceives me. I notice what the other thinks I am and they become aware of what I think they are. In this action, the other offers form as an aesthetic act and the self reacts to it. The reaction falls on a continuum of negation or acceptance of the image. Here again, power dynamics and critical awareness provide for the courageous step of awareness for the courage to present one's differences and to accept diversity in relationship and community where dialogue is present. This begins in a core philosophy of dialogue that does not seek consensus. "Lived life tends to recoil and hide deep inside itself, tends to withdraw into its own inner infinitude, is *afraid of boundaries* [author's italics], strives to dissolve them, for it has no faith in the essentialness and kindness of the power that gives form from outside; any viewpoint from outside is refused. And, in the process, the *culture of boundaries* [author's italics] (the necessary condition for a confident and deep

---

87. Clark and Holquist, *Mikhail Bakhtin*, 94.

88. Bakhtin, *Art and Answerability*, 137.

89. Green, *Mikhail Bakhtin and Biblical Scholarship*, 165.

90. Ibid., 169.

91. Bakhtin, *Problems of Dostoevsky's Poetics*, 59.

92. Green, *Mikhail Bakhtin and Biblical Scholarship*, 34.

style) becomes impossible."[93] A person's self definition and self-perception is formed through relations with others. [94]

Biblical scholar Barbara Green uses the image of the author drawing a self-portrait while at the same time drawing the other. Seeing oneself in the mirror is never the same as the drawing or observing of us by another.[95] *I-for-the-other* (how I look to others outside of me) is not identical to *I-for-myself* (I as I see myself on the inside). This allows the form known by the self and the form offered by another to go beyond what either is, creating open potential.[96] "To author in such a dialogic way is both to recognize the border between myself and an other and to sense that it is permeable, porous, repeatedly crossed in more ways than I can ever take in."[97] The process is reciprocal in that the self, through outsideness, also bestows form to others through *the other-for-me* (how outsiders appear to me).[98] "I enter as deeply as I am able the space of the other—their particularity—perceive it to some extent with their ear and eye—and then return to my own space, remembering, marking—integrating—what I have experienced."[99]

Dialogue, informed by the concepts heteroglossia, dialogue, outsideness, and authoring, carries implications for an anthropology that is relational.[100] Understanding a relational anthropology from the perspective of difference means multiple views and difference provide opportunity. People are most productive and reach their potential when accepting the responsibility to listen to a variety of views in dialogue, allowing the self to grow.[101]

93. Bakhtin, *Art and Answerability*, 203.

94. Ibid., 32.

95. Green, *Mikhail Bakhtin and Biblical Scholarship*, 166; Morson and Emerson, *Mikhail Bakhtin*, 74.

96. Morson and Emerson, *Mikhail Bakhtin*, 180–84.

97. Green, *Mikhail Bakhtin and Biblical Scholarship*, 35.

98. Bakhtin, *Art and Answerability*, 32.

99. Green, *Mikhail Bakhtin and Biblical Scholarship*, 34.

100. A choice not to dialogue turns an attempt for dialogue into monologue, where one voice is left unheard. Monologue is defined as finalized, abstracted, transcribed, and systematically dialectical. All of these value abstract control and order over the messiness of actual ordinary life and dialogue (Bell and Gardiner, *Bakhtin and the Human Sciences*, 221–24).

101. Morson and Emerson, *Mikhail Bakhtin*, 50. Bakhtin insists that learning is a reciprocal process progressing from the outside dialogic event to the inner self.

Critique of Bakhtin: Complex, Challenging, Critical

The sheer vastness of Bakhtin's work, not to mention its complexity, makes appropriating and pushing it to new areas such as practical theology daunting. The original Russian texts of Bakhtin's work render the concepts of some Russian words difficult to fully translate into English, leaving the scholar unaware of the layered contexts embedded in Bakhtin's work. This can make the concepts confusing and less rich in their implications. Bakhtin's work demands years of study to effectively use his work responsibly because of its sheer volume and because of the difficulty for non-Russian scholars to deeply appropriate the context and culture of Russia during the time of his work. Bakhtin's work, however, is rich in insight about relationship formed in dialogue, challenging, and inviting of deeper examination. His work is deeply ethical and he weaves his insights into literature, dialogue, and the reality of self.[102] "Ethics demands a match in word and deed, requires embodiment and particularity with all of its messy, painful, and joyful challenge, calls for a signature on a customized life: 'for him ethics [is] always generated from within and never imposed from without.'"[103] He is said to have utilized his insights about dialogue and communication in his own life, listening respectfully. Accepting of difference, he avoided blaming others for choosing viewpoints contrary to his own, finally saying when he could say nothing else, "That is very interesting."[104]

One person cannot mandate another's self-understanding. Authoring in dialogue speaks of independence and interdependence. This presents the dilemma of living the difference of our individualities, our histories, our cultures from the perspective of affirming both connectedness and independence.[105] It requires a rethinking of our tradition and history to take into account the particularity of our context and to respect the individuality of our history.[106]

Dialogue that Does Not Seek Agreement or Consensus

Dialogue that includes the necessity of constant and vital difference presents a dialogue that does not seek consensus. Bakhtin insisted that

102. Green, *Mikhail Bakhtin and Biblical Scholarship*, 3.

103. Ibid., 31.

104. Clark and Holquist, *Mikhail Bakhtin*, 254.

105. Pui-lan, *Hope Abundant*, 65.

106. Ibid., 4.

dialogue is not an instrument to be used to impose one's will on another, but rather is an active interaction between people in the world. Dialogue deconstructs monologues to identify the silenced voices and the nature of their otherness, realizing that both one's own and the other's voices are equally feasible value-orientations. It enables those in dialogue to listen mutually to the other, seeking creative understanding. Fusion and diffusion as well as order and disorder are of equal importance in dialogic encounters through the relationship of identity and difference.[107]

As dialogue authors the self and the other, it privileges outsider voices and calls for a relationship with those who are on the margins. "Within a Bakhtinian universe, it appears, dialogue *must* be primary—not because there is necessarily love or compatibility in that universe but because all participants are equally unprivileged: unity, plurality, and uniqueness are equally indigenous in each human personality, realized in an answerable act on the border and before the person of a unique other." [108] Dialogue is non-consensus seeking. The interconnectedness and difference in dialogue provides space for creative action, if dialogue and realtionship are nurtured and allowed to flourish. Bakhtin's work on authoring, dialogue and outsideness contributes to my practical theology methodology, informing the methods used, and the outcome of my research.

The non-consensus seeking dialogue of multiple voices, the doctrine of God as Trinity, and the scientific symbol of mirror neurons function as sources for my understanding of anthropology as relational and of the margins as relational, dialogic space. In the next chapter we turn to the Church and examine ecclesiology with an understanding that a relational dialogic anthropology is integral to welcoming diverse and different voices to the dialogue. For a sense of the Church as relational community we begin with discussion on a Trinitarian ecclesiology informed by pneumatology.

> For me Church is about a sense of community and the sense of change, the sense of the Gospel asks us to change things in the world we are in and not to rest and not to sit still, that sense of movement and momentum, I think is the most important thing about it to me. (Anne, dialogue)

107. Bell and Gardiner, *Bakhtin and the Human Sciences*, 221–25.
108. Ibid., 227–28.

4

Using Our Imagination, Our Intuition, Our Compassion

> Nothing draws me. I think what is missing is that invitation to grow deeply, spiritually outside of the familiarity of the liturgy, outside of kind of a safety that provides. Where is there an invitation for community at a shared dialogue level? I wasn't finding it. (Mai, dialogue)

THE TRINITY AS FOUNDATION for relationship grounds people as individuals and as community and invites all into the community and shared dialogue for which Mai hungers. Building on the discussion of Trinity from the last chapter, I begin with an examination of deep structures present in an identity as Catholic: sacramentality, mediation, and communion. Following this, I move to a focus on the anthropological foundation of an ecclesiology of Church based in Trinitarian theology. The polarity and diversity in the Church today springs from different viewpoints surrounding catholicity, communion, and dialogic communication as well as reactions to modernity and the social crises engendered by the existing polarity and division. Trinitarian ecclesiology summons the Church to a transformative vision of catholicity and communion that includes communion as koinonia, the praxis of the church, and dialogic communication. A discussion of several models of church pertinent to today's Church follows. These models, proposed by Dutch practical theologian Johannes van der Ven and Hebrew Scriptures scholar and theologian Walter Brueggemann, enable a look at church within the context of plurality, diversity, and difference. An examination of models allows for the acknowledgement of one's own model as one among many and provides impetus for assessment and rethinking of one's own model of the church and those seen in church communities.

> The official Church, the hierarchical Church, is crumbling from the center. Just listen to the idiotic policies they're coming out with. It is an insult to all of us. It's crumbling from the center, and it's going to come from the grassroots. I don't know if I'm going to see it in my lifetime, but I can see it dying around me. Our religious congregations are dying, and I feel bad for my own congregation because I think we brought something to society, to the world that will be lost. But that's the way life is on the planet. It's birth, it's chaos, and it's destruction, and it's rebirth. Right now it's the chaos, and the destruction is pretty alive and well, but still there's life. So the chaos and destruction is going on, but I believe it's balanced. I don't want to look at this in a negative way because God continues to be God. (Sarah, dialogue)

Sarah's struggles with the Church today, balancing her struggles with her faith in God and her hope for new life because "God continues to be God." Church is "a community of faith and struggle working to anticipate God's New Creation by becoming partners with those who are at the margins of church and society."[1] Its transformation is continually undergoing change. Structurally, as an organization, it aims at accomplishing its vision and mission as the People of God bringing about and proclaiming the kindom[2] of God.[3] The lenses of community and struggle allow the church to connect through action and reflection with those who are marginalized in the church and society.[4]

1. Russell, *Just Hospitality*, 12.

2. "Kindom" is a term used by *mujerista* (Hispanic) theologian Ada Maria Isasi-Diaz as a less hierarchical, less patriarchal alternative to "kingdom." Others would say "reign of God," and still others, like Van der Ven, use the original term *basiliea*.

3. Van der Ven, *Ecclesiology in Context*, xi–xii.

4. Russell, *Just Hospitality*, 12.

It's Just a Living Faith Model

I am pulling my suitcase through the streets of downtown as I head for a Sunday service at an Intentional Eucharistic Community. I arrive as a large group of people prepare the hall where it will be held. The room is abuzz with laughter and people calling greetings. I am welcomed by people with whom I dialogued over the last few days as well as by those who recognize me from a flyer that was distributed asking for dialogue partners. I help set up chairs in concentric circles, put out liturgy pamphlets, and watch as a simple table is prepared with a Bible and flowers. It seems everyone is helping. Musicians begin tuning their instruments and as the time for beginning approaches people start to settle in, waving at the "latecomers." The theme for this week is "Non-Violence: Dismantling Racism." During dialogue two days before, Shannon shares that she and her partner wrestled with a choice of Church community for themselves and their children. They settled first at the parish of St. ___ and now at its "offshoot," their Intentional Eucharistic Community "that re-invented itself as a community that worships together." She talks about finding and staying in the parish community. "I'm real glad we stayed because it was just the right community for us and they were very welcoming; they were very excited we were having kids. It was amazing how well we were accepted and welcomed and blessed and my parents were shocked when they came up for the Baptism of our oldest to know that he would be baptized in the Catholic Church and lightning didn't strike" (Shannon). The service is led by many people, and no one person stands out. The homily with the theme, "What am I afraid of?" is given by one of my dialogue partners who is an articulate young woman in her early thirties. She says, "You should have the kind of faith that would move mountains, but when I saw the 'mountain' it moved my faith." A dialogue with the community ensues. They then move to the prayers of the faithful and communion. As I participate, I shift to a deeper understanding of Andrew's comment the day before that the social justice aspects at this community all start as part of the liturgy, and Kate's comment that "they talk about issues and even more so than I because I had done so much demonstrating in the seventies that I was kind of done with that. It is spiritual and it is active politically. It is just a living faith model."

ECCLESIOLOGY:
INTEGRATING EXPERIENCES OF THE SPIRIT

Rapid cultural changes, increased globalization, plurality, rapid technological changes, and the blessings and curses these engender in the lives of
people lead to recurring questions. These along with changes in ecology,
medicine, and economics bring questions of social justice to the fore and
foster a renewed interest in the movement of the Spirit and the movement
of the Spirit in Jesus Christ. Ontological changes that once emphasized
objectivity, truth, and rationality are moving to an understanding of truth
as plural and imperfect that is formed in the context of historical time.
Epistemological changes are also moving knowledge to a theory of knowledge as created by humans and produced by human consciousness.

Added to these are changes in lay ministry within the Church. My
dialogue partners in an Intentional Eucharistic Community speak of
their present and past involvement in every area of ministry from liturgy
planning to social justice work. My dialogue partners continue their involvement in leadership and ministry in the variety of small Christian
communities of which they are a part. Such growth in lay ministry has
been the reality for the past few decades throughout the United States.[5]
Fox cites Thomas O'Meara, OP, concerning his work *Theology of Ministry*,
"His theological judgment of what is happening today is that there is an
explosion of ministry throughout the world which 'suggests that the Holy
Spirit is intent upon a wider service, a more diverse ministry for a church
life that will be broader in quantity and richer in quality.'"[6] These contribute to a renewed interest in a Trinitarian ecclesiology by emphasizing the
Holy Spirit.

The turn to a Trinitarian ecclesiology is informed by three historical
happenings. The first is a postmodern turn that questions modern epistemological and ontological bases of theology.[7] The second is the presence
of opportunities for ecumenical dialogue that provides relationship with
other Christian traditions as well as other faith traditions. The third critical development is the emergence of new charismatic movements in all
churches emphasizing the Spirit especially within evangelical and pentecostal churches.[8] The advent of charismatic experiences within mainline

5. Fox, "Discerning Meaning," 7.
6. Ibid.
7. Hinze and Dabney, *Advents of the Spirit*, 19–22.
8. Ibid., 19–21

denominations began to be heard in the 1950s.[9] Since then, Pentecostalism has spread globally, particularly in Latin America, Asia, and Africa. Hinze and Dabney explain, "These charismatic movements can be viewed as a part of a much larger renaissance of interest in spirituality and mysticism, and experiences of smaller Christian communities that emerged in the second half of the twentieth century. But taken as a whole, these various experiences of the Spirit have raised disturbing questions about how to integrate dynamic personal experiences of the Spirit of Jesus Christ within the doctrinal and liturgical life of the churches as well as the significance of these experiences for evangelization and catechesis."[10]

Ecumenical Dialogue

A renewed emphasis on ecumenical dialogue continues both within the Catholic Church since Vatican II (1962–1965) and within Protestant denominations. This ecumenical dialogue led theologians to question the use of a solely Christocentric approach to creation, cultures, and ecclesial matters and to begin a move to pneumatological approaches and a Trinitarian ecclesiology.[11] Pneumatology functions as a unifying source for the many communities of worship and their witness to Jesus Christ in the fellowship of the Spirit.[12]

With a focus on the doctrine of God as Trinity, new forms of spirituality became Spirit-centered. A turn from tradition and classical philosophy to interdisciplinary discussion with biologists, physicists, and philosophers continues to generate interest in a common language of Spirit that speaks of something more and something "other."[13] In this talk of the Spirit a renewed understanding of communion, koinonia, dialogue, and universality are providing a summons to understand the work of the Spirit in the Church both for those perceived in the center and for those on the margins. Gail's prayer group is an example.

> I was part of a prayer group in [place] and it was an interfaith prayer group. We would go to a prayer group at a Methodist church. We would meet beforehand to pray together. Those Wednesday nights were really significant. We were amazed at

9. Ibid., 18.
10. Ibid., 19.
11. Hinze and Dabney, *Advents of the Spirit*, 19–21.
12. Ibid., 19.
13. Ibid., 21.

how our prayers would be answered when we would pray for other people's concerns. We fasted that day too. We saw amazing things happen. God is Jesus for me, but "No one knows the Father except through me," so there's a separation of some sort there. And of course there's the Holy Spirit. My partner ___ cannot understand God in three ways, there's one God. That is so massive. Who knows how many parts there are to God? We call it three. (Gail, dialogue)

A TRINITARIAN ECCLESIOLOGY LOST AND FOUND

Loss of a Spirit-Centered Ecclesiology

In 1825 Johann Mohler, a Roman Catholic theologian, proposed a Spirit-centered ecclesiology stressing the presence and action of the Spirit as the beginning of Christian conversion and formation of Christian community.[14] The Spirit draws people into participation in communion with God and with each other. "He also identified the Spirit as source of a dynamic unity in diversity in the Church which disavows both a rigid uniformity and egoistic versions of diversity."[15] In later years he moved to the more doctrinal tradition of the hierarchy and espoused an incarnational ecclesiology setting the stage for an ecclesiology that was singularly Christocentric. He used this to justify the visible, sacramental, and hierarchical character of Church, restricting the dynamic role of the Spirit, while still emphasizing Pentecost and the Incarnation as defining moments of the Church.[16] Thus, he influenced the adoption of a neo-Scholastic paradigm by Roman Catholic theology and official doctrine that would stress the mystical Body of Christ and incarnational ecclesiology over a Spirit-centered ecclesiology.[17] The Thomist or neo-Scholastic movements emphasized the role of the Spirit in the decisions and teachings of the magisterium and each person's obedient participation in the life of the Church.[18] While these movements

14. Hinze, "Releasing the Power of the Spirit in a Trinitarian Ecclesiology," 345.

15. Ibid.

16. Ibid., 346.

17. Ibid.

18. Holland, *Modern Catholic Social Teaching*, 122–23. Thomists sought to provide moral guidance for the Church, the culture, and the state through papal authority, feeling that the Protestant rejection of the Church and objective authority from the pope undermined all authority and the social community and was the main root of the modern crisis (ibid., 120–21). They placed emphasis on hierarchical structure in

emphasized the Spirit, their philosophy made the active role of the Spirit in the entire Church and in the universal charisms of both lay people and clergy in ecclesial ministry difficult to be seen or heard. Yet, Mohler's early work on a Spirit-filled ecclesiology led to a fuller Trinitarian ecclesiology in the second half of the twentieth century.[19]

Recovery of a Trinitarian Ecclesiology

Three theologians helped initiate a fuller recovery of the doctrine of the Holy Spirit in Catholic theology leading to a Trinitarian ecclesiology: Yves Congar, OP, Heibert Muhlen, and Karl Rahner.[20] "Together these theologians set the Roman Catholic Church on a path away from a rigidly institutional and juridical vision of Church, and laid the groundwork for a renewed anthropology and ecclesiology that drew inspiration from pneumatology as well as Christology."[21] Congar challenged the judicial and institutional understanding of Church, insisting on the indwelling of the Spirit in each person and in each of the marks of the Catholic Church.[22] He affirmed the Christology of the Church, while also affirming the necessity of a strong focus on the Spirit, emphasizing ecclesial communion. [23] Muhlen "advocated thinking of the Spirit in personalist terms as the 'we' that is the bond between I and you, emphasizing the inner life and person to person relationship of the Trinity, as well as the corporate identity of the Church."[24] For Muhlen, *perichoresis* provides the basis for the understanding of the interconnectedness of the Trinity.[25] Finally, Rahner discussed the Trinity as the self-communication of God, providing the basis for a dialogic Church. Rahner not only recognized the communicative mission of the Spirit as the participation of the individual in the life of the Trinity, he also recognized that, as part of the Trinity, the Spirit provides the

---

society and reassertion of the values of human reason and freedom within the context of faith (ibid., 122–23).Thomists also stressed an understanding of the need for the human to be rooted in community under legitimate authority justifying a hierarchical ecclesial authority, and the need for religion to be restored to a public position (ibid., 122–23).

19. Hinze, "Releasing the Power of the Spirit in a Trinitarian Ecclesiology," 345.

20. Hinze, *Practices of Dialogue in the Roman Catholic Church*, 360.

21. Ibid., 360–61.

22. Ibid., 353.

23. Ibid., 353–55.

24. Ibid., 355–56.

25. Ibid., 357.

incarnational and pneumatological foundation of the Church.[26] Acknowledging that the Spirit bestows charismatic gifts of the Spirit on both the laity and ordained, he emphasized the need for recognizing the charisms of the Spirit, particularly as seen in new ecclesial forms and heard in prophetic critique of the Church.[27] Joe and Miriam's dialogue about the Church are examples of the fruit of this theology.

> Baptism is a source of all ministry. Not ordination, but baptism. We're all baptized. Ordination gives us a function within the Christian Church and certain responsibilities, but, uh, my ministries stem so much more from my baptism. (Joe, dialogue)

> One thing I do take offense at is that I don't like the word *laity*. I think laity is divisive. *What would you use?*

> People of God. We are the people of God; we are all the people of God. And we are all called by our baptism to be priests in our own way. Jesus calls us and God calls us to do different things. He gives us different talents so that we can grow and nurture each other. As I see it, beyond the central piece and the focal piece of the seven sacraments, we have a lot of room and a lot of room for creativity and understanding of how people, all people, can participate. (Miriam, dialogue)

CALLED TO CATHOLICITY, DIALOGUE, AND COMMUNION: A TRINITARIAN ECCLESIOLOGY

Deep Structures: Catholic Both-And Thinking

The deep structures of sacramentality, mediation, and communion enable a renewed awareness of the presence of the Spirit in the Church. The stories of Catholics on the margins of the Church describe religious identity as Church, the meanings one has of oneself and the community as well as the meanings others have of both. They also describe religious belonging involving commitment, participation and membership in a religious organization. "Personal and social identity [in the Church] are shaped and maintained not primarily by the specific differences that an individual or a society possesses over against others, which may be many but superficial, but by what might be called 'deep structures' which may be few and shared

26. Ibid., 358–59.
27. Ibid., 360.

with others."[28] Peter Phan, an Asian-American Catholic theologian, contends that these deep structures, which may contain doctrines but also contain ritual, art, and behaviors, help constitute Catholic identity.[29] Deep structures are often shared by others in other faith traditions. These deep elements include a "feel" and an "instinct" about catholicity. My dialogue partners refer to "what is in my bones," or "what is in my blood." For Catholics these include *sacramentality*—God revealed in the everyday including the cosmos, human love, and the experience of community. It also includes *mediation*—God's grace always available to all people, God present and active in daily life and people co-responsible with God for the common good of all. Finally, it includes *communion*—people's way to God and God's way to people is in community as relational people.[30] Also included is analogical imagination. "These structures are characterized by the inclusiveness of *both-and* rather than *either/or* thinking, a positive appreciation of their divine creator, a high regard for the community as the locus of God's self-communication, a basically optimistic attitude of hope for redemption of everything"[31]

Analogical Imagination

Phan points out that while analogical thinking is present in the Catholic imagination, it is not restricted to Catholics only. Analogical imagination understands the Catholic self through analogies to our own experiences and our analogous understanding of others' experiences and God's saving work in history.[32] Catholic identity is not effectively formed by accentuating differences from others including other denominations and religions, as long as these remain superficial, but rather by acknowledging and exploring these deep structures of sacramentality, mediation, and communion.[33] "The analogical imagination does not, however, cancel out

28. Phan, "'Reception' or 'Subversion' of Vatican II by the Asian Churches?," 178

29. Ibid., 179.

30. McBrien, *Catholicism*, 1192–1200. Phan, "Religious Identity and Belonging amidst Diversity and Pluralism," 179.

31. Phan, "Religious Identity and Belonging amidst Diversity and Pluralism," 14.

32. David Tracy, who has contributed much to practical theology, covers analogical imagination in his book *The Analogical Imagination: Christian Theology and the Culture of Pluralism*.

33. Phan, "'Reception' or 'Subversion' of Vatican II by the Asian Churches?," 14. This brings about the value of dialogue and ecumenical dialogue as a means of fortifying Catholic identity (Phan, "Religious Identity and Belonging amidst Diversity and

differences and dissimilarities in its search for ordered relationships and analogies; rather, it clarifies them, even intensifies them, as the particularity of each position-understanding gains in intensity and becomes clearer to itself and to others, in the course of the conversation."[34]

These deep structures and analogical imagination present in conversations from the margins, assist hearing similarities as well as differences in views. One dialogue partner, Colleen, speaks here about her experiences in her Church community. She innately understands the presence of the deep structures of *sacramentality* in the valuing of each member of the inclusive community and of *mediation* in the ways God works through the poor and the experiences of people's lives. She intuits *communion* in the way the community, through the Spirit, is able to realize God's presence in the community, and change itself to bring a just inclusive community.

> Yeah, what did we have that made us realize that no, God is not a word talked down? You know, I really think it was, I'm guessing now, we were located in the inner city and we had a lot of inner-city programs for poor people. You know, we listened to the "down and outers." We listened to the marginalized, you know. So there were people who were coming to that Church who were not talked down to. People knew, I think, you listened. You learned from the street people, from the poor, from the marginalized and all that they said. "If you want us here, then you have to take us as we are." Perhaps that was it. We were not just a white invader just out of the suburbs. I think we learned from the 'down and outers' and the marginalized and the poor and the derelicts. Well, we always had a ministry for the special needs. We always had a special needs program for people, whether the derelicts or the special needs people. If they are going to fit into Church, you have to give a little. You can't just say, "Stick your tongue out for communion," and somewhere along the line that changed. Someone caught on that was goofy. Thank God, somebody catches on along the way. (Colleen, dialogue)

Beside the deep structures of sacramentality, mediation, and communion required to provide renewed awareness of the Spirit, a relational anthropological approach is also needed. "An anthropological approach to the need for community and church considers the ways in which the invitation of the Spirit through the deepest aspirations of the human person toward identity and mission reflects the *imago Dei* in each person that can

---

Pluralism," 288).

34. Hunt, "Trinity and Paschal Mystery," 71.

be fully received, purified, and realized in the communion of persons."[35] The anthropological foundation for the human as relational is the doctrine of God as Trinity.[36] Likewise, a doctrine of God as Trinity provides a theological anthropological foundation for a Trinitarian ecclesiology.

A TRINITARIAN ECCLESIOLOGY

Trinitarian ecclesiology grounds the Catholic Church as a dialogic Church and a communion of God's people.[37] The foundation of the dialogic Church is the communication of God with God's self in the Trinity and with God to humans: listening, speaking, and acting.[38] This calls the Church to *catholicity*, an awareness of the inclusive nature of the Church and communion with all people. It actively seeks the inclusion of all the People of God as Church, encouraging *communication, dialogue*, and a way of being together that is genuine relationship with each other and with God.

Catholicity—The Working of the Spirit

Pentecost provides a look at the early Church communities in which God's gift of understanding through the outpouring of the Spirit enabled understanding and difference to transform people's lives and the lives of their communities. "The Spirit does not so much create the structures and procedures but rather breaks open structures that confine and separate people so that they can welcome difference and the challenges and opportunities for new understanding that difference brings."[39] The working of the Spirit is integral to many dialogue partners' understandings of the diversity in the Church and the ways church communities are enlivened by it.

> Well, I think in our world we need to communicate. We have a responsibility to communicate. I don't like the word *schism*. Schism to me is Pius X. Schism is closer to Opus Dei, closer to legionnaires, but actually is found in Pius X. But they are more acceptable to the institution because they are closer to the right.

35. Hinze, "Releasing the Power of the Spirit in Trinitarian Ecclesiology," 368.

36. LaCugna, *God for Us*, 289.

37. Hinze, *Practices of Dialogue in the Roman Catholic Church*, 11–12.

38. Ibid.

39. Russell, *Just Hospitality*, 61.

> But the institution will not reach out to the people in the left like us. They will not do that kind of thing, because it is too challenging.

So what do you think will change that?

New people. The Holy Spirit. (Dan, dialogue)[40]

A Call to Catholicity

An anthropological understanding of Church based on a Trinitarian ecclesiology leads to a deeper catholicity. It requires a broad understanding of the universality of the Church's nature and mission. In the past, the Church emphasized a high Christology stressing the divinity of Christ, making Jesus' humanity seem less central. This correlated with a high ecclesiology. This high ecclesiology emphasized hierarchical and clerical forms of Church. Genuine diversity of voices exists in Scripture and in the tradition. In conjunction with these voices, the identity and mission of Jesus Christ empowered by the Spirit facilitates a more comprehensive understanding of Church today.[41] This ecclesiology roots itself not only in a renewed understanding of Jesus empowered by the Spirit, but also in an understanding of the Spirit at work in today's Church, the Church throughout history, and the early Church.

An awareness of the risen Jesus who through the Spirit is free to unleash the power of the charisms of all God's people empowers the Church.[42] "Thus the reach of the cosmic Christ becomes the reach of the Church."[43] The cosmic Christ, seen in the diversity of our cosmos, through the power of the Spirit guides it to a greater catholicity. This catholicity is evident in the Second Vatican Council's teaching on the universal call to holiness as the Spirit works in each individual giving the Spirit's gifts to each person. It can be seen in the willingness of the Second Vatican Council to consider

40. Dan's reference is to the Society of Pius X, led by Archbishop Lefebvre, who consecrated bishops in a manner not in communion with Pope John Paul II. Pope Benedict XVI has recently offered a means to accept full communion.

41. Hinze, "Releasing the Power of the Spirit in Trinitarian Ecclesiology," 349–50.

42. Gaillardetz, *Church in the Making*, 94.

43. Ibid. Hans Kung, Edward Schillebeeckx, Leonardo Boff, and Roger Haight, contemporary Catholic theologians, have developed an ecclesiology from below, starting with the people of God, making charisms the foundation and starting point for ministries and order in the Church (ibid., 98). After Vatican II, this became a foundation for lay involvement in the Church (ibid.).

catholicity of the Church from the perspective of other religions, not just the Roman Catholic Church.[44]

Communication and Dialogue

The self-communication of God in history through the Word and the Spirit offers a model of effective communication in the Church.[45] Vatican II changed the understanding of communication within the Catholic Church, moving from a hierarchical communication espoused during the previous few centuries to an exploration of both the individual and the community's dialogue with God and dialogue within the Catholic Church.[46] Pope John XXIII's emphasis on aggiornamento focused on bringing the Church up-to-date in the modern world. It also laid the groundwork for a dialogic Church.[47] The Council's examination of the Church's identity and mission deepened its understanding of the identity and mission of God. The Church summons people to dialogue to work for the common good, to promote justice and God's kindom in communities and in the world.

Ecclesiologist Yves Congar argues that "the indwelling of the Spirit in the individual, accompanied by cognitive, affective, and moral fruits and gifts of the Spirit, needed to be more sufficiently integrated into an ecclesiological framework."[48] This understanding invites the Church to dialogue not demanding unity, but rather reveling in diversity with the inner faith that our deepest relationships with God and each other call us as a people to harmonious dialogue. "Once our internal geography recognizes that, however much we are center, we are not the only one, we have no choice

44. Ibid., 51.

45. Hinze, "Releasing the Power of the Spirit in Trinitarian Ecclesiology," 369.

46. Hinze, *Practices of Dialogue in the Roman Catholic Church*, 19–20. Catherine LaCugna started with the work of Karl Rahner and Rahner's insistence that the Trinity revealed God's self-communication. "LaCugna believed, in contrast, that the God revealed in the Incarnation and paschal mystery of Jesus Christ is a God who acts in the freedom of love (which cannot be reduced to a freedom of choice) and that this love is indistinguishable from the divine being" (Groppe, "Catherine Mowry LaCugna's Contribution to Trinitarian Theology," 736). Chapter 3 takes a closer look at Trinity and how our own human personhood is rooted in relationship because we are the *imago Dei*, created in the image of the Triune God.

47. Mannion, *Ecclesiology and Postmodernity*, 110.

48. Cited in Hinze, "Releasing the Power of the Spirit in Trinitarian Ecclesiology," 353. Hinze's later work in 2006 examines the role of dialogue in the pre-Vatican II and the Vatican II Church.

but to affirm the positions of others not as 'marginal' to our centers, but as centers of their own."[49]

> Vatican II it invited all of us to change, right? So that change was an instrument for further change and the following of that thread, the flow of that. The externals changed, the priests were now facing the people . . . But the internals, like who is Jesus to you, they were still there. Suddenly we were doing the handshake of peace, deep relationship, well, even revealing relationship. Jesus was the primary relationship and then the format the church took around that and the relationship with the diversity of people within the church. That was the whole underlying thing, unity and diversity. (Mai, dialogue)

Communion—Koinonia

A Trinitarian ecclesiology calls the Church to communion, that is, koinonia. This has both practical and social implications for the Church today. In his letter to Philemon, Paul speaks of sharing faith (Phil 4–7); the word used for sharing is koinonia.[50] In Scripture, koinonia is the participation of the community in the life of the Creator God, Jesus, and the Spirit—the participation in the Trinitarian relationship of God.[51] Koinonia emphasizes a vertical relationship with God, but also a horizontal relationship with the People of God and the world.[52]

In Harry's story of his Church community, the Spirit's presence presents herself in the life experiences of the Church and the prophetic actions of this community, in their communication, dialogue, and communion. This idea of Spirit relates to ecclesiology—the Spirit linking all Christians *in communio*—the communion between God and God's people and God's

49. Carroll, *Practicing Catholic*, 313.

50. Osiek, *Philippians, Philemon*, 135. Paul's writings to the various churches of Corinth, Thessalonica, Galatia, Rome, and Philippi reveal the early church as community struggling to understand itself as Church—in Christ—God's new community in which all were full citizens in the kindom of God (Roetzel, *Letters of Paul*, 3, 51, 79).

51. Fuchs, *Koinonia and the Quest for an Ecumenical Ecclesiology*, 12. Too often, people speak of the Trinity in terms of masculine imagery—God the Father, God the Son, and God the Spirit. Elizabeth Johnson, CSJ, a theologian who teaches at Fordham University in New York, suggests that the female imagery has been absent but that the triune God could be imaged as creator, spirit, wisdom. Additionally, the triune God may be imaged as mother, Sophia God, Sophia's child Jesus, Sophia spirit.

52. Gaillardetz, *Church in the Making*, 47.

people with each other.[53] Harry's story speaks about a community open to the multiple voices of the Church community who dialogue and theologically reflect on their experiences. This action moves them to action, and newness in their parish community.

> In the seventies they reinvented the parish and they said, "We're an urban parish, we've got all these poor people who are sleeping on our doorstep, let's figure out how we can help." I think it attracted people who believed it. I don't think it was the first two pastors, they weren't the nucleus of it, but they enabled it. In the Vatican II era there was lots of participation. The pastor was a firm believer that he had such a big job already running all this stuff that was going on at ___ that he pretty much let the community run the liturgy and the music and so on. When our next pastor came, there was a proposal from the Archdiocese called Clustering. They were investigating whether they would cluster parishes so that there would be two priests for six parishes. This terrified us for two reasons: one, we were worried that we would be left out in the cold because we were so small with three or four hundred people; and we were competing with communities with three and four thousand in the suburbs. We would just get shut down. So, we had parish assemblies, and we had surveys, and we had focus groups, and we had dinner events to talk about it. I think we way overreacted to it. One of the results of it was at a parish assembly they were sort of saying, "Well, (pastor) what do you think?" He's the pastor and he's just sitting in the pews like everybody else. He said, "We have to acknowledge that there probably will be a time when there is no priest, or not a regular priest, and we need to get prepared for that, and we want to continue." So, we started having lay prayer leaders and we started having more homilies by lay people. It used to be an unusual occurrence, and it became the norm. We started having the entire liturgy planning done by the worship committee. It was gradual. It was this idea that we've got this vision in the future that we may not have an ordained priest, and we've got to get ready because we don't want to lose what we've got. The people at (parish) are not shy, so there were some people who didn't want to stand up and preach, but they were happy to make the bread. Or there's somebody who loves making textiles, so they would do the decorations. Somebody would take communion to the nursing homes because the priest couldn't do it all. (Harry, dialogue)

53. Kärkkäinen, *Trinity Global Perspectives*, 47.

Koinonia as Body of Christ—Relating

A traditional understanding of the Trinitarian Church works to realize that a koinonia with God in communion with Jesus Christ and the Spirit is relational. [54]Koinonia involves the action of relating both to God and each other, the action of participating, and the action of dialogue with Triune God and with others. Ken understands this communion as a call to be Body of Christ.

> Well, Church . . . it's really tied into community, you know. Where do we contact the divine? Through the world you do, and through community you do, and through other people. It's like we are the Body of Christ and at the words of institution it's like, I think that's really strong that we are the Body of Christ and the bread is the symbol of us being the Body of Christ, not separate from us or Jesus made into a thing. (Ken, dialogue)

J. Y. Lee uses a Christocentric and Trinitarian approach to koinonia. The heart of the Church's life is Eucharist, drawing people together to form the Body of Christ. Eucharist allows people to experience in a unique way the presence of God in their midst. From an Asian perspective, Eucharist is a family affair, springing from respect for ancestors and an ancestral rite that is not only remembering, but also service to one's ancestors.[55] This adds a new dimension, revealing family as the primordial expression of koinonia.[56] Koinonia as family, in all of its forms, reveals the interconnectedness and relationship of all God's people that koinonia embodies.

Koinonia as Body of Christ—Acting

Koinonia begins in the understanding of the Church as Body of Christ.[57] The body of Christ acts throughout history as the People of God who make Christ present and dynamic in the world from the resurrection of Christ to the end of time.[58] This understanding brings the kindom of God here through the sacramental action of doing for others in the memory of Jesus, what Jesus does for us. "At the center of the Church's self consciousness as

---

54. T. Brown, "Personhood as a Tool to Reflect upon Koinonia," 167.

55. J. Y. Lee, *Trinity in Asian Perspective*, 184–85

56. Ibid., 197.

57. Schneiders, *Revelatory Text*, 41

58. Ibid.

Church is its experienced oneness with the risen Jesus who is Christ and Lord . . ."[59]

> I do like the idea of Eucharist and communion. And communion is bigger than a wafer, that's for sure. And the whole, "this is my body" that's the whole action. You all here [waves hands towards imagined people]—that's my body. So "this is my body" finally for me stood for more than this hunk of bread. "This is my body" was all inclusive. (Colleen, dialogue)

This action toward communion—koinonia—by the people and by the Church is transformative praxis. These actions, throughout history bring about a community of equal companions through the grace of the Spirit. "It is a kinship in hope that demonstrates the continuous movement of the Spirit of God in all times and places and peoples and cultures; a koinonia that demonstrates that the creed is not an abstraction but comes to birth in a continuous river of holy lives; a company of the friends of God and prophets today, in the past, and in the future."[60]

> I would say that we need to gather in community, whether you do that in an established Church, however you do this, this is what we need to do. Community is very, very important. Breaking the bread of our lives together, sitting down and saying, "What kind of a month did you have?" We need to pray together. We need to hear one another's stories. We need to be compassionate with one another. That's the most important thing for us to do in this day and age because we are so riddled by violence; people need to gather in a compassionate way. (Sarah, dialogue)

Koinonia as Body of Christ—Dialoguing

As people gather in a compassionate way, as Sarah encourages, the Church deals with diversity, divergence, and polarity. A positive response to these is dialogue. It is through the action of dialogue that the Church can strive to realize a greater communion. This returns the Church in its catholicity, communication, and koinonia again to the necessity of non-consensus seeking dialogue. Dialogue in the Church cannot happen without an ecclesial culture that wishes to listen, to discuss, and to become responsive

59. Ibid., 72.

60. Johnson and Brumbaugh, "Trinity: To Let the Symbol Sing Again," 138.

to all sides of the real questions and issues of all those in the Church, including those on the margins.[61]

Yet catholicity, dialogue, and koinonia raise questions as to their limits. What priority do structures within the Church have? Is priority given to the universal church, espousing an approach emphasizing a Christocentric approach rather than a Trinitarian approach? Should there be an emphasis on ecclesial authority, office, protection of official teaching of the Church, and obedient response of the faithful? Or is priority to be given to the communion of the local church and the communion of churches emphasizing subsidiarity and the exercise of authority in ways that do not destabilize the working of the Spirit in the life of the Church?[62] Can priority be given to a communion of churches that also include the margins in ways that do not suppress individual self-expression with authoritarianism? Diversity and polarity in the Church revolve around ideas of catholicity and communion, inclusion and exclusion and choice, authority and freedom. These are important questions in the Church today. They can be answered in both the affirmative and the negative depending on one's ecclesiology and model of Church.

Finding Common Ground

Cardinal Bernardin's Common Ground Project, founded in 1996 to address the acrimonious polarity present in the Church on a multitude of issues, is an example of the dialogic church. It gathered radical, conservative, liberal, and moderate Catholics together in dialogue to discuss pastoral issues in the Church in hope of coming to a consensus.[63] Through dialogue and learning it hoped to avoid the distrust, polarization, and inflexibility in thinking about issues that characterized debate in the Catholic Church during the past few decades.

61. Hinze, *Practices of Dialogue in the Roman Catholic Church*, 240–43.

62. Hinze, "Releasing the Power of the Spirit in a Trinitarian Ecclesiology," 379.

63 "Catholic Common Ground Initiative 2010." Cardinal Bernardin—Archbishop of Chicago and chair of the U.S. bishops' committee that drafted a pastoral letter on war and peace—articulated a consistent ethic of life from womb to tomb. "Those who defend the right to life of the weakest among us must be equally visible in support of the quality of life of the powerless among us: the old and the young, the hungry and the homeless, the undocumented immigrant and the unemployed worker" (Bernardin, *Consistent Ethic of Life*). After Bernardin's untimely death, the group continued to meet, and Bernardin's consistent ethic of life, a "seamless garment" in looking at the ethics of life from womb to tomb, continues to give an opportunity for Catholics to move from one-issue politics to a more systematic, consistent ethic of life.

Will the Catholic Church in the United States enter the new millennium as a Church of promise, augmented by the faith of rising generations and able to be a leavening force in our culture? Or will it become a Church on the defensive, torn by dissension and weakened in its core structures? The outcome, we believe, depends on whether American Catholicism can confront an array of challenges with honesty and imagination and whether the Church can reverse the polarization that inhibits discussion and cripples leadership. American Catholics must reconstitute the conditions for addressing our differences constructively, a common ground centered on faith in Jesus, marked by accountability to the living Catholic tradition, and ruled by a renewed spirit of civility, dialogue, generosity, and broad and serious consultation.[64]

In the twenty-first century, polarization has become even more intense in the Catholic Church, in the United States and throughout the world. The Church continues to be challenged to enter the next decade as a Church of promise, confronting polarization and difference with honesty, imagination, dialogue, and generosity. Terry and Colleen are anxious for the Church to be relevant and authentic in its approach to the challenges they see today.

What does the Church stand for in terms of its whole social justice, you know? The other thing I do appreciate about the Church, though, is not well publicized; again, we're not a one-issue Church. You know, one issue should not be the litmus. Nobody's for abortion. It is not the litmus test for every person. I have heard many, many priests and have read from other bishops that said we're not a one-issue Church. And there are plenty of issues out there, you know, womb to tomb, and the whole business. (Terry, dialogue)

Yeah, I think that clinched it when they started to say that the gays couldn't be Catholic; and then the divorced and the remarried, they couldn't be Catholic; and if you voted for someone who they did not agree with, you couldn't be Catholic. You know, it didn't make any sense. Gradually, they're kicking people out of the Church and then we set up programs for alienated Catholics. Well, we are alienating them. I thought, "There's something wrong here." (Colleen, dialogue)

64. "Catholic Common Ground Initiative 2010."

The Church is made for relationship; yet relationships are difficult. Because understandings of Church differ, people's expectations differ. Some call for unity at all costs understanding Church from one model. This model wishes to continue strict ecclesial authority with little freedom of choice. This is seen as necessary to protect and defend the collective wisdom of the Church tradition. Others are more comfortable in a diverse Church, dialogic practices that agree to disagree, and a unity in diversity. "In God there is unity in diversity and diversity in unity."[65]

Many Catholics on the margins love the Catholic Church, identify deeply with it, and are often pained by their alienation. Ted, one of my dialogue partners, is an example.

> So we got word that a couple of weeks after Easter that our pastor is going to be gone. It was this feeling of, we are the branches, the whole thing about the tree and the branches thing. But it felt like the hierarchy is who's really in charge here. You can talk all you want and do all you want, but when it comes down to it, it is the hierarchy and it is a monarchy, and there is somebody in charge that can do anything they want. That really upset me. I work in organizational development. I work with people with transitions all the time and they brought in a transition team that was doing stuff that was fifteen years old; they didn't listen to the people. We had these wonderful things we were implementing and they put this associate priest in the role of the pastor. He says, "I've got this parish and I'm gonna take it for a spin," to quote him. I think the Church in a way is—at least in the U.S. from what I can see—is missing an opportunity to engage in community at a deeper level. I don't feel like I'm a child of the Church. I think we're kind of taught that. I feel like I'm an adult, mature. I want a mature relationship with the leaders of my faith and I don't think it's a mature relationship right now. The hierarchy needs to listen and I don't feel they're listening. I feel disconnected from the community. And that's it, not just from the hierarchical Church, the bigger Church—the big c Church—but also disconnected from the little c church. (Ted, dialogue)

Ted describes churches needing authenticity and listening. He also uses the terms big c Catholic Church and the little c church, allowing a beginning appreciation of his understanding of Church.[66] This suggests a move to

65. Orsy, *Receiving the Council*, 5.

66. When talking about Church as part of society, Church as a large c can be understood as God's invisible creation. Church with a large c can also be understood as

consideration of the models of Church that arise in people's understanding of Church. This chapter uses a practical theological perspective rising from the praxis and experiences of Catholics. I write acknowledging the historical insight that the Church has continuously undergone change and is, in fact, undergoing change in this twenty-first century.

ECCLESIOLOGY: MODELS OF CHURCH

Institution, Denomination, Association

The Church as institution is one among many institutions in modern society. It can be seen as universal, encompassing all members of society. As a community of believers, with God as the source and destination of the Church, the Church is inclusive; made up of people who have not chosen each other, but rather ones who are brought together in solidarity and friendship as the Body of Christ.[67] The Church can also be understood as denomination that is one institution among many. It can also be seen as an association, open in freedom and choice to those who join, with autonomy to determine their closeness or distance in participation in the Church during their lives. Some on the margins of the Catholic Church, like Julia, understand the Catholic Church not only as Body of Christ, but also as an association, open to the freedom of choice.

> I wore something with bare shoulders and I was cold-shouldered by all these old Italian women. You know, like they were making frumping noises around me and staring at me like I was inappropriate. At one point, one woman dropped a jacket on me before I went to Communion. I was angry, humiliated, and infuriated. Because I wouldn't walk into a mosque with my shoes on. I respect other people's faith traditions. I was kind of like, this is my faith tradition; I know what's acceptable and what is not. The fact is Jesus doesn't care whether I'm wearing a tank top, and so I was so angry and really humiliated. I'm talking about

universal, encompassing all members of society and contributing to personal and social integration (Van der Ven, *Ecclesiology in Context*, 23). In the Catholic Church, the People of God are always seen as Church with a large *c* (Carroll, *Practicing Catholic*, 6). The Church with a small *c* is the visible institution. This Church can be understood as an association in which God is working in and through people who come together as a community expressing their engagement in the world (Van der Ven, *Ecclesiology in Context*, 140). Ted's use of big *c* Catholic Church is meant to refer to the hierarchical Catholic Church, and his use of small *c* to refer to the Church parish.

67. Van der Ven, *Ecclesiology in Context*, 43.

this because I feel it might be useful, but it's not something I talk about. I walked out of the Church when it was over; I spat on the steps. I was pissed and I left. From that point on I would tell people I left the Catholic Church to beat the rush. So, for awhile after that I just didn't go to Church. (Julia dialogue)

Many in the Church and on the margins call for dialogue and an adult relationship with Church officials and the wider Church community, despite the fact that sometimes their understanding of the Catholic Church is criticized by current twenty-first century official Church teaching and conservative Catholics.

I really would like Church to be more inclusive and I know that Catholic means universal and probably that is it was meant to be in the end. But something that accepts different perspectives would be good. You got to have structure, rules and guidelines but some of the arbitrariness that exists that we have discussed earlier, like women priests . . . A Church that looks at society and gives guidance to the current needs to the people involved in the Church, not necessarily based on whatever history or precedence told them to teach. I think that would be the main thing. A Church that looks at society and says this is what our followers need from us and we are going to give them that. Ultimately it will take a pope being appointed or voted on with the cardinals that has a more modern view. Ultimately it could be a decision could be made that individual communities could decide what to do within the framework of the larger teachings of the Church. (Terry, dialogue)

Well, I think the priest or the clergy in general, the hierarchy is teaching out of a fear mode rather than a freeing mode. I suppose a lot of it is fear of losing their status maybe, their bread and butter. I don't know, but I think there's a fear in them that I don't have. What priest would stand up there and not give you communion because you had a rainbow stole on. What would make them do that? I don't get it. I just don't get it. (Colleen, dialogue)

"It is self-evident to everyone, Christians and non-Christians alike, that the community which calls itself the Church of Christ never lives in a social, cultural, or political vacuum."[68] In this twenty-first century, the Church is no longer the center of society as it was centuries ago in an agrarian, pre-urban, and premodern time. The Church, along with other

68. Schillebeeckx, *Church: The Human Story of God*, 187.

aspects of society (social, political, economic, and cultural), is characterized by a certain specialization due to increased institutionalization and differentiation of functions of society and the rigidity and complexity of bureaucracy that emphasizes policies rather than personal loyalties.[69] A sense of individual autonomy and the leveling of social authority that arose with modernity in the nineteenth and twentieth century's combines with this increased institutionalization. The resulting polarization of the Church makes the Church, like every other institution in society, an object of discussion, criticism and protest, as well as the object of reflection, change, and conflict.[70]

MODELS OF CHURCH

Understanding One's Own Model of Church

The struggle with advances in technology and science and the resulting changes in society and their effects on religion pits both a liberal reaction and a conservative reaction rife with polarity, division, and diversity against each other. While diversity, polarity, and division are not new, struggling with individualism, globalization, pluralism, and the effects of moving to an urban, technologically advanced society make this a contemporary struggle. From this struggle models of Church arise.[71] "To survive in this skeptical world, theologians sought to make religion believable to rational, scientifically attuned minds—and offered a set of moral precepts more than any claims of miracle or transcendence. The liberal project, at least in the last century, has sought uniquely modern forms from religious faith and practice, updating old doctrine and ritual and eschewing any claims to timeless truth."[72] The conservative approach has often claimed that more isolated sectarian communities with strict rules and beliefs are necessary to endure the modern challenge. Yet, in this twenty-first century, another paradigm may be more beneficial, one that brings in the *both-and* leading the Church to the *in-beyond* understanding of being *in-both*. "The Church today is experiencing, more acutely perhaps than in former times, an uneasy tension; but it is a tension that ought to prove fruitful. Local Churches, and even certain groups within them, are becoming ever more

69. Jodock, ed., *Catholicism Contending with Modernity*, 338.

70. Van der Ven, *Ecclesiology in Context*, 18.

71. Ibid., xiv.

72. Ammerman, "Journeys of Faith," 42–43.

conscious of their distinctive characteristics within the universal Church. There is a growing conviction that the grace of catholicity cannot unfold to its full extent unless a genuine diversity exists between the ecclesial communities within the same communion."[73]

An examination of church models enables a consideration of the various understandings of Church, and a chance to identify one's own primary working model. "The Church is a mystery. It is a reality imbued with the hidden presence of God. It lies therefore within the very nature of the Church to be always open to new and ever greater exploration."[74] In the history of the Catholic Church, many images of church arise from Scripture.[75] "When an image is employed reflectively and critically to deepen one's theoretical understanding of reality it becomes what today is called a 'model.'"[76]

New paradigms for models of church develop in response to changes in the church and society, helping the church to find its identity in a changing world. No one model can effectively describe the church, as each has its weaknesses and its strengths. Questions of each model are pertinent to a discussion of models of church. In terms of this model, what are the relationships that unite the church? Who are the beneficiaries of the church's activities? What is the purpose of the church and its ministry?[77] These questions enable an understanding of the strength that weaknesses of each model and a deeper understanding of one's own model of church. Models of church can synthesize what is already known, as well as point out inconsistencies and incongruence reflecting problems in the models of church.

73. Pontifical Biblical Commission, *Interpretation of the Bible in Church*, 5.

74. Pope Paul VI, quoted in Dulles, *Models of the Church*, 18.

75. Among these are communities of disciples sent to the world (Rom 15, Mark 13), community of visible witness through faith and virtue (1 Pet, Rev, Acts), and community of healing and reconciliation (Matt, Luke, John) (Senior, "Correlating Images of Church and Images of Mission in the New Testament," 6–7). Paul Minear noted ninety-six images of church from the New Testament in his seminal work first published in 1960. These include members of Christ, communion of the Holy Spirit, unleavened bread, and the people of God. (Minear, *Images of the Church in the New Testament*, 268–69). "It was really the pastoral orientation of Vatican II, so refreshingly enunciated in the *Constitution on the Church* (*Lumen Gentium*) and the *Constitution on the Church in the Modern World* (*Gaudium et Spes*), that gave rise to a variety of different models with strongly biblical roots. Re-imaging the Church as the People of God, Body of Christ, Sacrament, Communion, Servant, were obvious departures from the previous notion of the Church as '*societas perfecta*' . . ." (Ciuba, "Impact of Changing Ecclesiological and Christological Models," 66).

76. Dulles, *Models of Church*, 23.

77. Ibid., 190–94.

Every model must be critically contextual. "Models of the church must not be dictated by cultural reality, but they must be voiced and practiced in ways that take careful account of the particular time and circumstance into which God's people are called."[78]

Models of Church in Context

Ted places his model of Church in the context of Vatican II, the turbulent sixties, and his family's experiences.

> I grew up in the sixties, Vatican II, and the social justice and the change in our communities. My parents started being right in the middle of that. They were older for that time period. But they were very much making that transition into the new Church. We grew up in [city, state] which was very conservative and it's the Mason-Dixon line of it in many ways. There's a lot of racism and bigotry. Not many African Americans live, well, they couldn't live in the community for very long. They would be chased out, I remember as a kid. The reason I brought that up is that my dad went through a metamorphosis of sorts in the sixties with Vatican II. Even before that, things were shifting. He was a teacher. At that time, as a little kid, we would have two Catholic brothers stay with us, and they were African Americans. And it was the first experience of being with somebody who's black and living with us for a couple of days probably. May have been longer. We would have people come visit with us, stay with us. We would kind of welcome people of different orders, usually Catholic. They were very much making that transition into the new Church. (Ted, dialogue)

VAN DER VEN'S FIVE MODELS OF CHURCH

Models proposed by Van der Ven are particularly interesting in the current context of today's Catholic Church in the United States. Ecclesial models range from church as the center of society and therefore coextensive with society to church as a subsection or part of society. Echoes of these models can be heard in both conversations about the Catholic Church and its needs in society from the margins of the Catholic Church in the United States, as well as in conversations within the hierarchical

78. Brueggemann, "Rethinking Church Models through Scripture," 129

Church as well. These ecclesial models because they are revealed in the context of economic, political, social, and cultural context can be seen in the Catholic Church throughout its history in the United States. The choice for a particular model suggests a preference for the position of the church in society.[79]

Van der Ven's five normative ecclesial models differ in their resistance or acceptance of modernity.[80] Three of the models—the amodern church, the amodern basic community, and the critical-modern basic community—critique modernity. The first two models are marked by required obedience to the authority of the church; a clear distinction between two classes in the church, that is, clergy and laity, based on the divine origin of its ministry; and an understanding that this church bears universal truth that cannot be questioned.[81] Echoes of these models can be heard as some within the Catholic hierarchy call for a smaller, holier Church and retrenchment toward a pre-Vatican II Church. In the amodern church, as the absolute bearer of faith, people want to return to a time when the church was the center of society. It is the only model to insist that the church must become the center of society again.[82] The amodern basic community's goal is to isolate the church from society as a small and holy few. Both the amodern and amodern basic communities resist modernization, turning away from society. Weaknesses in these models include a lack of dialogue with diversity, exclusion of those with differing views, and benefits to those in power in the church. The third model, the critical-modern basic community, does not turn away from society but rather engages actively and critically with society with the purpose of transforming it.[83] The critical-modern basic community, small in size, emphasizes the transcendence of the Gospel that the church proclaims and the apocalyptic time of the kindom of God is happening now. It is marked by demand for adherence to moral and religious principles and

---

79. Van der Ven, *Ecclesiology in Context*, 3–27. Models for church suggested by Avery Dulles, a Jesuit theologian in the Catholic Church, are widely used and include five models originally proposed in 1978 and a sixth additional model proposed by Dulles in 1987. These are: institution, mystical communion, sacrament, herald, servant, and school of discipleship. These models seek to understand church as community in terms of a basic paradigm drawn from ordinary human experience (Dulles, *Models of Church*, 15–33).

80. Van der Ven, *Ecclesiology in Context*, 27–31.

81. Ibid., 28.

82. Ibid.

83. Ibid., 30.

high personal and communal devotion. This is the model found in small Christian communities within larger parish communities. Bill and Lily speak here of their interaction with several of these models of Church.

> I would go to Mass and get angry at the priest for what he was saying to the children. About if they don't go to Mass, if they don't go to confession, if they don't go to confession before going to Communion. It's like Jesus didn't say that. He said, "Sit down, I'll feed you." He didn't ask how old you were, he didn't ask you what you believed. He just said, "Sit down and I'll feed you." And the priest was getting really angry with the kids. "This is how you behave, this is how you believe." I would leave Mass and the kids would walk back to school and I would drive and I would just pray, pray, pray that I would let that go before I got back to school. I didn't want the kids picking up on it. (Lily, dialogue)

> I think I get more energy from the small faith community. You know, our liturgies are a couple of hours or so and they go by in a flash. I think most people would recognize it for what it is. It's more, I think, in line with the early Church—you know, the home liturgies, the home sharing, a sharing of faith and spirituality and trying to tie what's going on in our lives with readings, and kind of supporting one another. (Bill, dilaogue)

In contrast, the final two ecclesial models—modern denomination and critical modern denomination—emphasize personal engagement and religious freedom and accept modernization.[84] These are marked by open communication between the individual and church tradition. In the modern denominational model, church is seen as one institution among many in a society that guarantees freedom in the church.[85] In the critical modern denominational model, the people of the church are aware of the negative consequences of modernization—economic injustice, social alienation, and loss of cultural meaning. Emphasis in this model is placed on the transcendence of the Gospel through metaphors of time.[86] God's presence in both the past and the future is revealed in the coming of Christ into the world that both interrupts the presence and allows it to retain some resemblance of consistency.[87] This model of church tries to contribute to the lessening of the needs and the suffering of the people. In these models

---

84. Van der Ven, *Ecclesiology in Context*, 22–23.

85. Ibid., 28.

86. Ibid.

87. Ibid., 27–30.

engagement with society and service to the world are key and create bonds within the church.[88] While emphasis in religious freedom is more congruent with modern American culture, the time needed to dialogue with diverse views requires a commitment from all involved. Response to its members and society and the community over church structures offers benefits to the church, but also requires introspection so that the church maintains its mission and identity.

Dialogue partners on the margins of the Catholic Church call for a Church with echoes of a critical modern denominational model. Anne and Harry describe their ideas of this model of Church.

> What do I think of when I think of Church? A sense of community and the sense of change. The sense that the Gospel asks us to change things in the world we are in and not to rest and not to sit still. That sense of movement and momentum, I think is the most important thing about it to me. Some of that is personal momentum and change. And maybe that's part of what I identify with being Catholic because I grew up in a service and justice Catholic place, to me that's what Catholic means. It wasn't until I got farther out that I understood that that's not everybody else's experience as Catholic but that's the only experience of Catholic that I'm interested in. (Anne, dialogue)

> I don't think we're returning to the roots intentionally by saying, "Ok, what are the roots? Let's go there." I think we're sitting there saying, "What's the right thing to do, Oh, look, we're just like a similar Christian community." I think it's more like we're choosing the things that are just, and the things we think are most empowering and most enlivening and they coincide with the early Church. So, we're not aiming to be a first-century community, I think we're aiming to be twenty-first century, and I think it has amazing correlations. (Harry, dialogue)

BRUEGGEMANN'S MODELS OF CHURCH

Because people on the margins are asking questions about tradition, texts, and living into new, communal ways of being church in a church marked by increasing polarity in conservative and progressive views Brueggemann's models of church provide a helpful perspective. Brueggemann explores the Hebrew Scriptures to suggest models of church that are deeply

88. Ibid., 22–30.

reflective of social crisis and historical circumstance and applicable far beyond the worldview of Hebrew Scripture worlds. For Brueggemann, an examination of church models requires thinking about the place where the person and the community are situated with God and what modeling is appropriate in the present time and circumstance.[89] The three models— a premonarchic model as a *new church start*, a monarchic model as *temple community*, and a post-exilic model as a *textual community*—appropriate the past traditions and reshapes the earlier traditions for its own use.[90]

A Temple Community

The *temple community* model is marked by a convergence of church and state, relative stability, members whose lives moved from the religious dimension into secularization, and a visible and funded leadership.[91] These were present in ancient Israel, particularly around the time of David, and are present now. For the Hebrew people the temple orders the civil imagination of the people of the time. In the temple community model established religion serves the powerful by stabilizing power and knowledge at the expense of others in the church and community.[92] Prophets exist in this model calling for a more radical and purer vision of faith. Analogies have been made between this time in the Hebrew Scripture and the Constantinian establishment of the Church. Brueggemann suggests that this is the governing model of modern established Christianity in the Western church.[93] Deb lives in an area where expected participation in a church is part of the fabric of the community. Sarah talks about being a prophet in today's Church.

> Coming down here, it's a very different dynamic from anywhere that I've been. I'm sure you've seen those differences, but you're

89. Brueggemann , "Rethinking Church Models through Scripture," 129.

90. Ibid., 136. In the Hebrew Testament, the temple community, at the center of society, existed from 1000 BCE to 587 BCE as Jerusalem established the monarchy and dynasty (ibid., 129). This is the core model for the people of the Hebrew Testament. The temple model is one in which the temple, the role of kings, the sages influential in the establishment, and the prophets all played a part in the temple's stability. Early Israel and the new church start model can be located at the time of Moses to David (1250 BCE to 1000 BCE) and incorporates the exodus period and a non-unified, socioeconomically marginalized community (ibid., 131–32).

91. Brueggemann , "Rethinking Church Models through Scripture," 130.

92. Ibid.

93. Ibid., 130–31.

in the Bible Belt where you can be washing the kitchen one day and your neighbor is banging on your door to offer you a Bible. There's just such a culture of religion and such a culture for even friendship around that religion. I've gotten multiple offers to come to this Bible study, come to church with us, come to this, that and the other thing. Do I want to make that my social outlet when I may not necessarily agree with a lot of the terms? I guess that has been something I've debated being down here. You're in such a dense environment, but I don't know that any part of being down here has led me to say, "Hey, I really want to do this like, I'll join the Church to fit in." (Deb, dialogue)

You know, I do believe that a prophet is one who stands up and speaks when everybody else is seated and silent, and who in their right mind wants to be called a prophet? My community knows that I stand in protest when we have these liturgies without inclusivity. I said to them, "If I am not present at the Eucharist would it be okay if I come to dinner?" "Of course." One on one, that's what I get all the time. However, Father _____ noticed that I wasn't there and I went over to greet him when we all sat down to dinner and he said, "Did you come to mass?" I said, "No." He said, "Why not?" I said, "It's another silent protest." He took my hands in his and said, "I get it." So, that's what I struggle with. (Sarah, dialogue)

A New Church Start

The *new church start* is a community birthed in marginality.[94] Such a community, while not having stable resources, is compelled by a shared commitment to a central story and a distinctive social passion.[95] Marked by improvisation and borrowing from the culture around it, what is borrowed is transformed by covenant and a passion for liberation and dependence on the movement of the Spirit. A *new church start*, such as Israel in the premonarchic period of Moses, "entails planting of an alternative community among people who were ready for risk and shunned established social relations because such resources and patterns inevitably led to domestication and bondage."[96]

94. Ibid., 133.
95. Ibid.
96. Ibid.

Yeah, I think that's where we were operating, on the margins of the traditional Roman Catholic Church. I picked my church because of what it was doing, and who the people were and what it stood for. It started an emergency shelter, a temporary emergency shelter in 1982 and it still is running. Its involvement in the neighborhood and its justice issues, and people committed and then the whole sense of an alive progressive community are important. Then the new priest wanted to see that we were regularized. What it meant is that they said we would have to cease the liturgy as it had been through three pastors. It would destroy our prayer, and destroy our community and no one, well, there are a few people, but the vast majority were like 'no.' We had three discussions. The second meeting we said, 'What would it mean if people went through every part of the mass and what that means, and what this means and what we'd have to do, the detail in the order of the mass etc.?' A couple of people went through that really, from their background. Ones who really knew it. So then, at the third meeting, because we were conscious that this is our decision, that we have to go one of two ways, we voted. And there were 119 people there and the vote was 113 to 6 that we keep going. Why would we want to regularize? So we moved the liturgy six blocks away. I mean it's not mass according to the rubric, the *GIRM* [*General Instruction of the Roman Missal*]. But sure, Rome defines what that word means. So, I don't need to use the word. But it's Eucharist. (Ken, dialogue)

A Textual Community

Brueggemann's final model, the *textual community*, works at the development of strategies and mechanisms for survival in a universalizing culture where the community has little influence over public policy.[97] As a community on the margins, recovery of memory and rootedness and connectedness is a primary task of such a community as is the intense practice of hope.[98] A textual community is engaged in formulating and interpreting text in a way that does note search for consensus. It rather struggles with the text, engages, and enters into the tradition of speech, reflection, discernment, and imagination as they witness to another reality. This textual community uses the materials of earlier models but constantly re-imagines and reinvents the earlier texts for the sake of its marginalized

97. Brueggemann , "Rethinking Church Models through Scripture," 133–34.
98. Ibid., 134.

community in its present crisis.[99] What happens is the textual community leads to a *new church start*. Brueggemann suggests that this is happening today.[100] This movement from temple to text is what some people in the margins of the Catholic Church are doing as they search for authentic ways of living out their Catholic faith.

> I'm a traditional Catholic. This generation is not new. As we are marching, we are pilgrims marching on the way to God. Every generation brings their own culture, their own understanding to the party. Jesus didn't say don't do that. Jesus said love one another. Be with one another. Care for one another, that's all Jesus said. What connects us is coming to the table and being included at the table, and I think we need to have an ongoing understanding of history. We need to have an ongoing understanding of what our rights and responsibilities are in this Church and we also have to have a healthy cynicism. We have to develop a healthy cynicism about what the hierarchy is telling us and how much we can buy, if anything at all we are going to bring out a new Church from the ashes. Because right now, what's happening? We're hospicing this old Church. It's very evident to me that this is a dying Church. People are disgusted with the secrecy; they are having a hard time buying into the old Latin that's coming back. The only ones that are, are the more conservative young people who've never even seen it before and it's interesting [to them]. (Miriam, dialogue)

Reimagining and Reinventing for the Sake of the Community

The movement to reimagining and reinventing the earlier texts for the sake of the community that is marginalized happens in this twenty-first century as the dominant models of church no longer hold. "A move from temple to text, requires a reconsideration of our social location, of the resources on which we can and must count, and of the work we have to do about the infrastructure that has largely collapsed."[101] This movement from temple to text requires that those on the margins recover memory, examining their roots and the ways in which they are connected. It requires practicing hope, studying and interpreting foundational texts

99. Ibid., 133.

100. Ibid., 134.

101. Brueggemann, "Rethinking Church Models through Scripture," 138.

imaginatively so that the community can engage and discern ways of living into another reality of church.[102]

Both Van der Ven's and Brueggemann's models of church speak to today's context. Van der Ven presents models seen within the church and within marginalized communities as they react to the stresses of postmodernity. Brueggemann describes how communities deal with and grow in their faithfulness to God as church models become more comfortable and a part of the center. Diversity gives rise to division, causing marginalization, and these marginalized communities begin to explore their faith commitment as a consequence. This gives rise to new ways of being church for that era. Brueggemann's textual community as the church today and a new church start provide one means of framing the experiences of my dialogue partners on the margins of the church.

The purpose of this chapter has been to elaborate a Trinitarian ecclesiology of church and examine models of church that may suggest ways of seeing church on the "margins" today. In this sense, a Trinitarian ecclesiology moves the church toward catholicity, dialogue, and communion through its understanding of itself as Body of Christ in union with the Spirit and as koinonia. Dialogue partners on the margins speak of these in their experience including within in small communities. An exploration of different models of church provides a route through a variety of models of church that can be seen within Catholicism within the United States today. It presents two very different lenses through which to explore the models of church on the margins. Both provide important information. Van der Ven's models orient models of church in relation to postmodernity, bringing with them the availability of choice, plurality, and diversity. Brueggemann's models provide a focus through the lens of social crisis.

The next chapter addresses choice, plurality and diversity within the context of practical theology. It focuses on praxis and the dialogical without consensus. Looking at practical theology as a field that welcomes a diversity of voices, it examines the significance of other knowledges in practical theology and the privileging of outside marginalized voices.

> The church is basically a group of people who come together because of a common belief. There is a common belief in the sense that God works through people. Nobody is in lock step and we're not all the same . . . You look at things in different ways but there is a common belief and we don't exist just by ourselves. (Luke, dialogue)

102. Ibid., 134–36.

5

Toward Pentecost Listening
A Trinitarian, Reciprocal Practical Theology

> On Pentecost it says they all spoke in different languages so that
> everybody understood. We need Pentecost listening for all these
> Pentecost voices. (Cindy, dialogue)

TODAY, WITH THE POLYPHONY of voices expressing a myriad of diverse
opinions, clamoring to be heard, how does one wade through the myriad
ideas, judgments, and feelings? How does one make sense of those voices
that are different or unusual because they have been rendered voiceless
in the past? One of the tasks of practical theological action is to welcome
all relevant voices as a part of the process of constructing the theological questions, voices that need to be part of suggesting and assessing the
alternatives.

> As far as I'm concerned one of the most important things for the
> Church today is to understand the importance of change. It was
> good in the first century; it might not be good in the fourth, so
> you change. And it might not be good in the eighteenth, and it
> might not be good today. And this is the very foundation. What
> they had in those days was important, and it was the best they
> had. They had a big thing up above and then the thing down
> below. As time came along, they begin to realize that the earth is
> not the center, and as time goes on we find out that we are part
> of a tremendous celestial organization. And we change. And

then, you get into the physics of the thing, the atomic structures and all of this kind of stuff and all of these things have to be integrated into what God brings to us; because God worked through the Jews of old, through mythology, and somehow now he works through us. We have to change. (Luke, dialogue)

Change, according to Luke, is not only imperative but also inevitable. Practical theology involves change that is transformation. As practical theology takes place in the praxis of everyday life, it becomes embodied and theologizes from the historical and material contexts of people and communities. Theology, once just concerned with the church, is expanding its theological spheres of action to the world and our local community.[1]

Peter Berger's book *The Heretical Imperative*[2] is very specific— one of the major characteristics of being a modern person is choice. And you can't get away from it. And no one, no group of people in the history of the world had, are faced with the kind of choices we have. My contention is that Bishops do not live in the context of the fact, of the same context that people do, or they're denying their own modernity and that people are faced with choice. And their job is to help them make choices through teaching and they've abandoned the role as teachers. (Dan, dialogue)

A METHODOLOGICAL UNDERSTANDING OF PRACTICAL THEOLOGY

In this chapter, I propose a practical theology that is relational, engaging other disciplines, listening to diverse voices, and seeking dialogue that does not require agreement or consensus. I center this discussion of practical theology within a framework offered by Richard Osmer.[3] Following a brief description of Osmer's task-based approach to practical theology, I explore how a Trinitarian theological rationale might situate practical

1. Davaney, *Pragmatic Historicism*, 168.

2. Peter Berger, a sociologist at Boston University, has written books on sociological theory, the sociology of religion, and Third World development. His work explores the relationship of the individual to society and understands that the social structure revolves around the idea that language is the most important sign system for human society.

3. Richard Osmer is a practical theologian affiliated with Princeton Theological Seminary. He proposes a cross-disciplinary model of practical theology especially suited for use in ministry.

theology in relationship. Van der Ven's model of empirical practical theology suggests that practical theology privilege the social sciences, but above all makes the case for a cross-disciplinary approach. This is followed by an exploration of the sources of justification of my practical theology work—experience, Scripture, tradition, and reason. I conclude the chapter with a discussion of the hybrid transformative-emancipatory theological and social science paradigm that underpins my practical theological work.

PRACTICAL THEOLOGY RATIONALE

A theological rationale includes the central theological principles about why a practical theologian works in a particular way. My theological rationale begins with a doctrine of God as Trinity informed by pneumatology. An anthropological understanding of the person made in the image of the Trinity reveals the person in relationship with God and others, interconnected, united yet diverse, and formed by each other's difference.[4] Practical theology' s foundation begins with both the understanding of God's presence with humanity and of God's acting in the divine economics of salvation in the world in the past, in the present, and in the future without collapsing those together.[5] Practical theology's appreciation of relationship fosters a welcoming of diversity, reciprocity in action, a freedom that realizes potential in difference.[6] This suggests practical theology includes other disciplines in the conversation, incorporates divergent voices, and involves those who would not normally be included in the theological conversation. It seeks the work of the Spirit in the world in these diverse conversations.

Engaged with the World

Practical theology's history encompasses a variety of meanings in diverse contexts, from merging "pastoral theology" to the interdisciplinary approach to practical theology that includes the social sciences. The task of practical theology is "to trace and think through the interactions or lack

4. Chapters 3 and 4 discuss an anthropology that is Trinitarian based and an ecclesiology that is Trinitarian respectively.

5. Purves, "Trinitarian Basis for a Chrstian Practical Theology," 224.

6. McDougall, "Return of Trinitarian Praxis?," 197. This could be understood in terms of Moltmann's notion of friendship in which a sharing of one's self and recognition of differences are the basis for reciprocity and equality.

thereof between Christianity inside the Church and that outside of it, as well as between religious and non-religious phenomena in society."[7] As it accomplishes such a task, it guides the Christian community theologically in its engagement with the world, helping it determine practices for Christian life in light of social, historical, and cultural conditions.[8]

A Dialogic Action

Practical theology is a theology concerned with action.[9] It can be described as a "practice" or a means of living life.[10] As a practice, it opens a dialogue bringing contemporary experiences, questions, and actions from the praxis of everyday life experiences into conversation with religious belief, tradition, and practice.[11] Its hermeneutic process of interpretation and reinterpretation situates practical theology's concern for action both in the church and in the world. This hermeneutical process engages with the complexity of multiple, shifting perspectives in this multicultural and pluralistic world concerned for the influence of power, culture, gender, and race on traditional theological methods.[12] This suggests the necessity of keeping all voices involved in the dialogue, and a need for a metacognitive and metalinguistic pause to critically take note of the progress of the dialogue, what is being said, how it is being said, and its effects.[13]

7. Van der Ven, *Practical Theology*, 38. Practical theology arose from experience and practice in the Church (Woodward and Pattison, eds., *The Blackwood Reader in Pastoral and Practical Theology*, 23). It has its basis, in part, within the Enlightenment's emphasis on reason and the turn to the subject that privileged experience as a source of knowledge. Thus, Schleiermacher was one of the first to suggest that human experience in religion connects the Christian faith and humanity (Heitink, *Practical Theology*, 19). Insisting that all theology is practical, he held together the two poles of description and evaluation as essential to hermeneutical understanding in theology, asserting the value of historical interpretation and knowledge of the person (Thiselton, *The Hermeneutics of Doctrine*, 124).

8. Holmes, "Interreligious/Interfaith Dialogue as Christian Praxis," 42. Practical theologian Nathaniel Holmes Jr. is an Assistant Professor of Religion at Florida Memorial University.

9. Purves, "Trinitarian Basis for a Christian Practical Theology," 222.

10. Veling, *Practical Theology*, 3.

11. Woodward and Pattison, eds., *The Blackwood Reader*, 7. James Woodward is canon of St. George Chapel, Windsor, England, and a Research Fellow of Cardiff University; Stephen Pattison is a practical theologian and professor of Religion, Ethics, and Practice at University of Birmingham, England.

12. O'Brien, "Practical Theology and Postmodern Religious Education," 317.

13. Ibid., 316–17.

Centered in Praxis and the Empirical

Practical theology roots itself in praxis, which is experience critically reflected upon in this global world. Praxis in practical theology is transformative action, involving both *poesis*—that is, making things—and *orthopraxis*—that is, authentic, transformatory action.[14] A critical praxis is the starting point for theorizing about God's communication and action. Practical theology's hermeneutic and theorizing involves an individual and communal dialogue with experience, tradition, Scripture, and the practical.[15] Being able to talk about God, in God's immanence and salvific work without collapsing the two together affirms that human experiences are of God. This affirmation of God's presence in experience points toward a practical theology rooted in a Trinitarian understanding which embraces the empirical, beginning with experience of the world and God's engagement with all humanity.[16]

A Public Endeavor

Practical theology is contextual. It understands context in its spatial and temporal dimensions by using both memory and anticipation of the present lived into the future to attend to its overall work.[17] Given its engagement with the world, practical theology situates itself as a public endeavor that is not relegated to a public few but incorporates all views, engaging in dialogue with the reality of this world, and addressing issues at the forefront of society.[18] As a public discipline, it tries to integrate theology into the weave and fabric of everyday living.[19] With the plurality and diversity in postmodern society, practical theology searches for insights in the 'orienting concerns' of a community's central stories.[20] This dialogue anticipates transformation with the intrinsic thankfulness

14. Forrester, *Truthful Action*, 7.

15. Heitink, *Practical Theology*, 7, 151; Browning, *A Fundamental Practical Theology*, 4.

16. Purves, "Trinitarian Basis for a Christian Practical Theology," 224.

17. Cahalan and Neiman, "Mapping the Field of Practical Theology," 80.

18. Forrester, *Theological Fragments*, 3–7.

19. Veling, *Practical Theology*, 3. Terry Veling is a practical theologian and head of McAuley School of Theology at Australian Catholic University.

20. O'Brien, "Practical Theology and Postmodern Religious Education," 318. Maureen O'Brien is a practical theologian and a professor at Duquesne University working in ministry education.

that grace is causing new insights for bringing God's kindom present in the experiences of life.[21]

Action in Service of the Common Good

The starting point of the praxis is the world as it should be. The essential purpose of practical theological action and reflection is to engage in a dialogue between a faith community's vision of the world, given whom God is and what the actual world is, leading to conversation and action that is both realistic and faithful to the faith community's vision.[22] "Practical theology is concerned for both the authentic appropriation of the communal religious story and the development of strategic commitment and action in service of the common good."[23]

Practical theology rooted in the Trinity and the life and action of Jesus includes emphasis on relationship and communion with the poor and those who suffer. "A trinitarian practical theology of communion is a socio-critical theology that names the lies behind the present experience of the denial of fullness of relational beings wherever that occurs."[24] A preference for the suffering and the poor compels an awareness of the politics of exclusion/inclusion not only present in the everyday experience, but also in the work of practical theology. Paying attention to power dynamics and questioning whose voices are included and whose are left out brings attention to what a belief means for the local community and all affected by the actions of the practical theological work. Practical theology with a trinitarian foundation calls for an eschatological disquiet when this communion is broken or not established in any area of human experience.[25] A practical theology that works for the common good in trinitarian ways suggests a politics of communion by seeking a life of communion with God and one another in the practices of the reality of the day to day.

---

21. Ibid., 317.

22. Cowan and Lee, *Conversation, Risk, and Conversion*, 71. Michael Cowan is a psychologist and practical theologian at Loyola University New Orleans, and Bernard Lee is a practical theologian at St. Mary's University in Texas.

23 O'Brien, "Practical Theology and Postmodern Religious Education," 316.

24. Purves, "Trinitarian Basis for a Christian Practical Theology," 238.

25. Ibid.

Practical Theology as Discipleship

Practical theology ultimately is the work of discipleship. The task of practical theology is to promote authentic discipleship in its concrete and contemporary situations.[26] Practical theologians Kathleen Cahalan and James Neiman suggest practical theology as discipleship functions as a field and a discipline containing a diversity of connected expressions including ministry, teaching, and research.[27] Practical theology practices its discipleship in communal, theological, and practical ways.[28]

MODELS OF PRACTICAL THEOLOGY

> We had a good background [when we were trained] in theology as young priests, but where did the background of theology come from? When we were in the ministry, we never looked at the Bible as the foundation of theology; we never did. Before we could study theology, we had to study philosophy, a basic introduction to the sciences, and when we were in high school we studied general science and we studied chemistry, and that laid a foundation for the world. So it gives you a foundation, it makes you realize that the world is a much bigger thing; that God is not bound in a box by the Bible or by the world by itself, he's much bigger than that. The world is his creation. (Luke, dialogue)

Practical theology differentiates into different categories in several ways. Focus can be on historical and philosophical underpinnings, as Luke suggests. It can also follow geographical location, and ways of dealing with multiple disciplines in practical theology, or methodology.[29] Practical theology is often categorized by the public to which

26. Cahalan and Neiman, "Mapping the Field of Practical Theology," 67–70.

27. Ibid., 64–78.

28. Ibid., 67–69.

29. Using a historical and philosophical focus, practical theology can also be categorized through studying the historical impact of the original sources, much as Johann Baptist Metz and Gerard West do. Within this category, a focus on systematic theology and a quest for truth is central in the practical theology of Clodovis Boff and Duncan Forrester, Johannes van der Ven, and Don Browning, respectively. In categorizing by geographical location, U.S. practical theologians focus on correlations and possible connections, European practical theologians search for possible distinctions and clarify differences, and Latin American liberation theologians give a central place to the position of the subject as an avenue toward knowledge. Ways of dealing with interdisciplinary issues in practical theology will be discussed later in this chapter. A

it speaks. Theologian David Tracy names three publics and divides theology into three categories, fundamental theology, systematic theology, and practical theology.[30] He suggests each category tends to speak most to a particular public: academia, the church, or society. Each helps theology approach its task of seeking to understand experience. These categories and publics examine three contexts for theological scientific work: the university, the church, and society and culture. Each public utilizes a corresponding mode and approach. The university follows an intellectual scientific mode and critical approach. The Church follows an ecclesial mode and dogmatic approach and society and culture follow an ethical mode and existential approach.[31]

Practical theology addresses all three publics. It engages with the Church's pastoral needs: preaching, catechesis, worship, spiritual and moral formation.[32] Practical theologians who speak to this public include Don Browning (1934–2010) and his fundamental practical theology, and James and Evelyn Whitehead.[33] Practical theology examines the public of society, including the technological, economic, political and cultural world, being mindful of the way in which the religious message is in relationship with public policy.[34] The public theology of Duncan Forrester, the social analysis model of Joe Holland and Peter Henriot,[35]

---

categorization by methodological focus used by Heitink yields four focuses: empirical-analytical, with an example in Van der Ven's work; political-critical, as seen in Forrester's work; normative-deductive, of which Don Browning's fundamental practical theology is an example; and pastoral-theological, with James and Evelyn Whitehead as an example (Heitink, *Practical Theology*, 171–78).

30. Tracy, *Analogical Imagination*, 56–57. Tracy is also known for his "revisionist" model for doing theology, expanding models of correlation. He espouses a postmodern framework that uses both critical reflection and reinterpretation of authentic Christianity and authentic secular thought in a revisionist model.

31. Tracy, *Analogical Imagination*, 22.

32. McBrien, *Catholicism*, 55.

33. James and Evelyn Whitehead gave practical theology and Christian ministry formation a method of theological reflection. It brings the Christian tradition, personal experience, and cultural resources into conversation with each other for theological reflection to address concerns in ministry. See Whitehead and Whitehead, *Method in Ministry*.

34. McBrien, *Catholicism*, 55.

35. Holland and Henriot employ a pastoral model of theology with roots in liberation theology. Their praxis model, a pastoral circle committed to story as the primary data of theology, centers all theological analysis in concrete, historical, and social experience which is always mediated. This social model begins with a commitment to the Gospel, to the poor, especially those whose situations constitute the lived reality of faith in the particular experience.

and the political theology of Johann Metz[36] are examples. The practical theologian who engages the public of the academy does so by justifying solutions through rigorous academic, empirical, and pragmatic means. Van der Ven's empirical theology is an example. A brief look at representatives from each of these practical theologies will be a foundation for my addressing all three publics in this book in chapter 6. The next section begins with a look at Osmer's development of a methodological understanding for practical theology.

METHODOLOGICAL UNDERSTANDINGS

The more you get involved with people's lives, the more horizontal the God concept is and your spirituality is involved with other people. So I think that is what happens: you become more involved with people's experiences. (Colleen, dialogue)

We are the people of God, we are all the people of God, and we are all called by our baptism to be priests in our own way. Jesus calls us and God calls us to do different things. He gives us different talents so that we can grow and nurture each other. As I see it, beyond the central piece and the focal piece of the seven sacraments, we have a lot of room, and a lot of room for creativity and understanding of how people, all people, can participate. (Miriam, dialogue)

Practical theology engages in human life through what Colleen describes as involvement in other's experiences. The resulting turn to experience makes room for the creativity and participation that Miriam describes by a myriad of people with talents who add to the work practical theology. A practical theologian's multiple perspectives, different questions, and use of a multitude of different lenses that heighten awareness proceed from a theory of how practical theology should be conducted and should proceed by a methodology.

36. These theologians are influenced by Karl Marx's critique of Christianity, its silence in the face of suffering, and his insistence on concrete analysis of economic, social, political realities. This gives rise to liberation theology's insistence that theology starts with the suffering poor and their concrete experience.

FOUR CATEGORIES FOR
METHODOLOGICAL REFLECTION

Osmer's four tasks necessary for interpretation in practical theology provide a basic structure for developing a practical theology process. The descriptive-empirical task undertakes a gathering of information about the practical theology problem in a systematic way. The interpretive task contains the theories and patterns of interpretation that might help answer the questions posed in the practical theological problem. The normative task asks the question about what ought to be going on in light of who God is in the world, and enunciates the theological ethic the practical theologian uses. Finally, the pragmatic task utilizes strategies and actions to answer the questions raised by the practical theological problem.[37] While Osmer proposes his approach to practical theology for congregational leaders, he offers a structure for viewing the tasks of practical theology. These tasks interact with and mutually influence each other.

To do these tasks well, the practical theologian must have an awareness of his or her own theological, thematic, and methodological understandings.[38] Osmer further suggests that practical theologians make decisions and form their theory of how they are to proceed around four necessary key areas for a methodological reflection in practical theology: a theological rationale, the theory/praxis relationship, sources of justification, and models of cross-disciplinary work.[39] Each mutually influences the other. Each nuance shapes the method employed and the tasks of practical theology and therefore the kinds of transformations and changes that can result from practical theology.

A CROSS-DISCIPLINARY DIALOGUE

Postmodernity—A Variety of Approaches

> To some extent I was probably questioning God, the existence of God, what makes people leave what we've been taught? At the same time, to this day, I do believe in God, but also, I think maybe, is my conception of God accurate? It doesn't matter if

37. Osmer, *Practical Theology*, 4–10.

38. Osmer, "Toward a Transversal Model of Interdisciplinary Thinking in Practical Theology," 305

39. Ibid., 306–7.

it is accurate, for that matter. The teachings that I've been told or exposed to, are they really the best way to live your life? Is that the best guidance that I could follow in terms of leading a good life and being happy and for those around me to be happy? (Terry, dialogue)

When I think back, life was so simple then. Things were black and white; I knew what was right and wrong and did my best to follow . . . thought I was following. And there's no black and white now. I don't know whether it's my age or my spiritual growth, but what does that mean? I don't know. (Judy, dialogue)

Judy and Terry's dialogue is about the difficulty of certainty and truth in a postmodern time. Theologian Paul Lakeland categorizes approaches to the crisis of modernity in theology as late modern, countermodern, and postmodern. Cahalan suggests these three approaches also exist within practical theology. The late modern continues to explore ethics and politics to find universal principles that can move toward truthful engagement with the world.[40] Cahalan identifies Browning as a late modern practical theologian. Countermoderns integrate concern with ethical relativism and loss of religious authority in the world. The countermodern Christian practice work of Dorothy Bass and Craig Dykstra is an example.[41] For those in a radical postmodern category, a return to the premodern or modern era is not an option because those discourses oppress people cultures and communities.[42] Political and liberation theologians are examples of a radical postmodern approach, addressing society and the problems encountered there.[43]

Van der Ven proposes an approach to postmodernity that moves practical theology out of walls of the university into dialogue with the church and Christian community. He suggests the use of an empirical theology to combat the problems of postmodernity which are individualism, secularization, church diversification, and privatism.[44] For Van der Ven, only an interdisciplinary model of practical theology that encompasses the social scientific sciences can address the questions of the postmodern age.

40. Cahalan, "Three Approaches to Practical Theology, Theological Education, and the Church's Ministry," 65.

41. Ibid., 64–67.

42. Ibid., 66.

43. Ibid., 64–67.

44. Van der Ven, *Practical Theology*, 91.

THE EMPIRICAL PRACTICAL THEOLOGY OF
JOHANNES VAN DER VEN

An Emphasis on Experience Through Empirical Means

For Van der Ven, no theology is complete without empiricism.[45] Empiricism emphasizes the primacy of experience and the application of observation and experimentation through the social sciences. Concerned with describing and explaining the hermeneutic, it grounds arguments in hermeneutic intention. This hermeneutic-communication stresses dialogue and merges social scientific and theological categories to unfold meaning.

Practical theology, as an academic discipline, involves theory and practice in a hermeneutic spiral. This hermeneutic-communicative approach functions as a frame of reference in investigating praxis. "By placing the height, breadth and length dimensions of religious experience and religious attitudes in a communication-theoretical framework, we seek to obtain not a product but a process. For communication which is the basis of the Church as a community of believers, consists of a dialogue between people sharing and discussing their different viewpoints."[46] The empirical theological approach uses both intra and interdisciplinary dialogue with other disciplines in the social and human sciences, and with theological disciplines, Scripture, and tradition.

Practical Theology—An Empirical Intradisciplinary Approach

The phases of Van der Ven's practical theology begin with the development of a theological problem and goal and proceed to theological induction, theological deduction, empirical theological testing, and finally theological evaluation.[47] Van der Ven's model proposes that empirical practical theology stand alongside literary, historical, and systematic approaches in practical theology not as a sub-disciplinary approach but rather an intradisciplinary approach. In this, practical theology borrows the methodology, concepts, methods, and techniques from the social sciences.[48] To Van der Ven, every theologian must be able to handle the theories, methods,

---

45. Ibid., viii–6. Empiricism, particularly that represented by Dewey, presents a style of thought that elevates the role of science as beginning in experience, subject to objective observation and experimentation.

46. Ibid., 24.

47. Ibid., 225.

48. Ibid., 2, 101.

and techniques of empirical science so that the methodology of this discipline is adopted by theology. This requires that theology itself become
empirical and expand its range of instruments beyond critical-historical
and systematic methods and techniques to empirical methodology. Thus,
practical theology as intradisciplinary, utilizing empirical methods, takes
up and critically assimilates these new methods and techniques developed
in other areas of science and develops these in practical theology work.
The adequacy of this approach is seen in the fact that practical theology
explains and develops theoretical presuppositions which are oriented
toward complimentary qualitative and quantitative approaches.[49] These
theoretical presuppositions, drawn from the critically reflected on praxis,
are in need of verification so there is not indirect falsification of theories.[50]

Critique

A basic epistemology that suggests that value free research methods can
obtain objective research findings and positivism are often associated with
empiricism.[51] However, feminist empiricists, countering this positivistic
understanding, improve the collection and interpretation of empirical
research by including women's voices, the voices of the oppressed, and the
other. They seek to overcome the shortcomings and omissions that render
past positivist findings as non-objective, non-neutral, and affected the
generalizability of them.[52] I find affinity with postmodern and poststruc-
turalist perspectives that emphasize bringing the 'other' into the research
process and reject notions of universality, objectivity, and universally applied truth. I understand interpretations of experiences as multiple, situated, and constructed.[53]

Van der Ven's inclusion of the social sciences is integral to practical
theology; however, his intradisciplinary use of social sciences can lead to
a separation of the empirical portion into its own cycle, separate from the
cycles of theological development, induction, deduction, and evaluation.

49. Ibid., 40.

50. Ibid.

51. Positivism, based on the scientific method, understands knowledge as formed
through logic and empiricism. It looks for truth that can be discovered if one can be
objective and neutral. It begins with deduction from a general theory, positing causal
relationships that depend on testing hypothesis deduced from that theory (Hesse-
Biber, ed., *Handbook of Feminist Research*, 7–8).

52. Hesse-Biber and Leavy, eds., *Feminist Research Practice*, 10–11.

53. Ibid., 10–21.

He uses a correlational approach to this intradisciplinary work. I suggest a different perspective allowing practical theology and social science to function as an intertwined discipline, each participating together toward the work of practical theology in cross-disciplinary ways.

Three Approaches Incorporating Other Disciplines for Interdisciplinary Practical Theology

There are three approaches to contemporary practical theology seeking to define the relationship practical theology and other disciplines including social science.[54] These three approaches address practical theology, and its relationship with other disciplines through the emphasis that they place on the importance of the practical theology. Each approaches the dialogue with other disciplines with a slightly different perspective and a slightly different weight given to practical theology.

A Correlational Model

Much of the interdisciplinary and intradisciplinary work of practical theology focuses on using the revised correlational approach of Browning, Tracy, and Van der Ven. The revised correlational model focuses on the praxis of each dialogue partner in a dialectic approach. Theology stands in a mutually influential relationship to the intellectual resources and emancipatory praxis of culture.[55] Tracy calls for a collaborative exercise of mutual critical correlation using the whole of human experience and language, both the questions and the answers, correlated with the religious texts.[56] This is done while staying in conversation with other theological areas, such as the confessional, symbolic, doctrinal expressions of the tradition.[57] Tracy's model for theological engagement functions in a pluralistic, theological, and cultural context, as a "philosophical reflection upon the meaning present in the common human experience and language, and upon the meanings present in the Christian fact."[58] It correlates secular thought with Christian thought, by investigating experience and

54. Osmer, "Toward a Transversal Model of Interdisciplinary Thinking in Practical Theology," 339.

55. Ibid.

56. Tracy, *Analogical Imagination*, 43–45.

57. Tracy, *Blessed Rage for Order*, 43–45.

58. Ibid., 43.

indentifying Christian symbols that will evolve into action to address the experience. For Tracy, culture and Christian symbols are important to the theological process. Browning takes Tracy's revised correlational method and applies it to practical theology that sees all theology as essentially practical. Fundamental practical theology is "critical reflection on the Church's dialogue with Christian sources and other communities of experience and interpretation."[59]

This approach, while welcoming the other disciplines, ends up incorporating and reducing their contribution to the dialogue to the single voice of practical theology. Additionally, Van der Ven's incorporation of the work of other disciplines into the work of the practical theologian means that the practical theologian needs to be versed in the discipline incorporated. Critiques of this method suggest that there are difficulties for the practical theologian in this method because each discipline enforces its own line of reasoning and the practical theologian must be versed in all of them.[60]

A Transformational Model

A transformational approach to the interdisciplinary work of practical theology, particularly that used by James Loder and Deborah Hunsinger, is based on a Christocentric understanding of the Trinity.[61] Loder proposes that practical theology and its interdisciplinary partners are situated in an asymmetrical, relational, bipolar unity that is analogous to the unity of humanity in relationship with Christ.[62] In this way, practical theology 'marginally' controls the other disciplines involved in an interdisciplinary approach. This model understands academic disciplines in a hierarchy by differentiating the disciplines in terms of their degree of complexity and comprehensiveness.[63] Each discipline uses it own internally generated objectives, methods, and linguistic conventions to interpret the practical theology phenomena.[64] Theology is judged the most comprehensive of the disciplines, as it is the only one that can

59. Browning, *A Fundamental Practical Theology*, 16.

60. Cartledge, "Empirical Theology," 6–10.

61. Osmer, "Toward a Transversal Model of Interdisciplinary Thinking in Practical Theology," 342.

62. Gilbert, "Prophetic and the Priestly," 129.

63. Latini, "Grief-Work in Light of the Cross," 1.

64. Ibid.

speak to questions about God and the ultimate purpose of human existence.[65] For Hunsinger, the theological work takes its bearings from God's self-communication in Jesus.[66]Any reliance on assumptions from non-theological fields that are inconsistent with Christian theology and Christian revelation must be negated, so that the positive contributions of these fields to religious practice can be appropriated.[67]

A Transversal Model

A final model, the transversal model, fits well with the practical theology methodology I advocate. The transversal model for cross-disciplinary fields, in dialogue with practical theological work, facilitates an embodied practical theology. It bases itself on a social doctrine of the Trinity in its relationality and focuses on the experience of embodied people. "In the dialogue between theology and other disciplines, transversal reasoning promotes different but equally legitimate ways of viewing specific topics, problems, traditions, or disciplines, and creates the kind of space where different voices need not always be in contradiction, or in danger of assimilating one another, but are in fact dynamically interactive with one another."[68] A transversal model for practical theology encourages thinking that is concrete, local, and contextual, but willing to reach beyond its own discipline into other trans-disciplinary concerns.[69] Because we enter cross-disciplinary conversations with individual beliefs, commitments, and prejudices, a transversal model enables realization that in a cross-disciplinary discussion there is much to share in terms of rational resources, as well as much that we can find that is radically different. While Hunsington's and Loder's approach allows Christian theology and Christian revelation privileged access to questions of God, in a transversal model other disciplines share in the discussion.[70] This interdisciplinary approach

65. Ibid.

66 Hunsinger, "Practicing Koinonia," 346–47.

67. Latini, "Grief-Work in Light of the Cross," 1–2.

68. Van Huyssteen, "Human Origins and Religious Awareness," 1.

69. Ibid.

70. An example of this is the contemporary use of cosmology, genealogy, biology, and sociology in the human search for meaning by cultural historian Thomas Berry and mathematical cosmologist Brian Swimme. Such work awakens us to God's relational work in creation and the universe, and calls us to be earth community. See Swimme and Berry's *The Universe Story: From the Primordial Flaring Forth to the Ecozoic Era.*

allows the practical theologian to identify shared resources in the many different forms of knowledge, permitting a cross-contextual, and cross-disciplinary practical theology.

The transversal cross-disciplinary model facilitates a reciprocal methodological understanding of practical theology. It also encourages accountability to the wider public of society and dialogue with the variety of voices coming from this public. This is undergirded by a Trinitarian understanding of practical theology. A reciprocal practical theology creates its own publics, movements, and discourse audiences in the twenty-first century.[71]

Reciprocal Practical Theology with a Transversal Cross-Disciplinary Approach

A reciprocal methodology in practical theology involves the people in making the practical theology knowledge without privileging one voice over the other. This reciprocal methodology invites dialogue partners into the practical theology conversation in a reciprocal give and take that shares and builds practical theology knowledge based on dialogue and shared, examined, and reexamined knowledge. This produces a collaborative, multilayered, and polyvocal understanding of practical theology that is not fixed because another understanding may appear with the next dialogue. This reciprocity in practical theology celebrates the individual narrative. It also celebrates the corporate narrative alive in the myriad voices of the narratives into which practical theology enters in dialogue. Practical theology, informed by a transversal cross-disciplinary understanding, thus provides another frame for practical theology as it searches for meaning within the academic, the Church, and society sectors. In so doing practical theology continuously and collaboratively interprets and integrates this meaning and transforms itself.

There are limitations to this approach. Because a practical theologian relates to the world through mediation of interpreted experiences, the theological and scientific modes of inquiry are affected by the practical theologian's perspective. This leads to a certain bias, and a selective emphasis on some subjects and neglect of others. As Osmer observes, "At present, no comparable principle of selectivity has been articulated

71. Elisabeth Schüssler Fiorenza envisions just such a move in Biblical Interpretation, moving the interpretation to the people (Fiorenza, *Wisdom Ways*, 5). I am grateful for her shared vision.

in the discussion of transversal interdisciplinarity."[72] The practical theologian can reduce these limitations by emphasizing context and contextual understanding. The use of a transversal, cross-disciplinary methodology requires the ability to dialogue with multiple disciplines. As the practical theologian uses the transversal methodology, rather than opening or closing the self off to other disciplines, the practical theologian pays attention to "what it means to discover an epistemic space that allows for the kind of interdisciplinary critical evaluation that includes a critical self-evaluation and optimal understanding"[73]

SOURCES OF JUSTIFICATION

I move now to Osmer's last area, that is, sources of justification. The practical theologian uses Scripture, tradition, theology, and reason to reveal insights for practical theological action. The methodological issue here revolves around how the sources are used and what weight is given to each.[74]

"Justification in the most general sense is simply a matter of being able to give good reasons for beliefs."[75] Experience, Scripture, tradition, and reason function as traditional sources of truth. I utilize these sources for justification, following Browning, within practical theology's understanding that they equally give insights into the practical theological problem and help the practical theologian undergird practical theological proposals.[76]

Dialogue between these four sources—Scripture, tradition, experience, and reason—formulates the theory in a practical theology that rises from praxis. Equal weight in dialogue with the practical theologian and the public with whom the practical theologian works helps all of these sources provide the hermeneutic material for speaking of God in the practical theological dialogue. There are limitations in assigning equal weight. Other methods claim their bias toward one or the other of the sources. Authenticity and fairness in assigning weight to each source for the particular practical theological context are necessary. Each source's

72. Osmer, "Toward a Transversal Model of Interdisciplinary Thinking in Practical Theology," 343.

73. Muller, "Transversal Rationality as a Practical Way of Doing Interdisciplinary Work," 226.

74. Osmer, *Teaching Ministry of Congregations*, 307.

75. Davaney and Frisina, eds., *The Pragmatic Century*, 84.

76. Browning, *A Fundamental Practical Theology*, 15–33.

input must be balanced dialogically in order for all the diverse voices to be heard. Over reliance on one source over the other will result in a silencing of the difference and diverse input that each source brings. If reason is given too much weight, then the faith aspect may be lost. If there is over reliance on the tradition, then faith practices that need changing may not be questioned. This reflects the need for the practical theologian to discern epistemological, ontological, and axiological groundings.

EXPLICATING A PRACTICAL THEOLOGY RECIPROCAL ETHNOGRAPHY METHODOLOGY

In social science as in practical theology, "A method is an interpretation."[77] Choosing a social science method for practical theology is a critical episte-mological decision. It is also an immensely theological decision.

My practical theology model can be broadly placed within a femi-nist model, informed by Trinitarian theology. It is informed by the work of Elizabeth Johnson, Mary Elizabeth Moore, Yvone Gebara, and Barbara Reid as feminist theologians as well as by the work of Sharlene Hesse-Biber, Patricia Leavy, and Elaine Lawless as feminist social scientists. Dialogue is an essential tool to build knowledge in feminist social sci-ence research. Dialogue empowers research by employing the strengths of diversity to produce more trustworthy and authentic research. "To dialogue means to 'invite in' ideas and interactions regarding points of view, to lay bare one's thinking about an issue and be willing to change course, be ready to make discoveries—be willing to entertain multiple points of view, not just similarities."[78]

> Because I don't feel as strongly that I only want feminine words and I only want feminine women—no, it's not like that at all. What I really want is inclusivity; I want to hear all the voices. If I've said anything about myself, I would say I'm a listener, and I want to listen to all the voices and it's just more and more obvi-ous that I don't hear all the voices. (Cindy, dialogue)

77. J. Marecek, quoted in Hesse-Biber and Yaiser, *Feminist Perspectives on Social Research,* 271. See Appendix C for detail on the method employed in this practical theology research.

78. Hesse-Biber, ed., *Handbook of Feminist Research,* 535.

Methodological Understandings of Epistemology, Ontology, and Axiology

Claiming My Bias

My epistemological and ontological underpinnings root my practical theology method in postmodernity, which is particularly a participative emancipatory paradigm.[79] This methodology seeks the empowerment of those on the margins and the redressing of the power imbalance for the marginalized. Its epistemology understands social knowledge and active construction as the co-creation of knowledge by human agents through the process of dialogue. Knowledge is embedded, never neutral, within value systems that are political, cultural, and historical. This understanding of knowledge basis it on difference, realizing that there are multiple constructions of knowledge.[80]

This paradigm sees praxis itself as a meaningful and important outcome of the inquiry process. In so doing, it folds ontology, epistemology, axiology, and methodology into one another. All become oriented toward seeking participants' genuine participation as a means of empowering a community through a redress of power imbalance for the marginalized. Thus, it advocates for forms of social actions in overturning unjust practices with the purpose of transforming society.

My practical theology method tries to ensure that a dialogic community is involved in the process of seeking practical theology theory. The welcoming of dialogue from all those who choose to respond is core. A practice of reflexivity, which was developed by feminist social scientists, places the beliefs and practices of the practical theologian (the subjective element) open to critical scrutiny so that the conditions where knowledge is constructed are transparent.

This paradigm proposes that there is no ultimate criterion for universal truth, only those agreed upon in certain times and under certain

79. Hesse-Biber and Leavy, *Feminist Research Practice*; Mertens, *Research and Evaluation in Education and Psychology*; Tashakkori and Teddlie, *Handbook of Mixed Methods in Social and Behavioral Research*; Denzin and Lincoln, *Collecting and Interpreting Qualitative Materials*—all discuss the participative emancipatory paradigm. Tashakkori and Teddlie refer to this as the Transformative/Emancipatory paradigm.

80. Davaney, *Pragmatic Historicism*, 23. Foucault notes that power produces knowledge. This necessitates that theories and conceptualizations "must be constantly confronted with praxis, reflexive thought aimed at action" (Flyvbjerg, *Making Social Science Matter*, 124–26).

conditions.[81] Rather than seeking truth in my practical theology work, I explore meaning and relationships with participants. Methodological suppositions about the validity, fairness, and authenticity of any practical theology work understand that this work is not merely a method that delivers one set of local and context grounded truths. This work also includes processes of interpretation, community consent, and reasoning to ensure rigorous, valid interpretation. It aims for methodological fairness by welcoming and hearing all voices, thus preventing further marginalization. Finally, I endeavor to bring authenticity, being aware of my own ontological suppositions.

In sum, the sources of justification for this practical theology work together equally. A transversal model of cross-disciplinary work allows multiple voices and a variety of disciplines to join the practical theology conversation. I engage this methodology in my practical theology work from these epistemological, ontological, and axiological presuppositions, grounding my practical theology methodology in a transformative-emancipatory model.

The next chapter looks at one final area of methodology—the relationship of praxis to theory—and examines a dialogical hermeneutic that does not seek agreement or consensus,[82] that forms the individual and the community through difference and the privileging of outsider voices.

> The growth and change in my spirituality, well, it's . . . it's really tied into community, you know. The divine, where we do we contact the divine? Through the world you do, and through community you do, and through other people. It's like we are the body of Christ. (Ken, dialogue)

---

81. Hesse-Biber and Yaiser, *Feminist Perspectives on Social Research*, 14.

82. This will be discussed in more detail in chapter 7. Bakhtin's concept of authoring and outsideness, from which this view grows, is discussed in chapter 3.

6

Practical Theology

A Dialogue Privileging the Voice of the Other

CONTINUING THE CONVERSATION— A METHODOLOGICAL UNDERSTANDING OF PRACTICAL THEOLOGY

DON BROWNING'S FUNDAMENTAL PRACTICAL theology and Duncan Forrester's public theology provide the foundation for my own practical theological approach. Johann Baptist Metz's work adds an additional foundation emphasizing the crisis of people's suffering and three basic categories of individual and corporate praxis: narrative, dangerous memories, and solidarity. Critically reflected praxis utilizes these individual and communal memories and stories in dialogic action to move toward new knowledge and transformation. This leads to an examination of hermeneutical understandings of dialogue that does not demand consensus, and a related privileging of outsider voices. A praxis orientation and non-consensus-seeking dialogue establishes a foundation for my practical theology understanding.

A PRACTICAL THEOLOGY UNDERSTANDING OF PRAXIS/THEORY

Practical theology's praxis/theory includes the philosophical, theological, and sociological decisions practical theologians make concerning praxis and its relationship with theory.[1] Praxis, purposeful critical action toward transformation, generates new knowledge, values, and social patterns. "Decisions about the theory-praxis relationship influence in fundamental ways the phenomena investigated in empirical work, the interpretive framework used to understand what is found, the norms offered to assess both Church and society and the models used to guide and reform present praxis."[2] Harry, below, narrates a story about his community that is praxis-oriented.

> One of the things we were asked to conform to was GIRM, that we had to serve communion in gold, silver, or platinum, and we estimated that we would need eight to ten chalices and it was going to cost $8,000 to buy these chalices. I said, "I was in the shelter last night as part of my volunteer stint for the month, and we don't even have enough cereal bowls, so are we supposed to buy $8,000 worth of gold chalices and these guys have to wash out their bowls so that they can have breakfast after the other guy?" How silly is that? And so we voted it down. We're not going to spend that money, and that got us in trouble. (Harry, dialogue)

Praxis Rooted in Alterity

The foundation of praxis is its disclosure of alterity.[3] This allows praxis to promote empathy and solidarity, expanding understanding and commitment to one another as people of God. Praxis rooted in alterity fosters the ability to broaden perspectives of the human experience and divine reality inspired by the doctrine of God as Trinity.[4] As practical knowledge, phronesis (practical wisdom), and habitus, praxis uses a hermeneutic of alterity that draws on the "dangerous memories" and individual and communal narratives that allow voices to be heard that have previously been

1. Osmer, *Teaching Ministry of Congregations*, 306.
2. Ibid., 307.
3. Graham, "Practical Theology as Transforming Practice," 106.
4. Ibid.

silenced. This appropriates Metz's work on dangerous memories and narrative.[5] Forrester's understanding of practical theology and its concern for the practice of what the Triune God in human behavior and in the world offers further nuance.[6] Affirmation of alterity, inclusivity, difference, and diversity leads to a unique understanding of the praxis of practical theology. It moves to an understanding of praxis as conversation, dialogue where we are formed individually and communally by difference and diversity.

FUNDAMENTAL PRACTICAL THEOLOGY —DON BROWNING

Conversation about Practical Practices

Browning's fundamental practical theology engages in critical conversation and dialogue between the Christian tradition and the experience of modern culture.[7] "We come to the theological task with questions shaped by the secular and religious practices in which we are implicated—sometimes uncomfortably. These practices are theory-laden . . . Christian theology should be seen as practical through and through and at its very heart, historical, systematic, and practical theology (in the more specific sense of the term) should be seen as subspecialties of the larger and more encompassing discipline called fundamental practical theology."[8] Browning identifies theology as primarily practical. His method puts the experience, reflection, and questions of Christian tradition with its sources into conversation with the experiences, reflections, and questions of Church communities for the purpose of transformation. Dialogue partners on the margins of the Church speak of varying experiences that question its practices.

> The Catholic community needs to watch its money. It's dying; the Catholic Church is dying because it's losing money. There was a time when it was supported by a lot of families; the support is dwindling, and I really don't know what's going to happen to all the Catholic churches when they don't have an influx of money coming in. There's going to be some kind of vacuum of power as the Churches get emptier and good priests don't take

5. Metz, *Faith in History and Society*, 105–6.

6. Forrester, *Forrester on Christian Ethics and Practical Theology*, 208.

7. Browning, *Fundamental Practical Theology*, 36.

8. Ibid., 7–8.

the place of the older ones that are just getting older. (Lance, dialogue)

I hope the Church will change in my lifetime, but what I think must happen [is] it has to burn down into ashes. I think so. They keep shooting themselves in the foot, everything that comes out of the hierarchy is distressed, is totally distressed. (Gail, dialogue)

I spoke with a man one time who was divorced many, many years and was an extraordinary minister and his pastor called him in and said, "We really need to talk and I know you have been divorced for a very long time and you've never remarried. Are you dating?" He said, "Yeah, I date here and there." And he said, "I'm going to have to tell you that you have to step down from being an extraordinary minister if you're dating." (Long silence) So, my whole thing kind of came up with this being divorced now. I'll go to other churches, it doesn't feel the same. It doesn't feel good. Do I still feel uncomfortable? Yes, literally. When I see my friends who are Catholic who wholeheartedly believe in all of it, I'm looking at them saying, "Doesn't this rub you wrong? Doesn't this bug you, any of it?" The Church is not my hangout anymore, because it's so family-based and my idea of what I wanted, you know, to be married in the Church, raise my kids in the Church, have a Catholic husband and do all that. I don't like to go to Church by myself. I don't know. It's painful. (Sade, dialogue)

Establishing Faith Assumptions and Theological Ethics

Practical theology that begins with praxis could start by describing and analyzing the experiences of my dialogue partners, declining Church enrollment, dissensus, the sadness that comes from divorce, or the alien feelings in one's own church. Fundamental practical theology moves from theory-laden practice experienced in the present to normative theory-laden practice to generating new theory-laden practices.[9] Core to the practical theology practice is the purpose of transformation, addressing the needs of the community in a creative way.

9. Ibid., 7.

Browning's method for practical theology lies within a narrative envelope and in theological ethics and moral theology.[10] The narrative envelope establishes faith assumptions that in turn give rise to narratives and metaphors that carry these assumptions. Theological ethics develops the criteria for testing the practical validity of claims of Christian faith. Theological norms develop in reflection about the practices and actions of the Church. Practical thinking rather than theoretical and abstract thinking, grounds the model as it works through Browning's four sub-movements.

MOVING THROUGH FOUR SUB-MOVEMENTS TO NEW THEORY-LADEN PRACTICES

Browning's first movement of descriptive theology using the hermeneutic context serves as the foundation for the next movements. It uses full descriptions of the psychosocial and religio-cultural histories pertaining to the practical theology problem, clarifying them as the ground of praxis.[11] Historical theology and systematic theology, the second and third movements, appropriate the normative theory-laden practice of the Church in relation to the experiences. They articulate and retrieve the Christian faith. The historical movement includes biblical studies, church history, and the history of Christian thought in its disciplines.[12] It questions the implication of the normative texts that are already part of our effective history for our praxis. The systematic movement investigates the broad thought of normative Christian texts in relation to the questions of the culture.[13] Finally, the strategic practical theology involves a thick description[14] of the problems involved in churches and critically examines the practices of the churches through the lens of the historical and systematic theology articulations and retrievals.[15]

10. Browning, *Fundamental Practical Theology*, 142–43.

11. Ibid., 62–63.

12. Ibid., 49.

13. Ibid. 52–53.

14. "Thick description" is a term used by Clifford Geertz, an anthropologist, to discuss not only the experience but also the context that helps give it meaning in a rich description (Geertz, *Interpretation of Cultures*).

15. Browning, *Fundamental Practical Theology*, 8, 58. Browning's work utilizes the thought of David Tracy, who emphasizes theology as springing from common human experience, informed by the Christian texts, and utilizing the methodologies of allied disciplines (ibid., 43–49). Tracy calls for a collaborative exercise of mutual critical correlation using the whole of human experience and language. Both the questions and

BROWNING'S HERMENEUTICAL FOUNDATION: HABERMAS, GADAMER, AND RICOEUR

Browning's practical theology method develops through the philosophy and consequences of hermeneutic philosophy and pragmatism. With a basis in the hermeneutic philosophy of Jurgen Habermas, Hans-Georg Gadamer, and Paul Ricoeur, Browning's practical thinking centers on his understanding of human thinking.[16] Habermas distinguishes communicative action as development of an action or understanding of a situation by subjects. This action or understanding develops through conversation that seeks agreement or consensus.[17] Communicative action involves experience, action, or practical knowledge and discourse. Discourse entails communication that expresses truth claims justifying them through reasoned argument. Habermas suggests that both action and discourse are necessary for social interaction and a democratic society. Gadamer, in turn, understands dialogue and conversation as the fundamental structure for human understanding. An understanding that starts with human practice is influential to practical theology.[18] Gadamer's insists on the role of effective history, bias, and preunderstandings, and the fusion of horizons in meaning-making.[19] This allows Browning to situate the human being as a being in language and opens Browning's hermeneutic to an understanding of dialogue as a process of interpreting texts, both individually and communally. This insight into the human as a being in language and the process of dialogue as important to practical theology is very much a part of my own understanding of practical theology. Ricoeur offers the understanding that interpretation begins when dialogue ends, suggesting that both dialogue and interpreting are necessary for understanding.[20] He also proposes an understanding of phronesis as communal practical moral reasoning.[21]

---

the answers correlate with the religious texts, while staying in conversation with other theological areas (Tracy, *Analogical Imagination*, 79–80).

16. Jurgen Habermas identifies four kinds of action: teleological (strategic), normatively regulated, dramaturgical, and communicative (Habermas, *Theory of Communicative Action*, 85–86).

17. Ibid., 2.

18. Kinast, *What Are They Saying about Theological Reflection?*, 53.

19. Ibid.

20. Schneiders, *Revelatory Text*, 140–41.

21. Thiselton, *Hermeneutics of Doctrine*, xix.

Critique

Browning's use of Habermasian and Gadamerian hermeneutics appropriates dialogue with the purpose of consensus as "a consensus that may break up and is reformulated repeatedly."[22] Browning encourages a critical hermeneutic dialogue for the sake of the common good by looking for positions mutually acceptable to all.[23] This move to consensus and agreement is consistent with Gadamer's argument that the ideal is "the transformation into communion in which we do not remain what we were."[24] The danger of this communion is that it is too often ignorant of the politics of power and can move to a false communal voice at the expense of those who lack voice and power.

A hermeneutical understanding forms life, thought, and concrete action. It includes difference and similarity and otherness in its formation.[25] Genuine conversation "occurs only when our usual fears about our own self-image die . . . Understanding happens in . . . intersubjective, shareable, public, indeed historical movement of authentic conversation."[26]

Browning's practical theology movements propel and call practical theology toward strategic action. Given its hermeneutic foundation and the fact that his practical theology work begins in descriptive, historical, and systematic movements, it appears to prefer an anthropology of the person as one who moves toward action through thinking. As a consequence, the privileging of thought over action allows the separation of the human person into a mind/body dichotomy that privileges the mind. This encourages dualism and seeing the person only as subject rather than as a person who acts, prizing thinking about something over acting in relationship. This dualism leads to objectification particularly of those who are different. From another perspective, I understand the person as a person always in relationship, who acts, and in this action forms thought.[27]

The task of reconstructing our faith experience and amending and reconsolidating a picture of the world when viewed privileging action and relationship begins in an understanding that action is the primary way a person understands. With knowledge starting within this action,

22. Browning, *Fundamental Practical Theology*, 50.

23. Ibid., 22.

24. Gadamer, *Truth and Method*, 341.

25. Thiselton, *Hermeneutics of Doctrine*, 114.

26. Tracy, *Analogical Imagination*, 101.

27. Bakhtin, *Problems of Dostoevsky's Poetics*, 293.

theology cannot continue to understand the self by separating the body from the mind/spirit. I understand *self* from several standpoints. The first is based on the foundation of a doctrine of God as Trinity that affirms the intrinsic nature of God as relational and humans as made in this image. Bakhtin's work on dialogue also shows that people need each other to most fully be themselves, to form themselves and their understanding in the action of dialogue.[28]

A practical theology with a foundation in relational dialogic action suggests that hermeneutical understanding include all voices and difference by welcoming them rather than reducing them to a single "truth." In the Christian tradition, response in faith to God's invitation of relationship through Jesus Christ and the Spirit begins individually but moves into a communal relationship. Such practical theology engages in dialogue, and dialogue necessitates listening to the other. Below, Kellie models such dialogue.

> I attended a rally at the cathedral about a year and a half ago and the people were coming out of Church and for woman's ordination what they did was, bought those miniature cupcakes from the grocery store and they put a toothpick with a little message on each one about the organization. It was very friendly because they weren't yelling when they came out so they said, "Hi, how are you? Have a nice day." I was holding up a banner, I wasn't actually handing out the cupcakes, and the people coming out of Church would nod, smile, and thank you and a lot of them would—I could just see in their faces. I can't believe we haven't ordained women yet. A lot of them, they're well educated and they know the stats. They know the history. But there's also people who walk by who didn't agree. There was this woman, who was probably in her late forties and had a thick accent, but spoke very intelligently on why it's not right in the light of the pope; or why the pope wouldn't agree. So she talked to someone else of our group who was just like, "I can't believe this woman, da, da, da." And this woman stood her ground very well, and I was very impressed. This was the first time that I was actually at an event, standing up for something in the Church politically. In fact, I remember keeping my sunglasses on because there were cameras and everything. So she walked away. She knew she had to walk away because she was so upset. And I just looked at this woman and I said, "I love the Church so much, which is why

28. See chapter 3 for more on each of these standpoints from a relational anthropological perception.

I choose to stay in the Church. And I really feel God and I really feel welcome in the Church a lot of the time. Do you feel that way?" And she goes, "Yeah, yeah." And I looked in her eyes and said, "Some women don't. Some Catholic women don't feel welcome because they feel this strong." She looked at me and it was the first time she actually stopped talking. She was a talker, and she kind of looked to the side and, well, "If the pope says it's okay, then I wouldn't mind." (Kellie, dialogue)

Browning brings together the use of the social sciences and humanities with theology. He situates practical theology in conversation that provides a clearly defined model that allows a conversation with the experiences of people, the church, and society. For Browning, practical theology's central task reconstructs our faith experience, amending and reconsolidating our more general picture of the world. Yet, as practical theology moves from theory-laden practice to normative practice and to new theory-laden practice, he uses hermeneutics that move to dialogue that seeks agreement. This model encourages a critical hermeneutic dialogue for the sake of the common good and looks for positions that are mutually acceptable to all.[29] Yet, consensus-seeking dialogue can mitigate the different voices and give preference to the most powerful, silencing the others. From another perspective, I propose the use of a hermeneutics that does not seek consensus and is rooted in an understanding of dialogic action as the epistemological ground of knowledge as the primary way a person grows to understand.

PUBLIC PRACTICAL THEOLOGY —DUNCAN FORRESTER

Action in the Public Sphere

Forrester defines practical theology as a study concerned with questions of truth in relation to action in the public sphere.[30] Practical theology that offers fragments of truth in the public debate moves from truth to action and from experience to a higher truth while continuing to work with and in the church.[31] For Forrester, all theology is public theology that is done in the reality of the whole world in face of the public. It dialogues

29. Browning, *Fundamental Practical Theology*, 22.

30. Forrester, *Truthful Action*, 23.

31. Ibid., 152–57.

with the greater public in the world. Theology engages in advocacy for and listening to the poor and the marginalized.[32] His practical theology approach looks to the past for wisdom in order to live a Christian life in the postmodern context. Crisis provides the context for discerning truth and summons the Church to a renewal of practice. An important part of the task of public theology is "to identify and address the deep underlying issues that are often too painful or awkward for politicians and others to address in public debate, and to identify the coming agenda, to articulate in the public square it convictions about truth and goodness, and to offer insights received from the tradition of which it is a steward."[33]

> There are multiple reasons that I wouldn't support the death penalty. Just the fact that sometimes innocent people are killed is huge. If you believe that people can forfeit their lives and that innocent people are being killed, that to me is enough to say with our human fallibility, it's not right. (Terry, dialogue)

> So, how are we really living out the social justice issues if we remain white centered? Where's our hypocrisy and how do we deal with that? So, that kind of thing that was going on whether there was a book group or children's education, whatever. (Andrew, dialogue)

> One of my early childhood memories from that place, it must have been in the mid-eighties, having voting booths set up in the social hall because they voted to become a sanctuary community for the refugees who were leaving El Salvador and Nicaragua and getting to Canada because they weren't allowed to stop here during the civil war. I found a community here and I also found political activism, which is really important. I got here, maybe in October, and they were already planning their trip to Fort Benning, to the School of the Americas, and that was sort of how I knew I found kindred spirits. So, I actually got on that trip and rode the bus all the way to Georgia from [city] with this group of people, and I actually made one good friend. Otherwise, it was a way to get to know these people; we rode in this bus for twenty-eight hours together. There was a fair amount of singing and sharing and thought process and whatever. It was very comfortable. It's very much like home. (Anne, dialogue)

32. Storrar and Morton, *Public Theology for the Twenty-First Century*, 26–27.
33. Forrester, *Truthful Action*, 128.

These narratives detail public, political issues that are also issues in the Church communities where my dialogue partners have found community: the death penalty, racism, immigration issues, and the US government's support and education of governments implicated in torturing their citizens. They also form a part of Tim, Andrew, and Anne's habitus which is their faithful practice. Forrester's model of practical theology addresses issues such as these by using social science. He put practical theology in dialogue with other disciplines, particularly social science. Yet, because of his belief that social science is not inherently theological, he utilizes it discriminately cautioning about leaving out a connection to Christian beliefs and a theological reflection.[34]

Offering Theological Fragments

Various levels of practice concern the practical theologian. Forrester articulates these concerns. "As a theologian she is necessarily concerned with the practice of the Triune God, with discerning what God is doing in the world; with human behavior considered theologically and with what God is calling us to do and be today; with the being and activity of the Church; with practice of Christians; and finally with what virtually monopolized the interest of practical theologians for far too long, the activities of the ordained ministry and other ecclesiastical agents."[35] This allows practical theology to be about attending to and arbitrating the voice of the other by hearing them tell their narratives and letting their voices speak.[36] Practical theology offers theological fragments that are relevant, true, illuminating, and helpful in the Church as it humbly looks for a just practice. Rather than proposing a whole system of truth, Forrester proposes glimpses or fragments of truth that are aimed at specific concrete situations as resources for action and understanding.[37] This interjection of theological fragments in the postmodern arena is a way to recover the Christian social vision in the public debate laboring in the world arena.[38] For Forrester, truth fragments are those fragments that do not consist of the whole truth, but may contain some truth for the particular situation. These fragments may be challenging and disturbing or encouraging and

34. Forrester, *Theological Fragments*, 7.
35. Forrester, *Truthful Action*, 7.
36. Ibid., 126.
37. Forrester, *Theological Fragments*, 4.
38. Forrester, *Truthful Action*, 152–54.

healing. They result from "a disciplined reflection on practices and happenings, on specific ethical dilemmas, life choices and experiences, all in the light of the great tradition of faith and the witness of scripture."[39] Forrester suggests that practical theology should first of all and above all be concerned with the practice of the Trinitarian God, with discerning what God is doing in the world.[40] For Forrester, the way to know the practice of a Triune God is to attend to the communicative practice of Jesus, to the actions of Jesus' life that are communicative of God and to the work of the Spirit in the Church. Practical theology as public theology is relational, not individualistic. It is a discernment of what God is calling people to do today, a discernment of where and who are about God's activity on the ground with real people and in real communities.[41]

Hermeneutical Understandings—Segundo and Habermas

A grasp of the hermeneutics underpinning Forrester's approach to practical theology allows for a deeper sense of his methodology. Forrester's hermeneutics appropriate a hermeneutic circle proposed by Juan Luis Segundo, who uses Habermas' hermeneutic philosophy. "In the hermeneutic spiral, engagement, action and understanding interact with one another to seek a strengthening of commitment, a reform of the Church, and a more just and caring social order, which all reflect the coming Reign of God."[42] Forrester's hermeneutic paradigm develops interpretation within a hermeneutic circle to bring about change by critiquing ideologies and helping to create new meaning more adequate for the poor and oppressed. This action enlivens the Church. Within this hermeneutic understanding, Habermas' philosophy contributes to Forrester's recognition of dialogue and argumentation as action. It seeks ways to reconcile pluralistic views with possibilities of reaching agreement or consensus. Forrester, understanding dialogue as ethical discourse, addresses the power and presuppositions involved in dialogic situations. He calls for dialogue in the academy and, ideally, conversation concerning the "signs of the times" rooted in the life of the ecclesial community as public theology. This communication holds up the universal "fragments" of truth that are part of a larger

39. Forrester, *Theological Fragments*, ix.

40. Ibid., 7–8.

41. Ibid., 11–12.

42. Forrester, *Truthful Action*, 30.

truth for public debate and beckons the practical theologian to continue to "mine" the tradition for truth.[43]

Critique

What is remarkable about Forrester's hermeneutical method is that while it calls for transformation to build God's kindom and for practical theology to move to the public square, it still moves toward consensus based on its hermeneutical model. This action also moves toward a consensus that presumes equality and shared goals.[44] Segundo's hermeneutics use Scripture to reduce power dynamics through ethical rules and truth, biblically based to address the power dynamic itself. Elisabeth Schüssler Fiorenza critiques Segundo's hermeneutic circle indicating that while Segundo's approach does not claim objectivity and an unbiased approach, it fails to be suspicious of the Scripture itself as interpreted text.[45] The use of a biblically based approach to power dynamics imposes a power dynamic itself. When the preunderstandings of Scripture interpretation are not exposed and defended, as in Segundo's model, Schüssler Fiorenza suggests that the failure to critically evaluate the interpretations of biblical texts comes close to using Scripture for proof texting.[46] It is necessary to expose and critique any preunderstanding of Scripture interpretation. This addresses the need for critical evaluation of the texts and their effects on the poor and oppressed.

Moving from Contextual Truth?

Forrester understands practical theology as theology moving from truth to action, and from experience to higher truth with shared goals. He understands the Christian faith as having the capacity for truth and being about truth. At the same time, normative truth often can move to exclusion. Looking for fragments of truth may take for granted that a truth found in the wisdom of the past traditions will be applicable universally to all Christians in this present time. This is particularly true if truth fragments are thought to exist only in the center of the Christian faith. For

43. Ibid., 154–55.

44. Peeren, *Intersubjectivities and Popular Culture*, 101.

45. Schüssler Fiorenza, *Bread Not Stone*, 101.

46. Ibid., 101–2.

Forrester, truth is not a matter of a complex thought system. It is rather an awareness that may challenge, encourage, or disrupt something that rises in the milieu of what is lived and loved within a community.[47] The word "fragment" indicates that these truth fragments may exist on the margins, reflecting not only a piece of the tradition in the center, but also a piece of the tradition in the margins.[48] I would propose that a "truth" offered for a particular public welcomes the *both-and*, being attentive and receptive to the multiple voices. It may offer options for action that are transformative. This mandates attentive listening and awareness of the contextuality of the truth offered for specific publics. As other voices are heard, the action and the truth offered changes with the context.

In sum, Forrester's theology is public theology seeking to address those issues too painful for politicians and others to address in the public debate. "It has a Gospel to share, good news to proclaim. Public theology attends to the Bible and the tradition of faith at the same time as it attempts to discern the signs of the times and understand what is going on in light of the Gospel."[49] While Forrester uses the term "truth," for Forrester truth, rather than being a complex thought system, is an insight appearing in fragments, hints, clues, and questions.[50]

THE POLITICAL THEOLOGY
OF JOHANN BAPTIST METZ

Narrative, Dangerous Memories, and Solidarity

Metz, too, looks to the past. He does so through dangerous memories and the narratives of suffering, offering hope to those who are marginalized. Metz's theology emphasizes the communal dimension of our faith. Theodicy—a defense of God's goodness despite the fact that evil exists in the world—is the question for theology for Metz.[51] According to Metz, practical theology is political theology.[52] The questions of catastrophic, massive, and systematic suffering in the world involve practical theology, knowing that humanity has the resources and the will to put an end to

---

47. Forrester, *Truthful Action*, 18.

48. Kee, "Exclusion," 368.

49. Forrester, *Truthful Action*, 128.

50. Ibid., 18.

51. Metz, *Faith in History and Society*, 119–21.

52. Ibid., 101.

it.[53] The task of theology is thus to give an account of hope that is within us. Metz turns to praxis, a critically reflected action, and suffering with a focus on eschatology. He proposes that theology needs to start from the fundamental categories of Christian praxis, narrative, dangerous memories, and solidarity.[54]

> Well, I think the priest or the clergy in general, the hierarchy is teaching out of a fear mode rather than a freeing mode. I suppose a lot of it is fear of losing their status maybe, their bread and butter. I don't know, but I think there's a fear in them that I don't have. What priest would stand up there and not give you communion because you had a rainbow stole on? What would make them do that? I don't get it. I just don't get it. (Colleen, dialogue)

Colleen stands in solidarity with people who are gay and lesbian and their supporters, who are refused communion each Pentecost in her area. Anne, below, is wrestling with the directive from the new pastor to their community that they must either conform to new liturgy guidelines or leave.

> This is another thing. The people who are actually living the Gospel, and actually serving the people, and feeding the poor, and finding ways to make life better for other people—those are the people you want to kick out? That makes me mad. I think I'm aware of how unlikely change is in that structure; it won't happen in this lifetime, and it probably won't happen in the next two or three, you know. And that makes me sad and not angry. This makes me feel, "You poor old men in your fanciful clothes, you don't really understand." I don't even know what Bible you're reading, 'cause the mandate is so obvious to me, the mandate of service is so obvious to me, that I don't know any other way to judge my faith except on action and I'm so lucky that I grew up that way. (Anne, dialogue)

These are stories of people and communities seeking to be embodiments of koinonia. These are also stories of pain and suffering, brought about by their marginalization in a Church that they love. My dialogue partners are typically socially active in peace and justice issues, progressively oriented, and liturgically centered. They are the lived reality of people on the margins living their faith and putting their "God-talk" into the reality of their context on the periphery of the Church.

53. Ibid., 123–27.
54. Ibid., 66–67.

The thing about the liturgy was that the lay person and the cleric would open the liturgy and call people to worship, welcome people, invite people to be recognized, would share in the opening prayers. They would move back and forth or pass the microphone back and forth so the priest would say one part and the lay prayer leader would say another. Then the gifts would be taken to the altar by lay people and they would be accepted by, actually the coordinator, who was a lay person. We had a team, we would accept the gifts, pour water into the wine,[55] wine into the cup and set the bread on the altar. Then after that the lay prayer leader and the ordained would come and do the prayers of consecration. The community would participate and speak those prayers in unison with the priest. Everybody would be welcome to Communion; everybody would help distribute Communion and then go on to the end. So, all through, lay people had a role to play next to the priest. Eventually the new young pastor was very concerned about the fact that lay people would say prayers that were reserved for the priest to say, so he did not want us to repeat the words of consecration as he repeated them, which we didn't stop doing, because it was a tradition we had grown accustomed to and felt we were part of the liturgy. It was the intention of the community that we are responsible, we are priests in many ways, baptized into the common priesthood of the faithful, yes. (Andrew, dialogue)

Andrew, Anne, and Colleen tell the narratives of an intentional eucharistic community. People acting in history are united by dangerous memories in solidarity with the suffering. This leads to praxis as discipleship, and the primacy of praxis speaking to the larger world. If the Church is to be the Church of the people, then our task as practical theologians is to listen to all people. "All men [sic] are called to be subjects in the presence of their God."[56] For Metz, all modern theologies do not take the turn to the

55. Symbolizing the union of humanity (water) and divinity (wine). When poured together, water and wine cannot be separated, nor can humanity be separated from God.

56. Metz, *Faith in History and Society*, 68. Metz's foundation for his theology includes *Gaudium et Spes*, the Second Vatican Council, and Vatican II's concerns for human rights and historical transformation. His conversation with Marxism included Marx's critique of power. This included Marx's thought on the historical and transformative nature of all action and his critique of the ownership model and the idea of exchange which eventually led to people being expendable (ibid., 114–16). This critique leads to a new understanding of history and anthropology and the demand for new political options, which figures in Metz's theology. Metz's theology also incorporates the modern theology of Karl Rahner and the theology of salvation mediated

subject seriously enough. While Metz uses the modern term "subject," he is arguing that the turn to the subject is too often privatized and idealized rather than focused more radically on the need to understand the poor and oppressed as people. Once the poor and oppressed are taken seriously, the Church unites all people, both the poor and the oppressed, and the spectators of the suffering together in the communion of the faithful.[57]

Critique

While Metz's method is incompletely detailed, Metz defines knowledge as practical knowledge evidenced and tested in the praxis of following Jesus that is nourished by dangerous memories of Jesus' suffering, death, and resurrection and the memories that allow humans to become subjects together in light of memories that connect them to their past.[58] Dangerous memories for Metz are challenging memories of suffering that interrupt the ways things are and reveal new and dangerous insights for the present.[59] Narrative, as the main genre for communicating human experience includes the faith experience and is particularly adept at allowing marginal movements to access the dangerous memories that connect the people with each other and their past. Anne and Harry continue their stories of connecting.

> When I started going to [Church], when it was still inside the parish—and this has changed dramatically since we left and took off, and the funding has just fallen through the floor—but at the time we left they had a homeless shelter with about forty-five men a night. They had a soup kitchen which fed three hundred people a night, an early childhood center for kids, crack babies, children with development disabilities. We still support a house for women leaving abusive and drug abusive relationships. I mean, we had outreach that just blew my mind, which was probably why I stayed. Since we left and we took the money with us, a lot of that has fallen away, which is extremely hard for us because we carry guilt. We know we were the lifeblood

by the historic self (ibid., 147–52; 198–207). These conversation partners led to Metz's critique of the neo-orthodoxy of the person asserting that the person is always social, leading to the eschatological nature of political theology (ibid., 81–84).

57. Ibid., 136.

58. Ibid., 226.

59. Ibid., 105.

of that, and because we were told we had to leave [there is] that suffering! (Anne, dialogue)

The Bishop sends us a letter saying how much he appreciated what [Church] does for the poor and, in the same letter, said, "Okay, the people that are going to the 9:00 Mass cannot be members of the parish anymore." It was such a non sequitur, like what we are doing for the poor is not charity, mister. What we're doing for the poor is because justice is demanded and we have the same demand for ourselves. So, how in one letter he could say, "Wow, what you're doing is so nice for people," and at the same time do something so unjust and so cruel. The people at [Church] demand justice because they believe God does. (Harry, dialogue)

The centrality of stories and storytelling give a sense that dialogue springs from our otherness, and then the sense that narrative is sacramental. This leads to a theory of the action of solidarity that is a category of assistance, support, and encouragement for each person in the face of their suffering. It acknowledges their dignity and personhood seeking to overcome their suffering and pain.[60] Narratives can be sacramental signs as they tell the story of the salvific event, stories of life, and suffering. In this they become themselves "a narrative of salvation within these stories."[61] The stories that Harry, Anne, Colleen, and Andrew narrate may well become the dangerous memories of this intentional eucharistic community. Their stories and the stories of their faith in Jesus the Christ connect their work for the poor, the homeless, and the marginalized with the larger community of the people of God. For Metz, memory and narrative become practical and Christian as they connect with global solidarity. Memory and narrative orient toward a future where all people can live together in God's kindom. They look toward the past for what is distinctive human experience and delve backward into the past for the humanitarian in Christianity.[62] Metz calls for the Church to be a Church of the people rather than for the people.[63] That is what Harry, Anne, and Andrew are seeking as well.

In summary, Metz brings a political and liberative approach to practical theology. With an emphasis on community, he understands that

60. Metz, *Faith in History and Society*, 208.

61. Ibid., 190.

62. Ibid., 208.

63. Ibid., 128.

dangerous memories told in the narratives of those who suffer result in discipleship that includes action for the poor and the suffering. Listening to the voices of the marginalized fosters plurality of meaning. It also provides a means of fostering justice and liberation and moves interpretation in practical theology to the task of transformation that uses the creative potential of dialogue on the margins.

Browning, Metz, and Forrester address various publics in their praxis. Browning does so by putting the experience, reflection, and questions of the Christian tradition with its sources into conversation with the experiences, reflections, and questions of Church communities for the purpose of transformation. Forrester addresses public issues by finding fragments of truth that helps in discerning action for the public good. Metz addresses the praxis for those who suffer through narrative, dangerous memories, and a preferential option for the suffering other.

A NEW HERMENEUTIC PARADIGM—DIALOGUE THAT DOES NOT SEEK CONSENSUS

Dialogue that Does Not Seek Agreement or Consensus

A hermeneutic understanding of dialogue most often designates dialogue for the purpose of reaching agreement or consensus. Yet, the differences and gaps in dialogue are as important as the harmonies and similarities. I suggest a dialogue rooted in alterity that does not seek agreement or consensus. A hermeneutic paradigm for non-consensus-seeking dialogue enables an understanding of practical theology dialogue from the standpoint of relationship. This enhances our effectiveness as practical theologians, and allows us to work in interdisciplinary, intradisciplinary, and cross-disciplinary ways. This is congruent with an understanding of the transversal model of cross-disciplinary practical theology.

Dialogue for the purpose of agreement has been examined by Martin Heidegger, Jurgen Habermas, Hans-George Gadamer, and Paul Ricoeur. An alternative dialogic hermeneutic paradigm for practical theology is informed by the work of Mikhail Bakhtin, a communication theorist. Bakhtin's work espouses a dialogue that does not necessarily seek agreement either in relationship or in truth claims. It emphasizes the ordinary rather than the ideal situation. Through an understanding of the contribution of heteroglossia (multiple conflicting voices in a text), it welcomes multiple voices as necessary for dialogue. Bakhtin's dialogic understanding resists control of meaning, providing a process of looking at alternative perceptions and emphasizing human freedom and responsibility of the individual while maintaining interdependence. Two Bakhtinian concepts discussed in chapter 3 are important for this dialogic hermeneutic in practical theology: dialogue (often called dialogism) and outsideness.

Bakhtin understands language as learned continuously through social contexts that demand a response. Dialogue, the constant starting point, begins with the act of communication itself. "We cannot break out into the world of events from within the theoretical world. One must start with the act itself, and not from its theoretical transcriptions."[64] Through dialogue as participatory experience, we enter into social interaction and relationship, and through this we are co-responsible in dialogue for shaping others, just as they are for shaping us. This is not a fusion but an engagement that results from traversing the porous and permeable boundaries between ourselves and the other in dialogue. In this encounter with the other in dialogue, the self is changed and knowledge and meaning are developed. Such dialogue is mutually constitutive, avoiding domination, control, and the collapsing of one self into another.

The sphere in which the self shapes and organizes in our expression is within the intersubjective space. Creative understanding is formed in the action of dialogue as dialogue partners respond to each other with some kind of meaningful exchange that checks and tests the other's talk for places of agreement or difference. This exchange is more than passive understanding or mere observation. It does not result in a merging or duplication of selves for consensus. Rather, engagement outside of the self, in creative understanding, reveals possibilities and educates each side about the other.[65] According to Bakhtin, the difference allows those in the dialogic encounter and away from that particular dialogic encounter to more fully know themselves. This process of creative understanding, positioned outside of the entity of understanding in time, space, and culture—outsideness—creates the possibility of dialogue and allows for new questions which generate new potentials.[66]

Bakhtin's dialogic understanding provides an important hermeneutic paradigm for practical theology in its awareness that dialogue is enhanced by the difference of the "other." [67] In fact, this difference is foundational.

64. Bakhtin, *Speech Genres*, 50.

65. Morson and Emerson, *Mikhail Bakhtin*, 55.

66. Ibid., 99–100.

67. There are challenges in Bakhtin's thought. He was a person of his time and did

The formative effects of multiple different voices and dialogue's social and historical contexts challenge all reductive meaning.[68] A dialogic hermeneutic paradigm moves a priority of thinking to the primacy of praxis.

A dialogic hermeneutic that does not seek agreement or consensus offers the practical theology dialogic community an opportunity for a change of consciousness. A dialogic hermeneutic interpretation is a commitment to practical theology and the multiple disciplines with which it is in dialogue. It is a commitment to thinking and validating theology though relationship and experience, and to different multiple-voiced dialogue of those participating in the transformation of practical theology.

An honoring of difference does not imply an indiscriminate stance of appreciation that leads to no action. Rather, it is in the reception of the other that one begins to act in relationship. It is in the action of hearing the difference, the edges, surfaces, and depths of the reality of one's self or a community, or a practical theology work that one enters into relationship with the reality of another. The difference in this reality critically generates an opportunity in the praxis to come to a new understanding. This new understanding helps each to reveal and actualize potential.[69] Those involved in the work of practical theology respond to images given by others through dialogue and allow themselves to mutually create a response and actively shape themselves from the response. Practical theology is compelled to wrestle with the difference and to actively engage with the alternative perspectives that may reveal new possibilities. This can happen even when these new possibilities appear as the opposite of the other's perspectives. With such openness, one may grow to understand one's own position more fully. Dialogue changes each person who participates in it. The privileging and honoring of difference allows for the chance to actively grow in *both-and* knowledge[70] and brings the opportunity for change to all who partake in the dialogue. This change may be an agreement that consensus cannot be found at this time or it may be something unforeseen or unanticipated. It might even be consensus, but it importantly encompasses all the voices without a demand for agreement, and without denial of someone's perspective.

not explicitly address gender issues in his writing. However, feminist scholars using his thought have found it to offer an impetus for embodied knowing and inclusion of excluded voices (Bell and Gardiner, *Bakhtin and the Human Sciences*).

68. Green, *Mikhail Bakhtin and Biblical Scholarship*, 59.

69. Morson and Emerson, *Mikhail Bakhtin*, 54–55.

70. J. Y. Lee defines *both-and* thinking as inclusive, open-ended, and creative (*Marginality*, 67). "This is a holistic and open-ended thought process" (ibid., 69).

CONCLUSION

I propose a cross-disciplinary reciprocal practical theology that uses a transversal model of interdisciplinary thinking and practical theology rooted in the Trinity. The practical theology I appropriate is deeply rooted in a theological rationale of the doctrine of God as Trinity, affirming relationship, difference, and diversity, and action for the world. I understand the practical theologian as a cross-disciplinarian who uses the tools and techniques from multiple disciplines to reveal the myriad ways the Christian faith acts within the context of everyday life to transform the world. Dialogue as dialogic praxis is generated in everyday experience forming theory through multi-voiced dialogue. Drawing from this methodology, chapter 7 considers the implications of this practical theology study in the voices of my dialogue partners in light of reciprocal ethnographic practical theology.

7

Pentecost Listening

THREE MAIN CONCERNS DRIVE this practical theology exploration of the margins of the Catholic Church. First and foremost, my interest is to explore the dynamics of the margins of the Catholic Church. The second concern is the implications of these dynamics on the relationships and meanings that emerge for others on the margins of the Catholic Church, for those today who talk about God and seek to understand God's relationship alive in their everyday experiences, and for those who minister in the Catholic Church. These are the topics of this chapter. My third concern is the use of dialogue that does not seek agreement, a welcoming of multiple voices, and a preference for the voice of the other in practical theology. This will be addressed in chapter 8.

Addressing the dynamics of the margins begins with dialogue. Dialogue conveys individual and communal understandings of the dynamics of the margins, the difficulties and problems my dialogue partners encounter with the Catholic Church, and the implications of these. Many envision an emerging Church within the Catholic Church itself. I use the voices of my dialogue partners in describing and highlighting all of these. Following each participatory account, I reflect upon their conversation by exploring the implications and meanings of their experiences both in the Church and on the margins. I then consider the implications of this dialogue and its meanings and relationships.

"I'LL TELL YOU WHO I AM AND YOU LISTEN!"

These reflections about meaning and dynamics reveal dialogue partner conversations. They also incorporate reflections made in a communal process of practical theology reciprocal ethnography. Dialogue partners insist on the importance of their voices being heard. Dan comments to those in the Church. "Don't you tell who I am. I'll tell you who I am and you'll listen. And, this is an exchange. I know who you are. I have some of who you are. You have no idea who I am. And you are trying to tell me who I am? You are wrong" (Dan, dialogue). Focus groups consisted of dialogue partners in two different regions. They volunteered their participation identified themes and sub-themes from the dialogues. They took these and linked them relationally in a way that expresses their own understanding of their experience of the margins in the Catholic Church. This chapter incorporates these reflections.

Naming Relationship and Feelings

Connections and hope for something new, albeit "maybe not in my life-time" (Gail, dialogue), present the margins as places where relationship is lived intentionally. My dialogue partners point to the margins of the Catholic Church as places of authenticity. "I feel I am a more authentic Catholic Christian now than I was when observing all the rules and regulations" (Sarah, dialogue). It is also a place of questioning. "Some theology classes I've taken, they had the depth that was so wonderful. They really made you think; you had to squirm around in your theology gut and see what do I really believe? It is good for me to do that kind of thinking" (Colleen, dialogue). "We went to Jerusalem, to Israel and listened at a mosque as part of the process. That was a real eye-opener. Hearing the stories my whole life and then going and actually seeing the place where many of these stories happened, something in me just shifted. There was a deepening that happened and a deepening in my questioning, too" (Ted, dialogue). And, finally, margins are a place of discernment: "Being Catholic is not about following the rules; it's about knowing what God's expectations for you are, and it's discernment, and learning throughout your life" (Harry, dialogue).

Dialogue partners feel themselves joined in relationship with a larger communion of Catholics who have gone before in history. Sarah observes, "There was a fork in the road and I had to make a decision, and I followed other Catholics who came to know God in this way, but we are all the same root" (Sarah, dialogue). Bill expresses himself as a person in relationship, even though he is on the margins: "In Chartres, there is a door, the image on it is that each person is holding on to the heel of the person above them . . . And it's just a reminder that we're not in this alone, we're holding on to our ancestors, and it's part of who I am . . . It's very much that we're in this together" (Bill, dialogue).

Marginality developed gradually for many of my dialogue partners in the context of their life experiences and spirituality. Most often these feelings of marginality are food for critical thought and prayerful reflection; as Jillian states, "I did debate with myself for awhile, is it better to stay a Catholic and try to change the Church as a Catholic? You know, try to make changes in the Church, because it's the only way you can change it, if you leave it no one is gonna listen. But then I went to my kids and thought whether I want to teach my daughter their stance on women, where women are not allowed to be leaders at the highest level" (Jillian, dialogue). Bea expresses, "I actually agonized a long time about what are the essentials." Sarah describes her process thus: "I see myself growing more deeply into what it means to be a Catholic. I feel I'm . . . I want to use the word *transforming*, and *growing* is very simplistic, I don't know what else to say, but it's like I'm becoming more Catholic in that I'm more authentic; maybe I could use the word *authentic*. I feel I'm a more authentic Catholic Christian now than I was when I was observing all the rules and regulations" (Sarah, dialogue).

Feelings about the Church are expressed by my dialogue partners. They speak of embarrassment and anger at the Church and its image. As Rita says, "I'll probably never leave the Catholic Church, but I am embarrassed at the image they have created for themselves." Jackie states, "Again I was embarrassed. Even recently, you shut your eyes and wince when the Pope was talking about the Islam and the Muslims being second class or whatever he said. I wanted to throw up" (Jackie, dialogue). Maria and Judy speak of the hurt and anger. "Being treated as if we were nothing! We didn't matter. 'We have our agenda.' That was very hurtful to realize that in spite of all that happened there, the people didn't mean a thing" (Maria, dialogue). Judy speaks of her anger. "In the beginning, my anger was at the church. And the women in my prayer group who had children abused by priests—their anger was at specific priests and how the church dealt with it, you know, because a lot of the anger was around the sexual abuse scandal" (Judy, dialogue). Anne explains, "This is the point at which

I get mad. Wait a minute, the people who are actually living the Gospel and actually serving the people and finding the poor and finding ways to make life better for other people, those are the people you want to kick out? That makes me mad" (Anne, dialogue). Cindy and Miriam describe not only feelings of marginalization, but also the feelings that arise from exclusion. They present very different reasons for this exclusion. Cindy remarks, "The priest is kind of very rigid, not really warm and open, and he approaches the church in a very rigid fashion. I feel like it's almost like a mini-inquisition. You're out, out, out, and so there's a lot of exclusion in the parish, absolutely" (Cindy, dialogue). Miriam describes her marginality as an ordained woman priest in the Woman Priest movement. "The church is exactly saying to me, I do not exist." She continues, "Well, I guess I'm a figment of my own imagination, and if I am, I can do anything I want, right? And what I want is to be God's witness, and so that's what I'm doing and I'm a priest. It was very important for me to be ordained. I'm a very traditional Catholic" (Miriam, dialogue). Here, ordination and her marginalization from the institutional Church is her choice. Perlman's findings that those who are excluded, are excluded from the benefits of the social system are pertinent here.[1] Not only are these dialogue partners excluded but the Church excludes itself from receiving the gifts that they offer willingly to the larger community of the people of God.

Assessment

Cindy and Miriam are not alone in speaking of exclusion in the Church. Numerous dialogue partners speak of the exclusion happening in the parishes of their diocese around voting issues, support of political candidates, and involvement in progressive Catholic organizations. Julia states, "So it's some of the real teaching that's going on that excludes people. I think these have a certain amount of shame or guilt that is tied to them and should we really feel that way?" (Julia, dialogue). Is the Church of the twenty-first century moving toward exclusion as an alternative to marginalization? From a perspective of Van der Ven's model of Church, this may be one sign of the amodern basic community. Some indications of this model are required obedience to authority, two classes in the church (laity and clergy), and the understanding that the universal truth the church bears cannot be questioned.[2] This model reacts to the plurality and difference in

1. Perlman, *Myth of Marginality*, 12.
2. Van der Ven, *Practical Theology*, 28.

postmodernity by striving to become a small and holy few, separating itself from society.[3] As this model turns away from society, it resists modernity. Dialogue partners note, as Mattie does, "Well, we're going backwards for sure, and the pope is saying if people leave we'll have a smaller, more pure Church." Andrew remarks, "Being judged against the 'pray, obey, and pay' model, we did not fit the mold." My dialogue partners note the same weaknesses in the institutional Church that Van der Ven identifies in this model: a lack of dialogue with diversity, exclusion of those with differing views, and benefits to those in power in the Church.

Remarkably, not one dialogue partner indicated that people in the center of the Catholic Church needed to be pushed out, ignored, or excluded for their opinions, beliefs, or practices. All suggested values of inclusivity prizing non-denomination. They often said, like Cindy, "We need to listen to all the voices."

Still, many dialogue partners expressed a disconnect between the hierarchical Church and the church as People of God. All but one of those who specify a difference between the institutional church and the Church as the People of God presently meet in some kind of spiritual community, whether it is a Small Christian Community, a prayer group, or an Intentional Eucharistic Community. Dialogue partners at all ages expressed this, suggesting a kind of unvoiced movement into Brueggemann's textual community model of Church. This textual community does not demand consensus but rather struggles and engages with the tradition to recover memory and rootedness while striving toward connectedness and the practice of hope as its primary action.[4]

Carrying the Good

Dialogue educates each person about him or herself, about the other, and about God. Dialogue partners find the benefits of dialogue in the struggle to understand God as a God of love, welcome, and plenitude. Sarah remarks, "So, through my experiences I began to become more and more aware that the God I'm coming to know is a God of openness and great love." This is the language of hope.

The practices of hope by those on the margins include a remembering of the traditions and memories of what they understand as good in their Catholic faith tradition. They "balance" their feelings of anger and

3. Ibid.
4. Brueggemann, "Rethinking Church Models through Scripture," 134.

embarrassment with these memories, letting them stand and harmonizing them with their "core values." One focus group stated, "We individually carry what is good and re-create [that] with like-minded people."

What is good is often expressed as something intangible. "It's like it's in my bones. It's like, I can't not be Catholic" (Judy, dialogue). "Being Catholic sorta gets into your DNA" (Jackie, dialogue). "It's so much woven into me, but not only history, but by some deep level of choice" (Mai, dialogue). Most often this dialogue topic generated a long pause and then a thoughtful answer when this intangible was explored. Dialogue partners Sarah, Sam, and Bill mention the sacraments, particularly Eucharist. Sarah explains, "I came to know God through the sacraments. I celebrate liturgy at the table, I make a thing out of having meals with folks." Bill suggests, "Maybe I'd be kinda poetic and just say bread, bread and wine, which is very much a part of who I am . . . Eucharist is not just something we do, but something we are" (Bill, dialogue).

Others mention liturgy and ritual, as Lily does: "It is the ritual that draws me." Mai says that what is in her bones is "something about regard for the transcendent which something in liturgy invites, promotes and provokes." For some dialogue partners, it is the teachings on how to live that they still find important. Sam declares that he was taught as a child about "not judging." Judy remarks, "The church gave me such a rich beginning; I have a foundation." Terry notes "the basic premises" that he maintains. "I truly believe that all life is sacred and I'm for the anti-death penalty."

Many dialogue partners point to a sense of family and being part of something larger. Dan suggests, "Well, my Grandma had the same belief, the same faith." Julia, like Lance, says, "I think it's like history, it's like family. You can't really cut yourself off from family ever, really" (Julia, dialogue). Anne comments on the history and being part of a tradition of "one of the first churches": "Part of it is family history. Knowing that we're part of something bigger that's been around for two thousand years, knowing that there have been mistakes; there's been healing; that the church isn't perfect; that it's evolving; that there's things that Catholics know that are different" (Anne, dialogue).

This sense of being Catholic also involves a cultural identity. As Julia explains, "It's very cultural; my mom is Hispanic too so, you know, it's part of that culture, part of her upbringing and part of my upbringing" (Julia, dialogue). Ted suggests, "I think there's the cultural identity of being

Catholic." Colleen states, "I can't not be Catholic as well as not be Irish, you know, I'm stuck with it, and Catholic is something in you."

Finally, dialogue partners identify with social justice traditions, as Jackie suggests: "The thing that I value most is the social justice perspectives, for sure." Maggy also remarks, "And the peace and justice tradition, I don't know, the good people and the good things that have come from the church."

Assessment

People on the margins, even though marginalized, value the Catholic tradition. J. Y. Lee's theology of marginality suggests that "what the contemporary and self-affirming definition of marginality attempts to do is to affirm the wholeness of its nature and shape a new creative image from the old image of disgrace and shame."[5] These "good things" that dialogue partners see as part of the wholeness of the Catholic faith reflect the deep structures of Catholicism, identified in chapter 4 as sacramentality, mediation, and communion. Whether it is a sense of the rich understanding of how to live their everyday lives with the "basic premises" they learned as Catholic, a sense of God's presence at work in the breaking of bread and the sharing of self, or the importance of inclusivity and connection to family, what is good about the Catholic faith continues to inform and influence my dialogue partners.

Brueggemann's model of church as a textual community becomes evident in these descriptions. As people on the margins, my dialogue partners are engaged in formulating and interpreting text in ways that struggle with the tradition, engage and enter into the through reflection, discernment, and imagination.[6] Through this engagement, they find what is sustaining about the tradition.

DELVING DEEPER: PERSONAL, STRUCTURAL, AND SYSTEMIC PROBLEMS WITH THE CHURCH

Dialogue partners also speak of what bothers them in the Church, including those disillusioning issues that contribute to their marginalization as well as deeper issues such as the cover-up of the clergy sex abuse scandal.

5. J. Y. Lee, *Marginality*, 50.
6. Brueggemann, "Rethinking Church Models through Scripture," 133.

Focus group discussion tended to see classify the problems in the Church as systemic, structural, or personal. Structural problems with the Church relate to the way it is put together such as its hierarchical or centrally organized structure. Systemic problems are widespread and affect the whole Church and its functioning, as well as those in it. My dialogue partners frequently indicate that systemic and structural problems in the history of the Catholic Church have caused successive systemic, structural, and personal problems. One group of dialogue partners in focus groups states, "The use of 'Church' on this sheet is often really the institutional Church. We don't want to give over the term 'Church' to those who would define it so narrowly." This is an important statement. In another area of the country, I even had to designate that I was looking for dialogue partners on the margins of the *institutional* Catholic Church in order to find volunteers.

Another focus group suggested that if Church problems had been addressed adequately, anger would not have caused people to be marginalized or to stop attending Mass. Still another group suggests the systemic and structural problems are leading to a dying Church, and they are hospicing this dying Church. "The background causes leading to the emerging Church involve the fact that they did not teach us to think before Vatican II, both priests and the people have a limited knowledge of contemporary post-Vatican II theological currents, and the Pope is in tension with the 'emerging church.'" They note, as Sarah does, "It's birth, it's chaos, and it's destruction and it's rebirth." They suggest, "We need this to happen and we need Pentecost listening and thinking and questioning for our becoming." In their listening to divergent views, they trust something new will rise from the ashes.

Yet another group suggests, "We are not hospicing this old Church. We have work to do on 'being Catholic,' discerning and dealing with identity, anger, the religious right, Vatican II teachings and the retrenchment from Vatican II teachings, priests, adult religious education, interconnections, and social justice." As they deal with these issues, this group sees a new paradigm growing that connects the early church with the emerging Church. They relate to Harry's comment: "We are not aiming to be a first-century community. I think we are aiming to be a twenty-first century church and I think it has amazing correlations."

One group remarks that the priests leaving the priesthood in the 1970s, "especially the ones we liked, who were the best with relevant homilies," the antiwar culture, and the cultural changes of this time led Catholics such as themselves to take more notice of the Church. This in turn led to thinking and questioning. This group feels that they are balancing the systemic and structural problems in the hierarchy and power structure of the church, which they term "the disruption of relationships which is sin," with their response of inclusivity, finding voice, and re-appropriation of the communion of saints. They see a relationship of counterpoint, as they carve something new. The current centralization of authority, lack of consultation and silencing of divergent views, and a male-centered church is being counterbalanced by thinking and questioning, an egalitarian and democratic way of being Church, inclusive language, and a movement to the margins. On the margins they find community, dialogue, relationship, and an inclusive space where "everyone is welcome at the table."

Focus groups all corroborate that systemic and structural problems are causal factors in their marginality. As one group said, "We are questioning all the negatives. We are breaking the silence."

The Church Is Out of Step with Its Own Purpose

Naming the Problems:
Personal, Structural, and Systemic in the Church

"There is growing disillusionment with the Church's attitude. The Church is out of step with its own purpose" (Joe, dialogue). "The church has a reputation for taking five hundred years . . . I don't hold out a lot of hope for the institutional church. I actually think the institution has a very good chance of going out of business or becoming irrelevant because, on the one hand, millions and millions of Catholics are becoming 'unchurched' because they don't see opportunities" (Harry, dialogue). Dialogue partners referred to the Church as sick and dying. "The church is alive and well here though it is a very sick place" (Jane, dialogue). Some, like Miriam, refer to hospicing a dying Church. "We are going to bring out a new church from the ashes. Because right now, what's happening is we're hospicing this old church." "They keep shooting themselves in the foot, everything that comes out of the hierarchy is distressed, is totally distressed. I don't think it will change in this generation—the church takes forever, just look at Vatican II . . . it will take hundreds of years" (Gail, dialogue).

RETRENCHMENT

Dialogue partners discuss the "retrenchment" they see happening. "I am suggesting that, the way that I experience the hierarchy today, I am expected to deny that vision and deny the culture that I live in and the kind of society I live in, to deny myths or the symbols of my vision. And I am supposed to leave it outside the Church as I walk in the Church door so that I can adapt a pre-seventeenth-century language. For example, when they defined homosexuality, they had no position in defining that. It is again, it is clearly Galileo revisited, and to me these are intelligent people" (Dan, dialogue). Mattie longs for Vatican II teachings: "Vatican II, well, they're going backwards, away from Vatican II, that's for sure!" Dan states, "I can understand what is going on today in the context of my own experience, which is pre-Vatican II."

Personal Problems

Personal problems are named as causing marginality; these include divorce, annulments encouraged by the Church for their husbands when they wanted the marriage to continue, the church's teachings on homosexuality and relationships, and abortion. Sometimes, as in Mike's case, a lack of knowledge about current Catholic teaching today exacerbated the problems. Matt speaks of the Church's teaching of no salvation outside of the Church and his love for his non-Catholic brother-in-law. "We learned as kids, like oh, my God, if you're not a Catholic then something is wrong. So, that's not fair. This guy is nice. And then I started wondering, that was the first big question I had. Why should he be punished?" (Matt, dialogue).

Dee speaks about getting pregnant as an eighteen year old and the mother of her boyfriend suggesting and then taking her to get an abortion. This has been a burden for Dee throughout her life. She says, "The really great thing about being Catholic is that I can go to confession; I've been to confession a few times, but haven't confessed this yet. This is how bad I feel about it. It is one of those things I still need to work on" (Dee, dialogue). Dialogue partners express a hesitancy to go to confession to priests they perceived as ultraconservative, authoritarian, and lacking empathy. These personal problems in the Church lead to feelings of marginalization and, according to one focus group, are "among the causal reasons for not going to Mass and for leaving the Church altogether."

Personal and family issues often were aggravated by Church communities, causing people to move to the margins. Janet was asked to leave her church as a young girl because her parents did not have the money to pay for school or the religious education. In her fifties, this incident still marginalizes her.

The church's teaching on homosexuality was mentioned by over half of my dialogue partners as unjust. "The church shames gay people" (Harry, dialogue). Pat and Steve agreed: "Like we said to you before, sexual equality is the civil rights issue of this generation, so that bothers us a lot." "I feel that something in the concept of religion gets incredibly screwed up when you disown your child for being gay" (Dee, dialogue).

Other personal issues also push people to the margins. The church's stance on annulment, irregular marriages, and the reception of Eucharist cause much pain and anger for those on the margins of the Church. "You know, there's still a certain amount of shame of not being an intact family" (Sade, dialogue). "I kind of left the church temporarily after I was divorced; actually, I got the marriage annulled, which I would never do again because I think the annulment process is meaningless" (Lily, dialogue). "What about divorced people? How about my aunt, who was in an abusive relationship for six years? The guy beat her bloody. She left him, found my Uncle Jack, they got married—they've been together for forty-five years, happy. She has been going to mass every weekend for forty-five years and not receiving communion because she's divorced. That's not fair" (Harry, dialogue). "I said at the annulment hearing I am going to read to you why the sacrament is valuable. The judicial vicar at the time said to me—his actual words were—'We don't care about the sacrament here, we only care about the law—Canon Law.' It's so hypocritical" (Jackie, dialogue). And James decided against annulment. "The only thing I would have got out of that is that I would tell the kids, 'We were never married, well, what does that make you? Ha, ha.' So, I said no" (James, dialogue). Kim speaks of being told that her parents' marriage was annulled. "I called my sister a bastard. It was a joke, but at the same time, wow, it ticked me off. How can you—you were married for twenty-five years—how can you say it's okay because you gave the church $2,000?" (Kim, dialogue).

Issues that decrease Mass attendance include boredom, irrelevant homilies, a difference in emphasis on worship style, and a loss of a sense of community. "But like at St. ____, it's just like it was growing up, the same thing, its routine, and it's kind of boring" (Sam, dialogue). "We had a Charismatic mass once every month and the Spirit just flowed. I still wonder what happened to it. I've asked a couple of priests, I don't get an answer" (John, dialogue). "If we're really going to take the essence of the Last Supper, we're so far away from it in Mass. I often say, the big cathedrals with people just sitting there doing nothing, that doesn't resemble the Last Supper to me at all. It was always meant to be community in sharing and action. How are we going to take care of the poor? That was the purpose of liturgy, [it] was to give you enough strength to go out and do what needs to be done" (Colleen, dialogue).

The single most mentioned personal problem for my dialogue partners is clergy sex abuse and its cover-up. Forty-six of my dialogue partners mentioned this as an issue that moved them to the margins of the church. Most knew people touched by the abuse personally speak of their friends' anger and sadness and their move to the margins of the Church. Many say that their friends have left the Catholic Church completely. Jane's experiences include getting physically sick at church concerning this issue. Jane says, "Abuse is never ancient history, people don't get that." James talks about his experiences with a priest who was a close family friend throughout the years his children were growing. "Absolutely, to me the Catholic Church lost all its common sense, they lost their integrity and this, I felt this before it got personal, and my kids might be involved" (James, dialogue). My other dialogue partners, like Sarah, demand that those responsible take personal responsibility. "That's one of the things that led me away, the hypocrisy of it all. And then we get this prayer card sent to each parish. The priest said we would pray this at the end of all the liturgies for this terrible crisis we're going through. Within that prayer card it was 'we have sinned.' So, fortunately, some people were saying, 'Wait a minute, we have sinned?' Take this prayer card and *hmm* with it because, we have all sinned but what you're talking about is not 'we'" (Sarah, dialogue). This problem in the Church is structural and systemic as well as personal.

Structural Problems

According to my dialogue partners, the Church is experiencing structural problems. These structural problems include an unhealthy hierarchical organization, too much control, and authoritarianism. "There are things that really bug the hell out of me. You know, the way the church flaunts its authority, the hierarchy, the way woman are treated, the way sexuality is hidden, the way homosexuals are ostracized" (Bill, dialogue). "Well part of my sense about that is we still have to address some deeper issues in the church around abuse, around power, around dispensation of the sacraments. Doesn't it bother people that we have few priests to do Eucharist, so they're going to do Communion Services where this poor priest will consecrate a bunch and dole them out. I mean, does that make any sense theologically to people?" (Jane, dialogue). "So, the church itself creates feet-of-clay people. They form dependent people in dependent ways, so that there is a lot of dependency in the mentality" (Jackie, dialogue).

Dialogue partners identify overall trends in the hierarchy of the Catholic Church toward retrenchment from Vatican II teachings, a lack of understanding of U.S. culture, and expectations about uniformity from Rome as having created a general disenchantment. There is growing disillusionment with the church's attitude. "It's power and structure, power through structure" (Dan, dialogue). "The rules are more important than the people. The Pope started saying you have to kneel here and then you have to bow there, and it was over and over again. We were told this is what you have to do. Who cares what we do? Who cares if I bow at the right time before I receive Communion? Who cares? Does God care?" (Cindy, dialogue). "This is the church that needs new thinking and we kind of thought there was hope for it, but I don't know after how many years of Pope John Paul's attitude and then Benedict; I still don't know what he wants to do besides make the church leaner and meaner" (Lily, dialogue). "The Catholic Church, I feel the big institution is very judgmental, exclusive, and focused on material things and not so much on social justice" (Shannon, dialogue).

Dialogue partners have concerns related to parishes as community, and pastoral effectiveness, and involvement. Issues of misuse of power and authority in the church, and related problems with young, conservative priests who want to exercise their power exclusively, are also part of structural difficulties driving people to the margins. Ted describes, "He says, 'I've got this parish and I'm gonna take it for a spin,' to quote him. Let's take it for a spin, totally shutting out people who had done wonderful work, and it felt like, 'I'm not welcome here'" (Ted, dialogue).

Finally, a lack of intellectual stimulation, a lack of spirituality in Church liturgy and community, as well as a lack of enrichment and discussion are also noted as structural problems. Judy remarks, "I think I got more and more disillusioned with them not listening to the laity or not realizing what our struggles were. When the GIRM (General Instruction for the Roman Missal) came out [in 2002], it just seemed that they isolated the priests further" (Judy, dialogue). Harry states, "To me the elements of the mass are being genuine and having integrity and being real and being true to the teachings of Christ, it's not whether you're following GIRM or not. And GIRM was sort of a retrenchment of previous rules." Tim remarks, "For the most part, I'll hear a sermon and a lot of times forget about it in a week or a day, or whatever." Luke states, "My kids don't go to church. They are good kids; they're both married. They're both strong in social justice, but when you talk about the church it doesn't resonate. Now, what went wrong? What was happening in the church did not make sense" (Luke, dialogue).

Personal and structural problems in the Catholic Church are connected with systemic problems. Joe indicates that systemic problems, in conjunction with a lack of leadership, add to a general disenchantment with the hierarchy, which causes people to move the margins (Joe, dialogue).

Systemic Problems in the Church

Systemic difficulties abound in the Church. Parish mergers and closing without any regard for the type of alternative leadership possibilities, limited connection by current Church hierarchy with Vatican II theological currents, and lack of leadership are just a few of the problems. In turn, lack of leadership leads to a lack of consultation and a silencing of divergent perspectives (Joe, dialogue). Exclusivism in belief, ritual, and attitudes, a culture of arrogance, and increased centralization are other systemic problems. The leadership maintains a sense of inequality and a canonical rigidity contrary to the Gospel (Bill, dialogue; Jane, dialogue; Joe, dialogue; Sandra, dialogue; Dan, dialogue).

Dialogue partners spoke to all of these issues. "No, no, it's systemic; it's a much bigger issue. I think the issues around priests and relationships are more a symptom of a bigger systemic issue of not being honest with naming—well, the abuse scandal is an example—the abuse scandal would be good, an example of not walking the talk, of saying one thing and acting in another" (Ted, dialogue). "I think the Church is determined to go back to old pre-Vatican stuff and they'll get it done cause that's who's in there right now" (Maggy, dialogue) "Well, I think the priest or the clergy in general, the hierarchy are teaching out of a fear mode rather than a freeing mode. I suppose a lot of it is fear of losing their status maybe . . ." (Colleen, dialogue).

Assessment

These systemic, structural, and personal problems in the Catholic Church produce tension within the present-day Church. For my dialogue partners, these result in a growing disillusionment with the church's teachings and demands for justice. Miriam suggests, "It is very evident to me that this is a dying church, people are disgusted with the secrecy." Rita explains, "The greed, the accumulated wealth while people die of starvation, the self-serving, arrogant attitude of the church—surpasses all other faith traditions in ego. The secrecy, I can no longer be one of the 'sheep'—one of the never-questioning, apathetic followers" (Rita, dialogue). Harry says, "You know you can't continue to oppress groups and expect people who demand justice to acquiesce."

Personal problems with the Church at times reflect Church teachings learned at an early age. Adult religious education with an emphasis on Vatican II teaching has enabled a many more to hear current understanding of the Church's teachings in question. Such education is needed by both laity and clergy alike due to inadequate education and retrenchment from Vatican II teachings.

Systemic and structural difficulties reflect issues in a Church that understands itself in a way that seems to be similar to Brueggemann's temple community model. Such a model is marked by a convergence of Church and state, relative stability, members whose lives moved from the religious dimension into secularization, and a visible and funded leadership.[7] Brueggemann suggests this is the governing model of Western Christianity. I would suggest it is the governing model of parishes to which my dialogue partners belonged before their move to the margins. Established religion in the temple community model serves the powerful by stabilizing power and knowledge at the expense of others in the Church and community.[8] This model "defaults" on its God-given vocation as Church and is eventually swept away by upheaval.[9]

Dialogue partners speak of the Church as dying, saying they are "hospicing this old Church." They point to a lack of social justice, a lack of meaningful liturgy opportunities, and an emphasis on rubrics and rules. Harry remarks, "I was in the shelter last night, as my volunteer stint for the month, and we don't even have enough cereal bowls, so are

---

7. Brueggemann, "Rethinking Church Models through Scripture," 130.

8. Ibid.

9. Ibid., 133.

we supposed to buy $8,000 worth of gold chalices and these guys have to wash out their bowls so that they can have breakfast after the other guy? How silly is that, and so we voted it down" (Harry, dialogue). Bea states, "This emphasis on things. The priest had all the Eucharistic ministers . . . come to a meeting, and so we did, and there was a five-page packet for us, lots of bold print, sacramental, thick, it was all about how to behave. Actually, at one point a friend of mine was a eucharistic minister, former Catholic, now she's retired, and she said, 'Bea, that place is toxic'" (Bea, dialogue). As the Church seems to focus power and control of knowledge, prophets keep calling it back to its roots. That is one of the roles my dialogue partners play in their communities.

In their analysis of the problems in the Church, some in my focus groups speak of those on the margins as if they are in conflict with some in the hierarchical church. Because of these problems and because of their experiences on the margins of the Church, they see an emerging church rising. While there is growing disillusionment, there is also hope.

WE CARVE OUT SOMETHING NEW: THE EMERGING CHURCH ON THE MARGINS

Those on the margins of the Catholic Church live and imagine creative new potential for an emerging Church in the liminal space of the margins. Dialogue with my dialogue partners and conversation in focus groups paint a picture of this emerging Church taking shape. One does not live into or imagine an emerging Church alone but rather in community. The envisioned emerging Church insists on relationship, dialogue, and community. One focus group of dialogue partners noted, "We don't go become Lutherans or Episcopalians, we don't stop being Catholic; we carve out something new." They state, "While some may consider the hierarchical Church as the more traditional church, the emerging Church more connects with the ancient tradition of our Catholic Church." One dialogue partner remarks, "People are leaving, but I think we are going to bring out a new Church from the ashes" (Gail, dialogue).

Another focus group images this emerging Church relationally as a "horizontal circle." Still another suggests that the emerging Church "is where we are and where we want to be. We have work to do." Another focus group indicates that as they "hospice this old Church, a new Church will emerge from the ashes of the present Church. There are conversations moving us forward to the emerging Church."

Relationship

The emerging Church that is marked by relationship is inclusive. Those on the margins call for inclusive community. This includes the GLBT community (gay, lesbian, bisexual, and transgendered), those with developmental disabilities, the poor, and the immigrant communities. They also want equal opportunities for women and married priest leadership. They suggest the use of inclusive language so all feel welcome. "You learned from the street people, from the poor, from the marginalized and all that they said. 'If you want us here then you have to take us as we are'" (Colleen, dialogue).

An inclusive faith community is seen as democratic and egalitarian. It is a place of divergent views that is open and welcoming. In its equality and acceptance of difference, communities are described much as Harry describes his old parish community before a change in pastoral leadership. "We were the place that if you were divorced and feeling unwelcome or you were gay, or you were radical or something, you would come to St. _____ because it was the place where you were accepted, you were nurtured, you were welcomed and cherished. I never felt that people tolerated me at St. ____. I felt that people just loved the fact that I was there" (Harry, dialogue).

Those on the margins of the Church describe a spirituality of relationship. Lily suggests this is "not being a child of God anymore, but being an adult in relationship with God." Spirituality involves vulnerability and sharing of everyday lives. Kate suggests that people can find a peace in relationship with God and others as they bring their bad experiences to a community where "people listen and they care." God is present on the margins. As James notes, "God isn't going to take you out of your situation; he'll leave you there, but he's going to be with you there and that is a huge difference, huge." Shannon suggests, "The phrase that I always remember that I like so much is 'bread for the journey,' which reminds me that this is not just a Sunday thing. This is your life; this is what you try to do all week. We know things about people's lives in our community that are so important to know. You know, whether it's their health or things they're going through or their kids or their jobs or people losing jobs, all kinds of things, you know things about people. And that kind of vulnerability brings a different level of spiritual understanding, I must say" (Shannon, dialogue).

Dialogue

Such actions involve dialogue. As one focus group notes, "The Spirit evolves in dialogue." Dialogue in the emerging Church is dialogue with God and each other, dialogue with the tradition, and dialogue with education partners such as the history of the Church, Scripture and theology. A Trinitarian theology suggests an understanding of a dialogic God in conversation with the world. Colleen notes, "I think the revelation of God is constant and I hope forever." Dialogue with God and each other includes as one focus group noted "ritual and liturgy, sharing spiritually through prayers and dialogic homilies that are lay led, and thinking and questioning."

A dialogue with tradition suggests "recovering and revaluing traditions." Jane states, "I love ritual, I love a lot of how the tradition addresses mystery and how the tradition, I mean the long tradition, even our mystics, there was very much a sense of universality and transcendence along with immanence that is not so much the rubrics and the high church and the funny hats and all of that, but just the tradition itself. This is a love affair with a God who loves us, you know, so immanently" (Jane, dialogue). Pat remarks, "Well, there are a number of things over the millennium that the Catholic Church has done very well; there happens to be a whole lot of Catholic music written that I happen to agree with. There is a whole lot of tradition which has dealt with social justice; there has been a whole lot about life" (Pat, dialogue). They include conversations about the experience with the hierarchy of the Church and conversations about how people "find their own authority to live in a relationship with their own self and other folks and in the universe with their God" (Sarah, dialogue).

Dialogue in the emerging Church allows people to speak, to have voice. One focus group suggests, "They did not teach us to think before Vatican II." As Ted and Sarah remark, "You've not converted a person if you silence them" (Ted, dialogue). "What's going to happen to us if people speak up and stand up and be counted?" (Sarah, dialogue).

Dialogue with education that facilitates continued spiritual growth is valued by my dialogue partners. They note that it needs to focus on "a more dialogic education rather than a spoon-fed education." Dialogue partners suggested education themes that I group into three areas: history of church, Scripture, and theology. They affirm the necessity of a continuing study of theology and ask the larger questions about their community's authenticity and relevance because of their studies. Dialogue partners note that Scripture study is necessary. Some believe that the use of the Bible in history has led to violence. Others such as Caroline note that further study allows a community to say, "This is what it says in the Bible . . . I know that it's going to be hard, but from my life experience these are the things you are going to face and let's do some practical work" (Caroline, dialogue). Bill suggests knowledge of Church history is needed. "I don't know if we're really honest with our own past, I think if we all knew history better I think the world would be a much different place, not just the church, but the world. If we all knew history better, I'm not sure there'd be much in the way of war, I'm not sure there'd be much in the way of poverty" (Bill, dialogue).

The need for listening as part of dialogue is suggested both for those on the margins and for the hierarchical Church. Colleen explains the results of her parish community listening. "Yeah, I think that's what saved us from becoming 'girminated' [following the GIRM guidelines]. That we have marginalized people telling us a thing or two. You know we listened to the 'down and outers.' People knew, I think you listened, you learned from the street people, from the poor, from the marginalized and all that they said" (Colleen, dialogue).

Community—Koinonia

The way dialogue partners speak about community seems to suggest a kind of koinonia, an invitation to communion beyond itself. "It is this communion of the Trinity that grounds the life and unity of the Church."[10] The emerging Church is envisioned as a Spirit-led community. Maria, Anne, and Bill who are all in different small communities, talk about the importance of these communities to their place on the margins. "That was the thing that kept us going and I think that we were together and experiencing the same things and encouraging each other. I don't know what would have happened if we would've been alone" (Maria, dialogue). "A sense of community and the sense of change, the sense of the Gospel asks us to change things in the world we are in and not to rest and not to sit still, that sense of movement and momentum, I think is the most important thing about it to me" (Anne, dialogue). And Bill notes "I think I get more energy from the small faith community. It's more I think, in line with the early church, you know the home liturgies, the home sharing, a sharing of faith and spirituality and trying to tie what's going on in our lives with readings, and kind of supporting one another" (Bill, dialogue).

10. Fuchs, *Koinonia and the Quest for an Ecumenical Ecclesiology*, 28.

Those on the margins who are living into this emerging Church describe themselves as educated and involved people who are also concerned with "what they do when they are not at the table." The array of social justice ministries my dialogue partners engage is impressive. Even for those who have grown to an age or health where active involvement is not an option, prayer ministries continue. Some are involved in political activism on behalf of the poorest of the poor in their communities. Others are involved in fighting the death penalty, war and instruments of war, hunger, and homelessness. This action involves giving of time, talent, and money. This social justice ministry arises from a spirituality sometimes nurtured in small communities, and sometimes when no community is available, nurtured in prayer with God alone. Anne suggests, "I found a community and I also found political activism which is really important." Bea states the importance of a community rooted in social justice. " The Gospel values were important . . . social justice, well it's justice, it's love, well it's just all the good stuff that comes out; justice, love, how to act in the world" (Bea, dialogue).

Assessment

The emerging Church on the margins provides new theological vision. This is similar to Brueggemann's model of a new church start. The new church start is a community birthed in marginality.[11] It has a shared commitment to a central story and a social justice passion. It borrows from the culture and community around it and transforms what it borrows with covenant and a passion for liberation. Lily remarks, "It's like, Jesus is here in this wine, you know, Jesus is not just there in Church, just because I have brought him here with my magic words, you know, I don't do that anymore. We have mass in our living room, and we have Jesus in our living room, we have bread and wine, we have the words of consecration and we all say them together" (Lily, dialogue). Sade states, "One thing I love within the Catholic Church is I love the saints because they are ordinary people who did extraordinary things. Very ordinary people." This gives hope.

J. Y. Lee theology of marginality suggests the concept of church begins on the margins. "The fellowship of God's marginal people is known as the Church or the body of Christ."[12] As my dialogue partners claim

11. Brueggemann, "Rethinking Church Models through Scripture," 133.

12. J. Y. Lee, *Marginality*, 4.

their name as Catholic, they imagine themselves as Church as the people of God. They realize that reconciliation is impossible without justice. They understand themselves as all made in the image of God and all invited into discipleship. As koinonia, they relate to God and understand their relationship with God demanding relationship with others. Thus, they call for women's leadership, for the respect for their GLBT brothers and sisters. Jane suggests that the Church needs "to include the gift of more people you're just going to have a greater sense of who's your leaders, a greater sense of role models for other people in the Church, and it empowers your people when you can see a woman priest, or a married priest, or somebody that connects with you, I mean, at least I felt I could talk to people from the pulpit and they got it" (Jane, dialogue). Luke notes, "The church is there to open us, to help us understand how God works through things." Thus, as dialogue partners talk about the Church, they also image God. They call for Church to be a "living faith model," understanding God present in everyday life. They call for community and relationship, understanding God present "where two or more are gathered" (Matt 18:20). As Mai suggests, "So justice is important and honoring the essence of who you are, people working together, supporting one another and asking the hard questions, studying them, probing them."

IMPLICATIONS OF THE DYNAMICS OF MARGINALITY

It is here—at the conclusion of the discussion of the emerging Church on the margins—that this study begins to express concrete implications of this dialogue for others on the margins, for those who are talking about God in their everyday experiences, and for those in ministry in the Church. People on the margins as well as those who are seeking God in their everyday experiences and those who are in ministry would benefit from this practical theology research. Dialogue in small groups, both on the margins and in the center of Church, could engage this work of practical theology and further allowing not only these voices to be heard but also generating new implications in the shared dialogue.

Additional suggestions arising from this dialogue on the margins of the Catholic Church are listed and addressed below:

- Social justice action is imperative.

- Liturgies that nourish and foster this action create bonds but also give witness to Jesus Christ in the fellowship of the Spirit.

- My dialogue partners on the margins call for ongoing formation as "on the margin discipleship" and continued education. Adult religious education is important in the areas of history of the Church, Scripture and theology. This education needs to be dialogic in its foundation, full of divergent voices and unafraid to act collaboratively in order to foster adult spiritual development. It is through this dialogue with another that spiritual formation happens and each person helps to author another. Education in history, Scripture, and theology allows for a critical understanding of the foundations and roots of the Catholic tradition. This exploration fosters connections of the individual and communal story with the larger Jesus story in tradition.

- A theological education is a necessity for those in ministry in this age of an educated laity. Education allows those in ministry to act as leaders. It collaboratively enables the minister to lead the church community in considering their context, the resources on which they can count, and the work necessary in a church rife with systemic and structural problems yet full of abundant hope.

- Making opportunities to dialogue is essential. Dialogue supports those who engage it. It is through dialogue that the each person epistemologically understands. It is in and through dialogue that each person is formed and assists in forming the other. We cannot see ourselves fully; it is only with another that we are fully seen so that this can be reflected back for growth and understanding. We do the same for others. This is a deeply spiritual action. Dialogue for those in ministry sustains not only the minister, but also the community of faith and struggle working to anticipate God's new creation in the world today.

- Dialogue is imperative as a part of community practice in Small Christian Communities, in Intentional Eucharistic Communities, and in Church parishes. Dialogue without seeking consensus is an art and an art that can be learned. A skill necessary in community, dialogue is particularly helpful for those dealing with the stresses of systemic and structural problems. Dialogue helps communities talk about issues, process them, and move to a new place. The ability to remember the history of the community, to dialogue about the community's rootedness and connectedness provides healing and hope.[13]

At the end, the purpose of this chapter has been to listen to the voices of those on the margins of the Catholic Church, exploring the dynamics of marginality, allowing them to name themselves, and listening as they describe the meaning and relationships they find emerging in the margins. The implications of these dynamics proposed for others on the margins for those today who are talking about God and seeking to understand God's relationship alive in our everyday experiences and for those in ministerial roles in the Catholic Church call for dialogue, education, and relationship. This dialogue rises from a practical theology model that is relational, engaging other disciplines, listening to diverse voices, seeking non-consensus dialogue. The next chapter will propose suggestions for what is next as I look to the future with hope.

13. These are the tasks of the textual community, one of Brueggemann's models of church. See chapter 4.

8

Faith that Good Does Not Die, Somehow Now God Works Through Us

Envisioning What's Next

TWO OBJECTIVES SET IN motion this practical theology research. The first is to understand the reasons why Catholics over the age of twenty-one, who were once active and involved in the Catholic Church but presently no longer attend Mass, find themselves on the margins of the Church and how they understand their own marginality. By bringing forth the voices of my dialogue partners, this study explores the dynamics of marginality and integrates these dynamics into the lived experience of Church. Systemic, structural, and personal problems cause disillusionment, anger, embarrassment, and pain leading to marginality. People on the margins continue to seek ways of expressing their spirituality through Small Christian Communities, Intentional Eucharistic Communities, prayer, and social justice activities.

The second objective, rooted in the experience of those on the margins, delves into the implications of the experiences of my dialogue partners for others on the margins of the Church, for all those talking about God and seeking to understand God's relationship in everyday experiences, and for those who minister within the Catholic Church. There are new ways of being Church emerging on the margins, marked by inclusive relationship in community as koinonia, non-consensus-seeking dialogue, a critical and thoughtful recalling of memories and narratives of the Catholic faith tradition, and appropriation of these in new and creative ways.

This practical theology research observed the consequences of a process of dialogue that does not seek agreement and consensus. This dialogue privileges the other and welcomes multiple voices. These contribute to practical theology method for the twenty-first century. Non-consensus-seeking dialogue allows centrifugal forces pushing towards unity and order and centripetal forces pushing towards multiplicity and diversity to stand together as practical theology. Thus, it finds new ways of transformative action.

Practical theology that takes seriously its work as discipleship uses dialogue that does not seek agreement or consensus as one primary means of encouraging relationship. The implications for the broader practical theological task begin in the transformative nature of dialogue. Dialogue forms all who appropriate the action. The goal of practical theology is transformation. Dialogue in itself is transformative. The welcoming of the unheard voices of my dialogue partners on the margins of the Roman Catholic Church to the conversation is the transformational aspect of this practical theology research. When the voices of people who have previously not been included in the conversation are heard the conversation changes. Dialogue that does not seek agreement provides opportunities to esteem God through relationship with a multitude of God's people. To be in relationship with God is to be in relationship with others. This creates a space for the creative potential of the margins to affect both the margins and the center for the good of all.

Yet, just to say practical theology seeks non-consensus-seeking dialogue does not assure it. A concerted effort to develop models that have a basis in dialogue that does not seek agreement requires attention to methodological presupposition, and the use of interdisciplinary modes of conversation. Ultimately, it requires an awareness of relationship, a perception of the plentitude and plurality of God, and attention to the practical theologian's own ability to sit with paradox. Practical theology as discipleship makes it an inherently relational discipline. A move to dialogue that does not seek consensus, a welcoming of multiple voices, and a privileging of the other are relational tasks. They are ones that should not and cannot be done alone.

This suggests two areas for further research. The first involves practical theology research for the Church. The second further possibility is to utilize dialogue that does not seek agreement or consensus in a variety of practical theology research opportunities. Further practical theology research in the Church that utilizes a dialogic practical theology that does not seek consensus will allow more in-depth conversations and support dialogue with both those on the margins and those in the center. Margins are fluid places becoming new centers as new margins are formed. As voices that have previously gone unheard join the conversation, there may be chance for face to face dialogue with all in the Church. Non-consensus seeking dialogue, a welcoming of multiple voices, and a privileging of the voices of the other can facilitate this fruitful conversation. More opportunities for those on the margins to state research topics in regards to the margins of the Church, and to continue the conversation about their experiences through practical theology research are needed.

Intentional eucharistic communities, such as the one with which I was associated through my dialogue partners, are developing as models of emerging Church. Their process, challenges, and journey as they seek authentic ways to live their relationship with God may provide insight into the ways we are Church in the twenty-first century. Participatory action research and more in-depth reciprocal ethnography could provide avenues to plumb the depths of these experiences.

The second area of research inquires into the use of a non-consensus seeking dialogue in practical theology method. Action research provides a method that intentionally probes the dynamics of experiences and could be helpful in exploring the benefits of a practical theology method that uses this non-consensus-seeking dialogue, welcoming of multiple voices, and privileging the other.

Finally, this dialogic account of the margins of the Catholic Church has redefined margins as fluid spaces where one can exist *both* in the margins *and* in the Church. With my dialogue partners, I have defined this space as a creative place where the reality of God can be seen and new ways of being Church for the twenty-first century are emerging. My dialogue partners honestly and graciously shared their journeys and this emerging vision. Realizing that God is more plural and multifaceted than can be imagined, there may be those who do see with the same lenses that either my dialogue partners or I use. They too are a part of the ongoing dialogue that exists today, in the past, and into the future. It is through this non-consensus-seeking dialogue that the People of God grow and change in relationship with God and each other. It is with faith that God's grace is beyond measure and the Holy Spirit is leading us that I close with Sarah's words.

How do we help people find their own authority—their own authority to live in a relationship with their own self and other folks and in the universe with their God? How do we help them to do that? Because life is all about relationships! (Sarah, dialogue)

Appendix A

May I Introduce You to My Dialogue Partners?

Andrew is sixty-nine years old with a master's degree in education.

Anne is thirty-two years old with a master's degree in costume design.

Bea is eighty years old and holds a BA. She is a librarian.

Bill is between fifty-five and sixty years old, is a priest, formally laicized to marry, and holds a master's degree in process theology. He is active in marriage ministry.

Caroline is thirty-one years old. She has a master's degree in professional sports administration.

Chloe is thirty-one years old and holds a master's degree. She is a CPA.

Cindy is sixty-one years old and is an executive secretary.

Colleen is in her seventies. She is a religious sister active in peace and justice work.

Dan is eighty years old and a priest formally laicized to marry. He holds a PhD in counseling and psychology.

Deb is twenty-four years old working on a master's degree in non-profit management.

Dee is forty-nine years old and is a lead business analyst.

Enzo is fifty-four years old.

Gail is in her sixties. She holds a BA and is an artist. She was a religious sister.

Hannah is twenty-four years old with a BA in English.

Harry is fifty-two years old. He is a computer consultant with a BA in architecture.

Jackie is in her sixties. She holds a PhD in counseling and a Master's of Divinity.

James is sixty-seven years old and is an electrical engineer.

Jane is between fifty-five and sixty years old. She has a Master's of Divinity.

Janet is in her fifties. She is a finance manager.

Jillian is thirty-five years old. She holds a PhD in cultural anthropology and works at a university.

Joe is eighty years old and a retired priest. He holds a PhD in Theology.

Judy is seventy-two years old with one year of college.

Julia is twenty-eight years old and has a BA. She is a journalist.

Kate is sixty-six years old with a master's degree in public health.

Kellie is twenty-nine years old and is working on MA sociology research. She has a BA in theology.

Ken is sixty-six years old and was a Christian Brother. He holds a master's degree.

Kim is thirty-five years old and holds a two-year associates degree.

Lance is twenty-nine years old with a BA. He is a social researcher.

Lily is seventy-three years old. She holds a JD.

Luke is eighty-four years old. He is a priest formally laicized to marry.

Maggy is between sixty-five and seventy-five years old. She holds a PhD.

Mai is in her seventies. She is a counselor with an MA in counseling.

Maria is in her seventies and is a retired teacher. She has an MA in Spanish.

Matt is forty-one years old and is an MD specializing in pain management.

Mattie is seventy-one years old. She is a former religious sister with a master's degree in religion.

Max is eighty-eight years old. He holds a BA in English.

Meredith is sixty-seven years old and holds a JD. She is in risk management.

Miriam is sixty-one years old. She has a BA in communications and is a hospital chaplain.

Pat is sixty-nine years old and has a master's degree in social work.

Ray is twenty-five years old. He is in college getting a BA.

Rita is seventy years old and is a spiritual director.

Sade is sixty-two years old. She has a BA in Art History.

Sam is twenty-six years old and holds a JD.

Samantha is fifty-two years old. She has a PhD in public health.

Sarah is between seventy-five and eighty years old. She is a religious sister and holds a master's degree in theology.

Shannon is sixty-one years old with a BA in education.

Steve is seventy years old and is a broker.

Susie is in her fifties. She has a college degree.

Ted is forty-six years old, with a BA in human services, and is a leadership group facilitator and life mapping coach.

Terry is twenty-six years old. He holds a JD and is active in pro bono work.

Appendix B
Dialogue Protocol[1]

PERSONAL INFORMATION

- Age
- Marital Status
- Education

FAITH JOURNEY

- Parent's religion and church participation
- Number of siblings and their church participation
- Personal participation during childhood, adolescence, young adulthood, and feelings about church during those periods
- Changes in belief and spirituality of any significance
- Partner's church history

PROCESS OF CEASING ATTENDANCE

- When and how did the process begin? What are the factors that influenced the decision?

1. This is a checklist for the interviewer serving as a guide for the semi-structured interviews.

- Was discontinuation gradual or abrupt? Was there a moment of decision or realization?
- Spouse/partner's attitude and whether it was a joint process
- Did other involvements in the church persist?

NAMING THIS SPACE

- What names or terms do you think of in relation to the religious or spiritual place you are currently in?

CURRENT ATTITUDES TOWARDS CHURCH

- Current assessment of factors that led to a change in attendance
- Feelings and attitudes toward parish and wider Church?
- Does self-identification as a Catholic continue? What is the level of importance of that self-identification?
- Does the faith journey continue? In what ways is it fostered and expressed?
- Is there any ongoing participation in church organizations or activities?
- Any factors that would lead to a return to regular Mass attendance?
- Involvement in community service, social advocacy, charity support, etc., and the relationship to faith?

Appendix C
Technical Appendix

THIS RESEARCH WAS CONDUCTED during my dissertation process for a PhD in Practical Theology at St. Thomas University. A brief outline of the research design and conduct is given in chapter 1. This appendix provides further details of the research methods used in this study. My practical theology methodology is detailed in chapter 6. A copy of the open-ended conversation guide used during the in-depth interviews can be found in Appendix B.

My practical theology research design is feminist reciprocal ethnography.[2] The knowledge shared and built in this method is based on dialogue in a collaborative, multi-voiced model. Reciprocal ethnography deepens the hermeneutical epistemology[3] and furthers knowledge construction rather than affirming what I think I know. Both interviews and focus group experiences provide phenomenological research data.

Advertisements helped me engage volunteers for dialogue. A snowball sampling strategy generated volunteers for dialogue.[4] Over 50 percent of my dialogue partners volunteered through this method. Venues included:

---

2. Lawless, *Holy Women, Wholly Women*. Elaine Lawless first used the term "reciprocal ethnography" to describe her research that involved the participants she was observing.

3 Epistemology studies the nature of knowledge, how knowledge is formed, its foundations, its range and limits, and its justification.

4. A snowball sampling strategy, a form of non-probability sampling, identifies a few people or organizations with relevant characteristics and then asks them for referrals (Berg, *Qualitative Research Methods for the Social Sciences*, 44).

- Craigslist advertisements were placed in the local area listings under the headings of community volunteers, community activities, and community events.
- Progressive Catholic organizations including Call To Action, CORPUS,[5] Association for the Rights of Catholics in the Church were contacted, and they graciously posted e-mails to their members concerning my research and the search for dialogue partners.
- Small advertisements were placed in local newspapers for a minimal charge.
- One advertisement was placed in National Catholic Reporter.

DIALOGIC LISTENING

My dialogue with dialogue partners consisted of semi-structured dialogues, audio-recorded, lasting approximately one hour.[6] I both exercised my own judgment and sought the participant's judgment about what is significant in both the interviews and the transcripts. Many dialogue partners came to the conversation having reflected on the question themes that I sent them, with points that they wanted to emphasize to me. I received e-mails after the interviews with additional thoughts about the questions from several dialogue partners.

PARTICIPATION LEVEL

The majority of dialogue partners who contacted me and set an appointment came to the appointment. Once consent was obtained, the dropout rate (8 percent) was low (N=5). There was a dropout rate of 7 percent (N=4) after obtaining consent prior to the appointment. Two people notified me of a change of vacation plans and two missed their scheduled appointments. Once the interviews were conducted, one person chose to ask for her conversation to be deleted from the study, expressing confidentiality concerns around divorce issues. This interview was deleted in accordance with my IRB (Institutional Review Board) agreement in working with human subjects.

5. CORPUS is a faith community affirming an inclusive priesthood, married and single men and women.

6. Appendix B contains the open-ended conversation topics used in the dialogues.

WORKING WITH THE DIALOGUE DATA

The interviews were recorded using a digital tape recorder. A choice was made not to use a typing service because of confidentiality issues. They were transcribed verbatim by two individually contracted transcribers who agreed to commit to confidentiality. The software Express Scribe, a free professional audio player software designed to assist in the transcription of audio recordings, was used. This program provides control of the audio playback using a transcription foot pedal or keyboard (with "hot" keys). This computer transcriber application also offers valuable features for typists, including variable speed playback and file management. Pedals were provided for both secretaries. Mediafire, a free data storage system that is password protected, was used to store and access the audio files.

Transcripts were uploaded to ATLAS.ti, a qualitative data analysis software. The choice to use a computer data software program is still debated in the social science field, particularly when the research uses only a small sample. Such a program can speed the coding process, and also provide interactive and flexible data coding and code management. The program facilitates grouping and filtering code management, allowing for visualization of the code schema. ATLAS.ti is a code and retrieve software designed to assist in theory building, creating higher-order more abstract classification schemes, semantically oriented typologies, and other ways of representing data. I chose ATLAS.ti because its schema is more intuitive rather hierarchical in the way it represents data and expresses relationships.

A computer-assisted system takes time to understand and use. The programs themselves do not do practical theology analysis. Rather, the practical theologian decides which tools to use, what and how to code and classify the data, and then does the analysis. There is a learning curve necessary with the software. While a CAQDA (Computer Assisted Qualitative Data Analysis System) may lead phenomenological researchers to overly objectify quantitative data, rendering it as less phenomenological quantitative data, this is less an issue with ATLAS.ti since it does not proceed in a hierarchical manner.

Using ATLAS.ti, I developed a list of key themes as they emerged from the data. I added to these key themes until dialogic analysis indicated no new themes were emerging. In this dialogic analysis I listened for the places where time and space come together in the narrative, helpful in identifying themes. Each key theme in turn has sub-themes. For example, systemic problems with the Church appear in all dialogues in a variety of ways among them: silencing of divergent views, a culture of arrogance, and exclusivism in ritual, beliefs, and attitudes.

MAKING KNOWLEDGE TOGETHER

As a final dialogue opportunity allowing dialogue partners to suggest their meanings and relationships in the themes, I facilitated two in-depth communal dialogues in focus groups, once in the South and once in the Midwest.[7] Once interview dialogue was coded for main themes and sub-themes, focus groups theologically reflected on these themes suggesting meaning and relationships.

ETHICAL CONCERNS

I recorded reflections after each dialogue, and kept a journal to identify biases and assumptions, thus practicing 'holistic reflexivity'.[8] I also explored how my own theoretical position and biography has affected my choice of dialogue partners and topics through journaling. I was attentive to my own structural, political, and cultural context and that of my participants throughout the dialogue process with my dialogue partners. My environment and context affects the research process and product. For that reason, I worked to be fully transparent regarding my environment and context, and to treat that as part of the data.[9]

Reflexivity provides for awareness of researcher bias. I took notes to record changes during the study and during the coding in an effort to be transparent. I utilized focus groups for feedback to assure credibility.

A pilot of the interview protocol in 2007 assisted in the development of a consistent use of dialogic interview techniques. Communicability was insured by member checks.

Every effort was made to address ethical issues in research related to this study. A participant permission form was utilized.

Dialogue partners are identified by pseudonyms. Places are identified generally by geographical location without specific names. See Appendix A.

---

7. This process is explained in chapter 1.

8. Hesse-Biber, *Handbook of Feminist Research.*

9. Ibid., 496

Appendix C

All dialogue partners participated voluntarily and could quit at any time. Both the purpose of the study and the procedures was explained on the permission letter.

Bibliography

Ahearne, Jeremy. *Michel de Certeau: Interpretation and Its Other*. Stanford: Stanford University Press, 1995.

Albright, Carol Rausch. "Neuroscience in the Pursuit of the Holy: Mysticism, the Brain, and Ultimate Reality." *Zygon* 36:3 (2001) 485–92.

Allen, John L., Jr. *The Future Church: How Ten Trends Are Revolutionizing the Catholic Church*. New York: Doubleday, 2009.

Ammerman, Nancy. "Journeys of Faith: Meeting the Challenges in Twenty-First Century America." In *Passing On the Faith: Transforming Traditions for the Next Generation of Jews, Christians, and Muslims*, edited by James L. Heft, 37–51. New York: Fordham University Press, 2006.

———. "Religious Choice and Religious Vitality: The Market and Beyond." In *Rational Choice Theory and Religion: Summary and Assessment*, edited by Lawrence A. Young. London: Routledge, 1997.

Anderson, Ray S. *The Shape of Practical Theology: Empowering Ministry with Theological Praxis*. Downers Grove, IL: InterVarsity, 2001.

Apfalter, Wilfried. "Neurotheology: What Can We Expect from a (Future) Catholic Version?" *Theology and Science* 7 (2009) 163–72.

Arens, Edmund. *Christopraxis: A Theology of Action*. Translated by John F. Hoffmeyer. Minneapolis: Fortress, 1995.

Bader, Christopher, et al. "American Piety in the Twenty-First Century." Baylor Institute for the Studies of Religion. 2006. Online: http://www.baylor.edu/content/services/document.php/33304.pdf.

Bae, Hyunju. "Dancing Around Life: An Asian Woman's Perspective." *Ecumenical Review* 56:4 (2004) 390–403.

Bakhtin, Mikhail. *Art and Answerability: Early Philosophical Essays by M.M. Bakhtin*. Edited by Michael Holquist and Vadim Liapunov. Translated by Vadim Liapunov. Austin: University of Texas Press, 1990.

———. *Dialogic Imagination: Four Essays*. Edited by Michael Holquist. Translated by Caryl Emerson and Michael Holquist. Austin: University of Texas Press, 1981.

———. *Problems of Dostoevsky's Poetics*. Edited and translated by Caryl Emerson. Minneapolis: University of Minnesota Press, 1984.

———. *Speech Genres and Other Late Essays*. Edited by Caryl Emerson and Michael Holquist. Translated by Vern W. McGee. Austin: University of Texas Press, 1986.

———. *Toward a Philosophy of the Act*. Edited by Michael Holquist and Vadim Liapunov. Translated by Vadim Liapunov. Austin: University of Texas Press, 1993.

Ballard, Paul, and John Pritchard. *Practical Theology in Action: Christian Thinking in the Service of Church and Society.* London: SPCK, 1996.

Barlow, Philip, and Mark Silk. *Religion and Public Life in the Midwest: America's Common Denominator?* Walnut Creek, CA: AltaMira, 2004.

Barna Group. "New Statistics on Church Attendance and Avoidance." March 2008. Online: http://www.barna.org/barna-update/article/18-congregations/45-new-statistics-on-church-attendance-and-avoidance?q=statistics+church+attendance.

Belcher, Jim. *Deep Church: A Third Way beyond Emerging and Traditional.* Downer's Grove: InterVarsity, 2009.

Bell, Michael Mayerfeld, and Michael Gardiner, editors. *Bakhtin and the Human Sciences: No Last Words.* London: Sage, 1998.

Bellah, Robert N., et al. *Habits of the Heart: Individualism and Commitment in American Life.* Berkeley: University of California Press, 2008.

Bendyna, Mary E., and Paul M. Perl. "Young Adults in the Context of Other Catholic Generations: Living with Diversity, Seeking Service, Waiting to Be Welcomed." *Center for Applied Research in the Apostolate.* June 2000. Online: http://cara.georgetown.edu/Publications/workingpapers/Young_Adult.pdf.

Benner, Patricia. "A Dialogue between Virtue Ethics and Care Ethics." *Theoretical Medicine and Bioethics* 18 (1997) 47–61.

Berg, Bruce L. *Qualitative Research Methods for the Social Sciences.* 6th ed. Boston: Pearson/Allyn & Bacon, 2007.

Bernardin, Carndinal Joseph. *A Consistent Ethic of Life: An American-Catholic Dialogue.* December 6, 1983. Online: http://www.priestsforlife.org/magisterium/bernardingannon.html.

———. *A Consistent Ethic of Life: Continuing the Dialogue.* March 11, 1984. Online: http://www.priestsforlife.org/magisterium/bernardinwade.html.

Bien, Nina, et al. "The Brain's Intention to Imitate: The Neurobiology of Intentional versus Automatic Imitation." *Cerebral Cortex* 19 (2009) 2338–51.

Bigwood, Carol. "Renaturalizing the Body (with the Help of Merleau-Ponty)." *Hypatia* 6:3 (1991) 54–73.

Bliss, Frederick M. *Catholic and Ecumenical: History and Hope.* 2nd ed. Lanham, MD: Rowman & Littlefield, 2007.

Boff, Clodovis. *Theology and Praxis: Epistemological Foundations.* Translated by Robert R. Barr. Maryknoll, NY: Orbis, 1987.

Bong, Sharon A. "The Suffering Christ and the Asian Body." In *Hope Abundant: Third World and Indigenous Women's Theology*, edited by Kwok Pui-lan, 186–93. Maryknoll, NY: Orbis, 2010.

Børtnes, Jostein. "The Polyphony of Trinity in Bakhtin." 2002. Online: http://www.hum.au.dk/romansk/polyfoni/Polyphonie_V/Bortnes5.pdf.

Bowe, Barbara. *Biblical Foundations of Spirituality: Touching a Finger to the Flame.* Oxford: Rowman & Littlefield, 2003.

Bracken, Joseph A. *The Divine Matrix: Creativity as Link between East and West.* Maryknoll, NY: Orbis, 1995.

Bray, John N., et al. *Collaborative Inquiry in Practice: Action, Reflection, and Making Meaning.* Thousand Oaks, CA: Sage, 2000.

Brown, Delwin, Sheila Greeve Davaney, and Kathryn Tanner, editors. *Convergence on Culture: Theologians in Dialogue with Cultrual Analysis and Criticism.* New York : Oxford University Press, 2001.

Brown, Raymond E. *An Introduction to the New Testament*. New York: Doubleday, 1997.

———. *The Community of the Beloved Disciple*. New York: Paulist, 1979.

Brown, Terry. "Personhood as a Tool to Reflect upon Koinonia." *Anglican Theological Review* 88:2 (2006) 163–79.

Browning, Don S. *A Fundamental Practical Theology: Descriptive and Strategic Proposals*. Minneapolis: Fortress, 1996.

Brueggemann, Walter. *The Land: Place as Gift, Promise, and Challenge in Biblical Faith*. Philadelphia: Fortress, 1977.

———. "Rethinking Church Models through Scripture." *Theology Today* 48:2 (1991) 128–38.

———. *Texts Under Negotiation: The Bible and Postmodern Imagination*. Minneapolis: Fortress, 1993.

———. *The Word Militant: Preaching a Decentering Word*. Minneapolis: Fortress, 2007.

Caggiano, Vittorio, et al. "Mirror Neurons Differentially Encode the Peripersonal and Extrapersonal Space of Monkeys." *Science* 324 (2009) 403–26. Online: http://www.sciencemag.org/content/324/5925/403.abstract?sa_campaign=Email/toc/17-April-2009/10.1126/science.1166818.

Cahalan, Kathleen A. "Three Approaches to Practical Theology, Theological Education, and the Church's Ministry." *International Journal of Practical Theology* 9 (2005) 63–94

Cahalan, Kathleen A., and James Neiman. "Mapping the Field of Practical Theology." In *For Life Abundant: Practical Theology, Theological Education, and Christian Ministry*, edited by Dorothy C. Bass and Craig Dykstra, 62–91. Grand Rapids: Eerdmans, 2008.

Camille, Alice L., and Joel Schorn. *A Faith Interrupted: An Honest Conversation with Alienated Catholics*. Chicago: Loyola, 2004.

Carey, Patrick W. *Catholics in America: A History*. Westport, CT: Praeger, 2004.

Carroll, James. *Practicing Catholic*. Boston: Houghton Mifflin Harcourt, 2009.

Cartledge, Mark. "Empirical Theology: Inter- or Intra-disciplinary?" *Journal of Beliefs and Values* 20 (1999) 98–104.

Case, Jonathan P. "Faithful and Effective God-Talk: Trinitarian Theology for the People of God." *Word and World* 18:3 (1998) 272–81.

"Catholic Common Ground Initiative." 2010. Online: http://www.catholiccommonground.org/content/about-catholic-common-ground-initiative.

Center for Action and Contemplation. "The Emerging Church—Conversations, Convergence and Action." 2009. Online: http://www.docstoc.com/docs/20497398/Post-Conference-Group-Reports.

Center for Applied Research in the Apostolate. *Frequently Requested Catholic Church Statistics*. 2009. Online: http://cara.georgetown.edu/CARAServices/requestedchurchstats.html.

———. *The Impact of Religious Switching and Secularization*. Winter 2008. Online: http://cara.georgetown.edu/Winter%202008.pdf.

———. *Methodological Notes*. January 10, 2005. Online: http://cara.georgetown.edu/CARAServices/FRStats/massattendweek.pdf.

———. *The Nuances of Accurately Measuring Mass Attendance*. September 22, 2009. Online: http://nineteensixty-four.blogspot.com/2009/09/nuances-of-accurately-measuring-mass.html.

———. *Sacraments Today: Belief and Practice Among U.S. Catholics.* February 2008. Online: http://cara.georgetown.edu/sacraments.html.

———. *Self-Reported Mass Attendance of U.S. Catholics Unchanged during Last Five Years.* 2005. Online: http://cara.georgetown.edu.

Certeau, Michel de. *Heterologies: Discourse on the Other.* Translated by Brian Massumi. Minneapolis: University of Minnesota Press, 1986.

———. *The Practice of Everyday Life.* Translated by Steven Rendall. Berkeley: University of California Press, 1980.

———. *The Writing of History.* Translated by Tom Conley. New York: Columbia University Press, 1988.

Cheyne, J. Allan, and Donato Tarulli. "Dialogue, Difference, and the 'Third Voice' in the Zone of Proximal Development." *Theory and Psychology* 9 (1999) 5–28.

Chopp, Rebecca. *The Power to Speak: Feminism, Language, and God.* New York: Crossroad, 1989. Reprint, Eugene, OR: Wipf & Stock, 2002.

———. *The Praxis of Suffering: An Interpretation of Liberation and Political Theologies.* Maryknoll, NY: Orbis, 1986. Reprint, Eugene, OR: Wipf & Stock, 2007.

Chryssavgis, John, editor. *Cosmic Grace and Humble Prayer: The Ecological Vision of the Green Patriarch Bartholomew I.* Grand Rapids: Eerdnmans, 2003.

Chung, Hyun Kyung. *Struggle to Be the Sun Again: Introducing Asian Women's Theology.* Maryknoll, NY: Orbis, 1990.

Ciuba, Edward J. "The Impact of Changing Ecclesiological and Christological Models on Roman Catholic Seminary Education." *Theological Education* 24:1 (1987) 57–72.

Clark, Katerina, and Michael Holquist. *Mikhail Bakhtin.* Cambridge: Belknap Press of Harvard University Press, 1984.

Clarke, John I. *The Human Dichotomy: The Changing Numbers of Males and Females.* New York: Pergamon, 2000.

Colyer, Elmer M., editor. *The Promise of Trinitarian Theology: Theologians in Dialogue with T. F. Torrance.* Lanham: Rowman & Littlefield, 2001.

Cornwell, John, editor. *Consciousness and Human Identity.* New York: Oxford University Press, 1998.

Cowan, Michael A., and Bernard J. Lee. *Conversation, Risk, and Conversion: The Inner and Public Life of Small Christian Communities.* Maryknoll, NY: Orbis Books, 1997.

Creswell, John W. *Research Design: Qualitative, Quantitative, and Mixed Method Approaches.* 2nd ed. Thousand Oaks, CA: Sage, 2003.

Crossan, John Dominic. *Jesus: A Revolutionary Biography.* San Francisco: HarperSanFrancisco, 1994.

Culpepper, R. Alan. *The Gospel and Letters of John.* Nashville: Abingdon, 1998.

Curran, Charles E. *Catholic Moral Theology in the United States: A History.* Washington, DC: Georgetown University Press, 2008.

Danow, David K. *The Thought of Mikhail Bakhtin: From Word to Culture.* New York: St. Martin's, 1991.

D'Antonio, William V., et al. *American Catholics: Gender, Generation, and Commitment.* Walnut Creek, CA: AltaMira, 2001.

Davaney, Sheila Greeve. *Historicism: The Once and Future Challenge for Theology.* Minneapolis: Fortress, 2006.

———. *Pragmatic Historicism: A Theology for the Twenty-First Century.* Albany: State University of New York Press, 2000.

Davaney, Sheila Greeve, and Warren G. Frisina, editors. *The Pragmatic Century: Conversations with Richard J. Bernstein.* Albany: State University of New York Press, 2006.

Davaney, Sheila Greeve, and Larry Laderman. "Introduction: Contesting Religion and Religions Contested: The Study of Religion in a Global Context." *Journal of the American Academy of Religion* 73:4 (2005) 979–85.

David, Harvey. *The Condition of Postmodernity: An Enquiry into the Origins of Cultural Change.* Oxford: Blackwell, 1989.

Davie, Grace. "Believing without Belonging: Just How Secular Is Europe?" 2005. Online: http://pewforum.org/events/?EventID=97.

———. *Religion in Britain since 1945: Believing Without Belonging.* Oxford: Blackwell, 1994.

Dean, William. "Humanistic Historicism and Naturalistic Historicism." In *Theology at the End of Modernity: Essays in Honor of Gordon D. Kaufman*, edited by Sheila Greeve Davaney, 41–59. Philadelphia: Trinity International, 1991.

Dentith, Simon. *Bakhtinian Thought: An Introductory Reader.* London: Routledge, 1995.

Denzin, Norman K., and Yvonna S. Lincoln, editors. *Collecting and Interpreting Qualitative Materials.* 2nd ed. Thousand Oaks, CA: Sage, 2003.

———. *The Landscape of Qualitative Research: Theories and Issues.* 2nd ed. Thousand Oaks, CA: Sage, 2003.

Dillon, Michelle. *Catholic Identity: Balancing Reason, Faith, and Power.* New York: Cambridge University Press, 1999.

Dixon, Robert, et al. *Research Project on Catholics Who Have Stopped Attending Mass.* Melbourne: Australian Catholic Bishops Conference Pastoral Projects Office, 2007.

Doak, Mary. "Feminism, Pragmatism, and Utopia: A Catholic Theological Response." *American Journal of Theology and Philosophy* 24:1 (2003) 22–33.

Donaldson, Laura E. "Postcolonialism and Biblical Reading: An Introduction." *Semeia* 75 (1996) 1–14.

———. "A Response: When Jesus Rewrote the Corn Mothers: Intertextuality as Transnational Critical Practice." *Semeia* 69/70 (1995) 281–92.

Donaldson, Laura E., and Kwok Pui-lan, editors. *Postcolonialism, Feminism, and Religious Discourse.* New York: Routledge, 2002.

Dube, Musa W. *Postcolonial Feminist Interpretation of the Bible.* St. Louis: Chalice, 2000.

Dulles, Avery Cardinal. *Church and Society: The Laurence J. McGinley Lectures, 1988–2007.* New York: Fordham University Press, 2008.

———. *Models of the Church.* Expanded ed. New York: Doubleday, 1987.

Elizondo, Virgilio. *Galilean Journey: The Mexican-American Promise.* Maryknoll, NY: Orbis, 1983.

Ellway, Peter. "Shopping for Faith or Dropping Your Faith?" May 2005. Online: http://www.csa.com/discoveryguides/religion/overview.php#st.

emerging church. 2010. Online: http://www.emergingchurch.info.

Emerson, Caryl. *The First Hundred Years of Mikhail Bakhtin.* Princeton: Princeton University Press, 1997.

Felch, Susan M., and Paul J. Contino, editors. *Bakhtin and Religion: A Feeling for Faith.* Evanston: Northwestern University Press, 2001.

Ferguson, Margaret, and Jennifer Wicke, editors. *Feminism and Postmodernism.* Durham: Duke University Press, 1994.

Flyvbjerg, Bent. *Making Social Science Matter: Why Social Inquiry Fails and How It Can Succeed Again.* Translated by Steven Sampson. New York: Cambridge University Press, 2001.

Fogassi, Leonardo, and Pier Francesco Ferrari. "Mirror Neurons and the Evolution of Embodied Language." *Current Directions in Psychological Science* 16:3 (2007) 136–41.

Forrester, Duncan B. *Forrester on Christian Ethics and Practical Theology: Collected Writings on Christianity, India, and the Social Order.* Farnham, UK: Ashgate, 2010.

———. *Theological Fragments: Explorations in Unsystematic Theology.* London: T. & T. Clark, 2005.

———. *Truthful Action: Explorations in Practical Theology.* Edinburgh: T. & T. Clark, 2000.

Foskett, Mary F., and Jeffrey Kah-Jin Kuan, editors. *Ways of Being, Ways of Reading: Asian American Biblical Interpretation.* St. Louis: Chalice, 2006.

Fox, Thomas C. *Pentecost in Asia: A New Way of Being Church.* Maryknoll, NY: Orbis, 2003.

Fox, Zeni. "Discerning Meaning: The New Lay Ecclesial Minsters." *Theological Exploration* 1 (2010). Online: http://www.duq.edu/theology/_pdf/faculty-publications/theological-exploration1.pdf.

Froehle, Bryan T., and Mary L. Gautier. *Catholocism USA: A Portrait of the Catholic Church in the United States.* Maryknoll, NY: Orbis, 2000.

Fuchs, Lorelei F. *Koinonia and the Quest for an Ecumenical Ecclesiology.* Grand Rapids: Eerdmans, 2008.

Fulkerson, Mary McClintock. *Changing the Subject: Women's Discourses and Feminist Theology.* Minneapolis: Fortress, 1994. Reprint, Eugene, OR: Wipf & Stock, 2001.

———. *Places of Redemption: Theology for a Worldly Church.* New York: Oxford University Press, 2007.

Gadamer, Hans-Georg. *Truth and Method.* Translated by William Glen-Doepel. 2nd ed. London: Sheed & Ward, 1979.

Gaillardetz, Richard R. *The Church in the Making: Lumen Gentium, Christus Dominus, Orientalium Ecclesiarum.* New York: Paulist, 2006.

Gallese, Vittorio. "Embodied Simulation: From Neurons to Phenomenal Experience." *Phenomenology and the Cognitive Sciences* 4 (2005) 23–48.

———. "Mirror Neurons, Embodied Simulation, and the Neural Basis of Social Identification." *Psychoanalytic Dialogues* 19 (2009) 519–36.

———. "The 'Shared Manifold' Hypothesis: From Mirror Neurons to Empathy." *Journal of Consciousness Studies* 8 (2001) 33–50.

———. "We-ness, Embodied Simulation, and Psychoanalysis: Reply to Commentaries." *Psychoanalytic Dialogues* 19 (2009) 580–84.

———. "Intentional Attunement: The Mirror Neuron System and Its Role in Interpersonal Relations." Paper presented at the European Science Foundation Conference, Paris, November 15, 2004.

Gallese, Vittorio, et al. "Action Recognition in the Premotor Cortex." *Brain* 119 (1996) 593–609.

Gallup. "Americans Believe Religion Is Losing Clout." Gallup. December 23, 2008. Online: http://www.gallup.com/poll/113533/americans-believe-religion-losing-clout.aspx.

———. "Americans' Church Attendance Inches Up in 2010." February 2010. Online: http://www.gallup.com/poll/141044/americans-church-attendance-inches-2010.aspx.

———. "Churchgoing Among U.S. Catholics Slides to Tie Protestants." April 9, 2009. Online: http://www.gallup.com/poll/117382/church-going-among-catholics-slides-tie-protestants.aspx.

———. "Religion." 2009. Online: http://www.gallup.com/poll/1690/religion.aspx#1.

Ganzevoot, R. Ruard. "Van der Ven's Empirical/Practical Theology and the Theological Encyclopedia." In *Hermeneutics and Empirical Research in Practical Theology: The Contribution of Empirical Theology by Johannes A. van der Ven*, edited by Chris A. M. Hermans and Mary E. Moore, 53–74. Leiden: Brill, 2004.

Gardiner, Michael E. *Critiques of Everyday Life*. New York: Routledge, 2000.

———. *The Dialogics of Critique: M. M. Bakhtin and the Theory of Ideology*. New York: Routledge, 1992.

Gebara, Ivone. *Longing for Running Water: Ecofeminism and Liberation*. Translated by David Mollineaux. Minneapolis: Fortress, 1999.

———. *Out of the Depths: Women's Experience of Evil and Salvation*. Translated by Ann Patrick Ware. Minneapolis: Fortress, 2002.

Geertz, Clifford. *The Interpretation of Cultures: Selected Essays*. New York: HarperCollins, 1973.

Gilbert, Kenyatta R. "The Prophetic and the Priestly: Reclaiming Preaching as Practical Theology." *Koinonia* 16 (2004) 118–39.

Gilroy, Paul. *Against Race: Imagining Political Culture beyond the Color Line*. Cambridge: Belknap Press of Harvard University Press, 2000.

Goodnough, Angelique Montgomery. "A Treasure Buried: Catholic College Student's Experience of Catholic Identity." PhD diss., St. Thomas University, 2010.

Graham, Elaine. "Practical Theology as Transforming Practice." In *The Blackwell Reader in Pastoral and Practical Theology*, edited by James Woodward and Stephen Pattison, 104–17. Malden, MA: Blackwell, 2000.

Gray, Mark M., and Paul M. Perl. *Sacraments Today: Belief and Practice among U.S. Catholics*. Center for Applied Research in the Apostolate, 2008. Online: http://cara.georgetown.edu/sacraments.html.

Greeley, Andrew. *The Catholic Imagination*. Berkeley: University of California Press, 2001.

Green, Barbara. *Mikhail Bakhtin and Biblical Scholarship: An Introduction*. Atlanta: SBL, 2000.

Grieb, A. Katherine. "People of God, Body of Christ, Koinonia of Spirit: The Role of Ethical Ecclesiology in Paul's 'Trinitarian' Language." *Anglican Theological Review* 87:2 (2005) 225–52.

Groody, Daniel G. *Globalization, Spirituality, and Justice: Navigating the Path to Peace*. Maryknoll, NY: Orbis, 2007.

Groome, Thomas H. *Educating for Life: A Spiritual Vision for Every Teacher and Parent*. Allen, TX: Thomas More, 1998.

Groppe, Elizabeth T. "Catherine Mowry LaCugna's Contribution to Trinitarian Theology." *Theological Studies* 63 (2002) 730–63.

Habermas, Jürgen. *Theory and Practice*. Translated by John Viertel. Boston: Beacon, 1973.

———. *The Theory of Communicative Action*. Vol. 1, *Reason and the Rationalization of Society*. Translated by Thomas McCarthy. Boston: Beacon, 1984.

Haers, Jacques, and Peter De Mey, editors. *Theology and Conversation: Towards a Relational Theology*. Leuven: Leuven University Press, 2001.

Hammond, Mary Tuomi. *The Church and the Dechurched: Mending a Damaged Faith*. St. Louis: Chalice, 2001.

Harper, Phillip Bryan. *Framing the Margins: The Social Logic of Postmodern Culture*. New York: Oxford University Press, 1994.

Harris, Maria. *Dance of the Spirit: The Seven Steps of Women's Spirituality*. New York: Bantam, 1989.

Hassan, Ihab. "Beyond Postmodernism: Toward an Aesthetic of Trust." *Angelaki* 8:1 (2003) 3–11.

Heitink, Gerben. *Practical Theology: History, Theory, Action Domains: Manual for Practical Theology*. Translated by Reinder Bruinsma. Grand Rapids: Eerdmans, 1999.

Held, Virginia. *The Ethics of Care: Personal, Political, and Global*. New York: Oxford University Press, 2006.

Henold, Mary J. *Catholic and Feminist: The Surprising History of the American Catholic Feminist Movement*. Chapel Hill: University of North Carolina Press, 2008.

Hesse-Biber, Sharlene Nagy, editor. *Handbook of Feminist Research: Theory and Praxis*. Thousand Oaks, CA: Sage, 2007.

Hesse-Biber, Sharlene Nagy, and Patricia Leavy, editors. *Emergent Methods in Social Research*. Thousand Oaks, CA: Sage, 2006.

———. *Feminist Research Practice: A Primer*. Thousand Oaks, CA: Sage, 2007.

Hesse-Biber, Sharlene Nagy, and Michelle L. Yaiser. *Feminist Perspectives on Social Research*. New York: Oxford University Press, 2004.

Hilkert, Mary Catherine. "Feminist Theology: A Review of the Literature: Key Religious Symbols: Christ and God." *Theological Studies* 56:2 (1995) 341–52.

———. *Naming Grace: Preaching and the Sacramental Imagination*. New York: Continuum, 2000.

Himes, Michael J., and Kenneth R. Himes. *Fullness of Faith: The Public Significance of Theology*. New York: Paulist, 1993.

Hinze, Bradford E. *Practices of Dialogue in the Roman Catholic Church: Aims and Obstacles, Lessons and Laments*. New York: Continuum, 2006.

———. "Releasing the Power of the Spirit in a Trinitarian Ecclesiology." In *Advents of the Spirit: An Introduction to the Current Study of Pneumatology*, edited by Bradford E. Hinze and D. Lyle Dabney, 345–79. Milwaukee: Marquette University Press, 2001.

Hinze, Bradford E., and D. Lyle Dabney. *Advents of the Spirit: An Introduction to the Current Study of Pneumatology*. Milwaukee: Marquette University Press, 2001.

Hoge, Dean R., et al. *Young Adult Catholics: Religion in the Culture of Choice*. Notre Dame: University of Notre Dame Press, 2001.

Holland, Joe. *Modern Catholic Social Teaching: The Popes Confront the Industrial Age, 1740–1958*. New York: Paulist, 2003.

Holland, Joe, and Peter Henriot. *Social Analysis: Linking Faith and Justice*. Rev. ed. Maryknoll, NY: Orbis, 1985.

Hollenbach, David. "Catholic Ethics in a World Church." In *Catholic Theological Ethics in the World Church*, edited by James F. Keenan, 140–46. New York: Continuum, 2007.

Holmes, Nathaniel C., Jr. "Interreligious/Interfaith Dialogue as Christian Praxis: A Practical Theology of Religious Pluralism." PhD diss., St. Thomas University, 2010.

Holquist, Michael. *Dialogism: Bakhtin and His World*. London: Routledge, 1990.

hooks, bell. *Feminist Theory: From Margin to Center*. Boston: South End, 1984.

———. *Yearning: Race, Gender, and Cultural Politics*. Boston: South End, 1990.

Hopkins, Dwight N., and Sheila Greeve Davaney, editor. *Changing Conversations: Religious Reflection and Cultural Analysis*. New York: Routledge, 1996.

Hudnut-Beumler, James David. *Looking for God in the Suburbs: The Religion of the American Dream and Its Critics, 1945–1965*. New Brunswick: Rutgers University Press, 1994.

Hulit, Lloyd M., and Merle R. Howard. *Born to Talk: An Introduction to Speech and Language Development*. Boston: Pearson/Allyn & Bacon, 2006.

Hunsinger, Deborah van Deusen. "Practicing Koinonia." *Theology Today* 66:3 (2009) 346–67.

Hunt, Anne. "Trinity and Paschal Mystery." In *Theology and Conversation: Towards a Relational Theology*, edited by Jacques Haers and Peter De Mey, 69–97. Leuven: Leuven University Press, 2003.

Hurley, Susan. "The Shared Circuits Model: How Control Mirroring and Simulation Can Enable Imitation and Mind Reading." Paper presented at the European Science Foundation Conference, Paris, February 15, 2005.

Immink, F. Gerrit. *Faith: A Practical Theological Reconstruction*. Translated by Reinder Bruinsma. Grand Rapids: Eerdmans, 2003.

Intentional Eucharistic Communties. "Embracing and Shaping Our Future." May 2009. Online: http://www.intentionaleucharisticcommunities.org.

Isasi-Diaz, Ada Maria. "'Mujerista': Definition." Online: http://users.drew.edu/aisasidi/Definition1.htm.

Jeeves, Malcolm. "Neuroscience, Evolutionary Psychology, and the Image of God." *Perspectives on Science and Christian Faith* 57:3 (2005) 170–86.

Jenkins, Philip. *The New Anti-Catholicism: The Last Acceptable Prejudice*. New York: Oxford University Press, 2003.

Jodock, Darrell, editor. *Catholicism Contending with Modernity*. Cambridge: Cambridge University Press, 2000.

John Paul II. "General Audience." September 9, 1998. Online: http://www.vatican.va/holy_father/john_paul_ii/audiences/1998/documents/hf_jp-ii_aud_09091998_en.html.

Johnson, D. Paul. "From Religious Markets to Religious Communities: Contrasting Implications for Applied Research." *Review of Religious Research* 44 (2003) 325–40.

Johnson, David H. "Emerging Churches: Reflections from a Traditionalist Seminary Dean." *Didaskalia* 19:1 (2008) 161–77.

Johnson, Elizabeth A. *Quest for the Living God: Mapping Frontiers in the Theology of God*. New York: Continuum, 2008.

———. *She Who Is: The Mystery of God in Feminist Theological Discourse*. New York: Crossroad, 1992.

———. "To Let the Symbol Sing Again." *Theology Today* 53:2 (1997) 299–311.

———. *Truly Our Sister: A Theology of Mary in the Communion of Saints.* New York: Continuum, 2003.

Johnson, Elizabeth A., and Julia H. Brumbaugh. "Trinity: To Let the Symbol Sing Again." *Scripture from Scratch.* 1999. Online: http://www.americancatholic.org/Newsletters/SFS/an0599.asp.

Johnson, Elizabeth A., and Susan Ross. "Feminist Theology: A Review of Literature." *Theological Studies* 56:2 (1995) 327–52.

Johnson, Kristen Deede. *Theology, Political Theory, and Pluralism: Beyond Tolerance and Difference.* Cambridge: Cambridge University Press, 2007.

Johnson, Luke Timothy. *Hebrews: A Commentary.* Louisville: Westminster John Knox, 2006.

Jones, Arthur. "Her 1979 Plea Unanswered." September 8, 2000. Online: http://findarticles.com/p/articles/mi_m1141/is_39_36/ai_65774931/.

Kaplan, E. Ann. *Postmodernism and Its Discontents: Theories, Practices.* New York: Verso, 1988.

Kärkkäinen, Veli-Matti. *Pneumatology: The Holy Spirit in Ecumenical, International, and Contextual Perspective.* Grand Rapids: Baker Academic, 2002.

———. "Trinity as Communion in the Spirit: Koinonia, Trinity, and Filioque in the Roman Catholic-Pentecostal Dialogue." *Pneuma: The Jornal of the Society of Pentecostal Studies* 22:2 (2000) 209–30.

———. *The Trinity: Global Perspectives.* Louisville: Westminster John Knox, 2007.

Kärkkäinen, Veli-Matti, and Moltmann, Jürgen. *The Spirit in the World: Emerging Pentecostal Theologies in Global Contexts.* Grand Rapids: Eerdmanns, 2009.

Kaufman, Gordon. *An Essay on Theological Method.* 3rd ed. Atlanta: Scholars, 1995.

Kee, Alastair. "Exclusion." In *Public Theology for the Twenty-First Century: Essays in Honor of Duncan B. Forrester,* edited by William F. Storrar and Andrew R. Morton, 351–64. London: T. & T. Clark, 2004.

Keenan, James F., editor. *Catholic Theological Ethics in the World Church.* New York: Continuum, 2007.

Killen, Patricia O'Connell, and John de Beer. *The Art of Theological Reflection.* New York: Crossroad, 1995.

Killen, Patricia O'Connell, and Mark Silk, editors. *Religion and Public Life in the Pacific Northwest: The None Zone.* Walnut Creek, CA: AltaMira, 2004.

Kinast, Robert L. *What Are They Saying about Theological Reflection?* New York: Paulist, 2000.

King, Ursula. *Christ in All Things: Exploring Spirituality with Teilhard de Cardin.* Maryknoll, NY: Orbis, 1997.

Klages, Mary. "Postmodernity." 2007. Online: http://www.colorado.edu/English/courses/ENGL2012Klages/lecturelinks.html.

Kosky, Jeffrey L. *Levinas and the Philosophy of Religion.* Bloomington: Indiana University Press, 2001.

Kosmin, Barry A., and Ariela Keysar. "American Religious Identification Survey (ARIS)." *American Religious Identification Survey (ARIS) Report 2008.* March 2009. Online: http://www.americanreligionsurvey-aris.org/reports/ARIS_Report_2008.pdf.

Kroeger, James H., MM. "Inculturation in Asia: Directions, Initiatives, and Options." 2005. Online: http://www.ucanews.com/html/fabc-papers/fabc-115.htm.

Kysar, Robert. *John: The Maverick Gospel.* 3rd ed. Louisville: Westminster John Knox, 2007.

LaCugna, Catherine Mowry. *God for Us: The Trinity and Christian Life*. San Francisco: HarperSanFrancisco, 1991.

———. "The Practical Trinity." *Christian Century* 109:22 (1992) 678–82.

Latini, Theresa F. "Grief-Work in Light of the Cross: Illustrating Transformational Interdisciplinarity." June 2009. Online: http://findarticles.com/p/articles/mi_hb6566/is_2_37/ai_n32146074/.

Lawler, Michael G. *What Is and What Ought to Be: The Dialectic of Experience, Theology, and Church*. New York: Continuum, 2005.

Lawless, Elaine. *Holy Women, Wholly Women: Sharing Ministries of Wholeness through Life Stories and Reciprocal Ethnography*. Philadelphia: University of Pennsylvania Press, 1993.

Lawrence-Lightfoot, Sara. *The Third Chapter: Passion, Risk, and Adventure in the 25 Years after 50*. New York: Farrar, Straus & Giroux, 2009.

Lee, Bernard. *The Galilean Jewishness of Jesus: Retrieving the Jewish Origins of Christianity*. New York: Paulist, 1988.

———. *Jesus and the Metaphors of God: The Christs of the New Testament*. New York: Paulist, 1993.

———. "Practical Theology as Phronetic." 1997. Online: http://203.10.46.30/mre/702/bleepractheol.htm.

Lee, Jung Young. *Marginality: The Key to Multicultural Theology*. Minneapolis: Fortress, 1995.

———. *The Theology of Change: A Christian Concept of God in an Eastern Perspective*. Maryknoll, NY: Orbis, 1979.

———. *The Trinity in Asian Perspective*. Nashville: Abingdon, 1996.

Lévinas, Emmanuel. *Existence and Existents*. Translated by Alphonso Lingis. Pittsburgh: Duquesne University Press, 2001.

Lillis, Theresa. "Student Writing as 'Academic Literacies:' Drawing on Bakhtin to Move from Critique to Design." 2008. Online: http://www.writing.ucsb.edu/wrconf08/Pdf_Articles/Lillis_Article2.pdf.

Lim, Chansoon. "Suffering, Change, and Marginality: Postmodern Implications of Jung Young Lee's Theology." PhD diss., Drew University, 2003.

Lindsey, William D., and Mark Silk. *Religion and Public Life in the Southern Crossroads: Showdown States*. Walnut Creek, CA: AltaMira, 2005.

Lui, Wai Ying. "Rethinking Cultural Marginality in a Postmodern Age." Master's thesis, University of Jyväskylä, 2009.

Lyotard, Jean-Francois. *Toward the Postmodern*. Edited by Robert Harvey and Mark S. Roberts. Amherst, NY: Humanity Books, 1999.

Lysaught, M. Theresa. "Eucharist as Basic Training: The Body as Nexus of Liturgy and Ethics." In *Theology and Lived Christianity*, edited by David M. Hammond, 257–88. Mystic, CT: Twenty-Third Publications/Bayard, 2000.

MacMurray, John. *Persons in Relation*. New York: Humanity Books, 1961.

———. *The Self as Agent*. New York: Humanity Books, 1957.

Magnus, George. *The Age of Aging: How Demographics Are Changing the Global Economy and Our World*. Singapore: John Wiley, 2009.

Malloy, Richard G. *A Faith that Frees: Catholic Matters for the Twenty-First Century*. Maryknoll, NY: Orbis, 2007.

Mandelker, Amy, editor. *Bakhtin in Contexts: Across the Disciplines*. Evanston: Northwestern University Press, 1995.

Bibliography

Mannion, Gerard. *Ecclessiology and Postmodernity: Questions for the Church in Our Time*. Collegeville, MN: Liturgical, 2007.

Manuel, Paul Christopher, Lawrence C. Reardon, and Clyde Wilcox, editors. *The Catholic Church and the Nation-State: Comparative Perspectives*. Washington, DC: Georgetown University Press, 2006.

Marcus, Paul. *Being for the Other: Emmanuel Levinas, Ethical Living and Psychanalysis*. Milwaukee: Marquette University Press, 2008.

Martos, Joseph. *Doors to the Sacred: A Historical Introduction to Sacraments in the Catholic Church*. Exp. ed. Liguori: Liguori/Triumph, 1991.

Massa, Mark S. *Catholics and American Culture*. New York: Crossroad, 1999.

Matera, Frank J. *New Testament Christology*. Louisville: Westminster John Knox, 1999.

McBrien, Richard. *Catholicism*. New ed. New York: HarperCollins, 1994.

———. *Report on the Church: Catholicism after Vatican II*. New York: HarperCollins, 1992.

McDougall, Joy Ann. "The Return of Trinitarian Praxis? Moltmann on the Trinity and the Christian Life." *Journal of Religion* 83:2 (2003) 177–203.

McFague, Sallie. "An Earthly Theological Agenda." *The Christian Century* 108 (1991) 12–15.

———. *Models of God: Theology for an Ecological, Nuclear Age*. Philadelphia: Fortress, 1987.

———. *A New Climate for Theology: God, the World, and Global Warming*. Minneapolis: Fortress, 2008.

McLaren, Brian D. *Everything Must Change: Jesus, Global Crises, and a Revolution of Hope*. Nashville: Thomas Nelson, 2007.

McNamara, Patrick, editor. *Where God and Science Meet: How Brain and Evolutionary Studies Alter Our Understanding of Religion*. 3 vols. Wesport, CT: Praeger, 2006.

Medley, Mark S. "God for Us and with Us: The Contributions of Catherine LaCugna's Trinitarian Theology." *Lexington Theological Quartely* 35:4 (2000) 219–36.

Meier, John P. *A Marginal Jew: Rethinking the Historical Jesus*. Vol. 1, *The Roots of the Problem and the Person*. New York: Doubleday, 1991.

———. *A Marginal Jew: Rethinking the Historical Jesus*. Vol. 2, *Mentor, Message, and Miracles*. New York: Doubleday, 1994.

Meme, Kevin, and Jeffrey Joseph Guhin, editors. *Young and Catholic in America*. Mahwah: Paulist, 2010.

Merleau-Ponty, Maurice. *The Visible and the Invisible: Followed by Working Notes*. Edited by Claude Lefort. Translated by Alphonso Lingis. Evanston: Northwestern University Press, 1968.

Mertens, Donna M. *Research and Evaluation in Education and Psychology*. 2nd ed. Thousand Oaks, CA: Sage, 2005.

Mette, Norbert. "Exclusion—A Practical Theological and Pastoral Challenge." Paper presented at International Academy of Practical Theology conference on Religion, Diversity, and Conflict, Chicago, 2009.

Metz, Johann Baptist. *The Emergent Church: The Future of Christianity in a Post-Bourgeois World*. Translated by Peter Mann. New York: Crossroad, 1981.

———. *Faith in History and Society: Toward a Practical Fundamental Theology*. Translated and edited by J. Matthew Ashley. New York: Crossroad, 2007.

Metzler, Norman. "The Trinity in Contemproary Theology: Questioning the Social Trinity." *Concordia Theological Quarterly* 67:3/4 (2003) 270–87.

Mich, Marvin L. Krier. *Catholic Social Teaching and Movements.* Mystic, CT: Twenty-Third Publications, 2000.

Migliore, Daniel L. *Faith Seeking Understanding: An Introduction to Christian Theology.* 2nd ed. Grand Rapids: Eerdmans, 2004.

Miles, Margaret R. "Sex and the City of God: Is Sex Forfeited or Fulfilled in Augustine's Resurrection of the Body?" *Journal of the American Academy of Religion* 73:2 (2005) 307–27.

Miller, Robert J. "Why Catholics Don't Attend Sunday Mass Catholic Research Forum." 1994.

Minear, Paul S. *Images of the Church in the New Testament.* Louisville: Westminster John Knox, 2004.

Moltmann, Jürgen. *The Spirit of Life: A Universal Affirmation.* Translated by Margaret Kohl. Minneapolis: Fortress, 1992.

Moore, Mary Elizabeth. "Dynamics of Religious Culture: Ethogenic Method." In *International Handbook of the Religious, Spiritual and Moral Dimensions in Education,* edited by Marian de Souza et al., 415–31. Dordrecht: Springer, 2006.

Morris, Pam, editor. *The Bakhtin Reader: Selected Writings of Bakhtin, Medvedev, and Voloshinov.* London: Arnold, 1994.

Morson, Gary Saul, and Caryl Emerson. *Mikhail Bakhtin: Creation of a Prosaics.* Stanford: Stanford University Press, 1990.

Mudge, Lewis S., and James N. Poling, editors. *Formation and Reflection: The Promise of Practical Theology.* Philadelphia: Fortress, 1987.

Muller, J. C. "Transversal Rationality as a Practical Way of Doing Interdisciplinary Work, with HIV and Aids as a Case Study." *Practical Theology in South Africa* 24:2 (2009) 199–228.

National Pastoral Life Center. "Called to Be Catholic." *Catholic Commmon Ground Initiative.* 1996. Online: http://www.catholiccommonground.org/called-be-catholic.

Newport, Frank. "Church Attendance Lowest in New England and Highest in the South." *Gallup.* April 2006. Online: http://www.gallup.com/poll/22579/Church-Attendance-Lowest-New-England-Highest-South.aspx.

———. "A Look at Religious Switching in America Today." *Gallup.* June 23, 2006. Online: http://www.gallup.com/poll/23467/Look-Religious-Switching-America-Today.aspx.

Ng, David. *People on the Way: Asian North Americans Discovering Christ, Culture, and Community.* Valley Forge, PA: Judson, 1995.

O'Brien, Maureen R. "Practical Theology and Postmodern Religious Education." *Religious Education* 94:3 (1999) 313–28.

———. "Reconciling Identity: Emerging Convictions in Religious Education and Practical Theology." *Religious Education* 104:3 (2009) 233–38.

O'Conner, Kathleen. "Let All Peoples Praise You: Biblical Studies and a Hermeneutics of Hunger." *The Catholic Biblical Quarterly* 72 (2010) 1–14.

Okure, Teresa. "The Church in the World: A Dialogue on Ecclesiology." In *Theology and Conversation: Towards a Relational Theology,* edited by Jacques Haers and Peter De Mey, 393–408. Leuven: Leuven University Press, 2003.

O'Meara, Thomas F. *Theology of Ministry.* Mahwah: Paulist, 1999.

Orevillo-Montenegro, Muriel. *The Jesus of Asian Women.* Maryknoll, NY: Orbis, 2006.

Orsy, Ladislas M. *Receiving the Council: Theological and Canonical Insights and Debates.* Collegeville, MN: Liturgical, 2009.

Osiek, Carolyn. *Philippians, Philemon.* Nashville: Abingdon, 2000.

Osiek, Carolyn, and Margaret Y. MacDonald with Janet H. Tulloch. *A Woman's Place: House Churches in Earliest Christianity.* Minneapolis: Fortress, 2006.

Osmer, Richard R. *Practical Theology: An Introduction.* Grand Rapids: Eerdmans, 2008.

———. *The Teaching Ministry of Congregations.* Louisville: Westminster John Knox, 2005.

———. "Toward a Transversal Model of Interdisciplinary Thinking in Practical Theology." In *The Evolution of Rationality: Interdisciplinary Lectures in Honor of J. Wentzel van Huyssteen,* edited by F. LeRon Shults, 327–45. Gran Rapids: Eerdmans, 2006.

Owens, Robert E. *Language Development: An Introduction.* Boston: Pearson/Allyn & Bacon, 2005.

Oxford University Press. *Oxford Dictionary Online.* 2010. http://oxforddictionaries.com/publicstart.

Oztop, Erhan, Mitsou Kawato, and Michael Arbib. "Mirror Neurons and Imitation: A Computationally Guided Review." *Neural Networks* 19 (2006) 254–71.

Patke, Rajeev S. "Benjamin and Bakhtin: The Possiblity of Conversation." *Journal of Narrative Theory* 33 (2003) 12–32.

Pechey, Graham. *Mikhail Bakhtin: The Word in the World.* New York: Routledge, 2007.

Peeren, Esther. *Intersubjectivities and Popular Culture: Bakhtin and Beyond.* Stanford: Stanford University Press, 2008.

Perlman, Janice E. *The Myth of Marginality: Urban Poverty and Politics in Rio de Janeiro.* Berkeley: University of California Press, 1976.

Perry, John. *The Problem of the Essential Indexical and Other Essays.* Oxford: Oxford University Press, 1993.

Peters, Karl E. "Neurotheology and Evolutionary Theology: Reflections on the Mystical Mind." *Zygon* 26:3 (2001) 493–500.

Pew Forum on Religion and Public Life. "Many Americans Mix Multiple Faiths: Eastern, New Age Beliefs Widespread." December 9, 2009. Online: http://pewforum.org/newassets/images/reports/multiplefaiths/multiplefaiths.pdf.

———. "How Religious Is Your State?" December 21, 2009. Online: http://pewforum.org/docs/?DocID=504.

———. "A Portrait of American Catholics on the Eve of Pope Benedict's Visit to the U.S." 2008. Online: http://pewforum.org/docs/?DocID=293.

———. "U.S. Religious Landscape Survey." March 2008. Online: http://religions.pewforum.org/.

Phan, Peter Cho. "Betwixt and Between: Doing Theology with Memory and Imagination." In *Journeys at the Margin: Toward an Autobiographical Theology in Asian-American Persepctive,* edited by Peter Cho Phan and Jung Young Lee, 113–34. Collegeville, MN: Liturgical, 1999.

———. "The Christ of Asia: An Essay of Jesus as the Oldest Son and Ancestor." *Studia Missionalia* 45 (1996) 25–55.

———. *Christianity with an Asian Face: Asian American Theology in the Making.* Maryknoll, NY: Orbis, 2003.

———. "Jesus the Christ with an Asian face." *Theological Studies* 57:3 (1996) 399–430.

————. "'Reception' or 'Subversion' of Vatican II by the Asian Churches? A New Way of Being Church in Asia." *Australian eJournal of Theology* 6 (2006). Online: http:// aejt.com.au/2006/vol_6,_no_1,_2006/.

————. "Religious Identity and Belonging amidst Diversity and Pluralism: Challenges and Opportunities for Church and Theology." In *Passing on the Faith: Transforming Traditions for the Next Generation of Jews, Christians, and Muslims*, edited by James L. Heft, 162–86. New York: Fordham University Press, 1996.

Phan, Peter Cho, and Jung Young Lee, editors. *Journeys at the Margin: Toward an Autobiographical Theology in American-Asian Perspective*. Collegeville, MN: Liturgical, 1999.

Phillips, Gary A. "'What Is Written? How Are You Reading?' Gospel, Intertextuality, and Doing Lukewise: Reading Luke 10:25–42 Otherwise." *Semeia* 69/70 (1995) 111–47.

Pinnock, Sarah K., editor. *The Theology of Dorothee Soelle*. Harrisburg, PA: Trinity, 2003.

Pontifical Biblical Commission. *The Interpretation of the Bible in Church*. Boston: Pauline Books and Media, 1993.

————. "Unity and Diversity in the Church." 1988. Online: http://www. catholicculture.org/culture/library/view.cfm?id=3737&CFID=38184398&CFTO KEN=71519668.

Pontificium Consilium ad Christianorum Unitatem Fovendam. "Directory for the Application of Principles and Norms on Ecumenism." *Letter to the bishops of the Catholic Church on Some Aspects of the Church Understood as Communion*. March 25, 1992. Online: http://www.vatican.va/roman_curia/pontifical_councils/ chrstuni/documents/rc_pc_chrstuni_doc_25031993_principles-and-norms-on- ecumenism_en.html.

Pui-lan, Kwok, editor. *Hope Abundant: Third World and Indigenous Women's Theology*. Maryknoll, NY: Orbis, 2010.

————. *Postcolonial Imagination and Feminist Theology*. Louisville: Westminster John Knox, 2005.

Purcell, Micahel. *Levinas and Theology*. Cambridge: Cambridge University Press, 2006.

Purves, Andrew. "The Communicative Practice of a Humble Church." *Inaugural Lecture for the Oxford Centre for Ecclesiology and Practical Theology*. Cuddesdon: Oxford Centre for Ecclessiology and Practical Theology, 2007. 1–14.

————. "The Trinitarian Basis for a Chrstian Practical Theology." *International Journal of Practical Theology* 3 (1998) 222–39.

Rathgeber, Benjamin, and Mathias Gutmann. "What Is Mirrored by Mirror Neurons?" *Poiesis and Praxis* 5 (2008) 233–47.

Rausch, Thomas P. *Being Catholic in a Culture of Choice*. Collegeville, MN: Liturgical, 2006.

Reid, Barbara E., OP. *Choosing the Better Part? Women in the Gospel of Luke*. Collegeville: Liturgical, 1996.

————. *Taking Up the Cross: New Testament Interpretations through Latina and Feminist Eyes*. Minneapolis: Fortress, 2007.

Reinharz, Shulamit, with Lynn Davidman. *Feminist Methods in Social Research*. New York: Oxford University Press, 1992.

Ress, Mary Judith. *Ecofeminism in Latin America*. Maryknoll, NY: Orbis, 2006.

Ribbens, Jane, and Rosalind Edwards, editors. *Feminist Dilemmas in Qualitative Research: Public Knowledge and Private Lives*. Thousand Oaks, CA: Sage, 1998.

Richard, Nelly. "Postmodern Disalignments and Realignments of the Center/Periphery." *Art Journal* 51 (1992) 57–59.

Rizzollatti, Giacomo, and Laila Craighero. "The Mirror Neuron System." *Annual Review of Neuroscience* 27 (2004) 169–92. Online: http://www.annualreviews.org/doi/abs/10.1146/annurev.neuro.27.070203.144230?journalCode=neuro.

Robinson, Geoffrey. *Confronting Power and Sex in the Catholic Church: Reclaiming the Spirit of Jesus.* Collegeville, MN: Liturgical, 2008.

Roebben, Bert, and Leo van der Tuin, editors. *Practical Theology and the Interpretation of Crossing Boundaries: Essays in Honor of Professor M. P. J. van Knippenberg.* London: Transaction Publishers, 2003.

Roetzel, Calvin J. *The Letters of Paul: Conversations in Context.* 4th ed. Louisville: Westminster John Knox, 1998.

Rohr, Richard. "Things Hidden: Scripture as Spirituality." Lecture given at St. Thomas University, Miami, FL, January 30, 2010.

———. *The Naked Now: Learning to See as the Mystics See.* New York: Crossroad, 2009.

———. *Things Hidden: Scripture as Spirituality.* Cincinatti: St. Anthony Messenger Press, 2008.

Rorty, Richard. *Philosophy and Social Hope.* London: Penguin, 1999.

Rosales, Gaudencio B., and C. G. Arevalo, editors. *For All the Peoples of Asia: Federation of Asian Bishops' Conferences.* Vol. 1, *Documents from 1970–1991.* Maryknoll, NY: Orbis, 1997.

Ruether, Rosemary Radford, editor. *Feminist Theologies: Legacy and Prospect.* Minneapolis: Fortress, 2007.

———. *Integrating Ecofeminism, Globalization, and World Religions.* Lanham, MD: Rowman & Littlefield, 2005.

———. *Sexism and God-Talk: Toward a Feminist Theology.* Boston: Beacon, 1983.

———. *Women-Church: Theology and Practice of Feminist Liturgical Communities.* San Francisco: Harper & Row, 1985. Reprint, Eugene, OR: Wipf & Stock, 2001.

Ruiz, Jean-Pierre. "Four Faces of Theology." In *Teaching the Bible: The Discourses and Politics of Biblical Pedagogy,* edited by Fernando F. Segovia and Mary Ann Tolbert, 86–101. Maryknoll, NY: Orbis, 1998.

Russell, Letty M. *Church in the Round: Feminist Interpretation of the Church.* Louisville: Westminster John Knox, 1993.

———. *Just Hospitality: God's Welcome in a World of Difference.* Edited by J. Shannon Clarkson and Kate M. Ott. Louisville: Westminster John Knox, 2009.

Sabin, Marie Noonan. *Reopening the Word: Reading Mark as Theology in the Context of Early Judaism.* New York: Oxford University Press, 2002.

Saldarini, Anthony J. *Matthew's Christian-Jewish Community.* Chicago: University of Chicago Press, 1994.

———. *Pharisees, Scribes, and Saducees in Palestinian Society: A Sociological Approach.* Wilmington, DE: M. Glazier, 1988.

Sarup, Madan. *Identity, Culture and the Postmodern World.* Edited by Tasneem Raja. Athens: University of Georgia Press, 1996.

Scharer, Mattias, and Bernd Jochen Hilberath. *The Practice of Communicative Theology: Introduction to a New Theological Culture.* New York: Crossroad, 2008.

Schillebeeckx, Edward. *Church: The Human Story of God.* New York: Crossroad, 1994.

———. *God Is New Each Moment.* Translated by David Smith. Edinburgh: T. & T. Clark, 1983.

Schneiders, Sandra Marie. *The Revelatory Text: Interpreting the New Testament as Sacred Scripture.* Collegeville, MN: Liturgical, 1999.

Schreiter, Robert J. *Constructing Local Theologies.* Maryknoll, NY: Orbis, 2007.

Schüssler Fiorenza, Elisabeth. *Bread Not Stone: The Challenge of Feminist Biblical Interpretation.* Boston: Beacon, 1986.

———. *But She Said: Feminist Practices of Biblical Interpretation.* Boston: Beacon, 1992.

———. *The Power of the Word: Scripture and the Rhetoric of Empire.* Minneapolis: Fortress, 2007.

———. *Rhetoric and Ethic: The Politics of Biblical Studies.* Minneapolis: Fortress, 1999.

———. *Sharing Her Word: Feminist Biblical Interpretation in Context.* Boston: Beacon, 1998.

———. *Wisdom Ways: Introducing Feminist Biblical Interpretation.* Maryknoll, NY: Orbis, 2001.

Schweitzer, Friedrich L. *The Postmodern Life Cycle: Challenges for Church and Theology.* St. Louis: Chalice, 2004.

Scott, Joan W., and Debra Keates, editor. *Going Public: Feminism and the Shifting Boundaries of the Private Sphere.* Urbana: University of Illinois Press, 2004.

Second Vatican Council. *Dogmatic Constitution on the Church (Lumen Gentium).* November 21, 1964. Online: http://www.ewtn.com/library/councils/v2church.htm.

Segovia, Fernando F., and Mary Ann Tolbert, editors. *Teaching the Bible: The Discourses and Politics of Biblical Pedagogy.* Maryknoll, NY: Orbis, 1998.

Seidel, J. "Method and Madness in the Application of Computer Technology to Qualitative Data Analysis." In *Using Computers in Qualitative Research*, edited by Nigel G. Fielding and Raymond. M. Lee, 107–16. London: Sage, 1991.

Seidman, Irving. *Interviewing as Qualitative Research: A Guide for Researchers in Education and the Social Sciences.* New York: Teachers College Press, 1998.

Senior, Donald. "Correlating Images of Church and Images of Mission in the New Testament." *Missiology* 23 (1995) 3–16.

———. *The Gospel of Matthew.* Nashville: Abingdon, 1997.

———. "Matthew's Gospel and the Jewish Context of Early Christianity." Lecture given at St. Thomas University, Miami, FL, October 16, 2009.

Shipps, Jan, and Mark Silk, editors. *Religion and Public life in the Mountain West: Sacred Landscapes in Transition.* Walnut Creek, CA: AltaMira, 2004.

Silk, Mark. "Defining Religious Pluralism in America: A Regional Analysis." *The Annals of the American Academy of Political and Social Science* 612 (2007) 62–81. Online: http://ann.sagepub.com/content/612/1/62.full.pdf+html.

Silk, Mark, and Andrew Walsh. *One Nation, Divisible: How Regional Religious Differences Shape American Politics.* Lanham, MD: Rowman & Littlefield, 2008.

Simcox, Kate D. "Performing Postmodern Christian: Communication in the Emerging Church and the Renegotiation of Divine Knowledge." PhD diss., Bowling Green State University, 2005.

Smith, Timothy L. *Thomas Aquinas' Trinitarian Theology: A Study in Theological Method.* Washington, DC: Catholic University of America Press, 2003.

Soelle, Dorothee. *The Silent Cry: Mysticism and Resistance.* Translated by Barbara and Martin Rumscheidt. Minneapolis: Fortress, 2001.

Song, Choan-Seng. *Tell Us Our Names: Story Theology from an Asian Perspective.* Maryknoll, NY: Orbis, 1984.

Soskice, Janet Martin, and Diana Lipton, editors. *Feminism and Theology.* New York: Oxford University Press, 2003.

Soulen, R. Kendall. "Who Shall I Say Sent Me? The Name of God in Trinitarian Perspective." *Journal of Scriptural Reasoning Forum.* June 2001. Online: http://etext.lib.virginia.edu/journals/jsrforum/writings/SouWhos.html.

Spezio, Michael. "Interiority and Purpose: Emerging Points of Contact for Theology and the Neurosciences." *Theology and Science* 7 (2009) 119–21.

Spong, John Shelby. "From the Tribal Deity to Universal Love." Sermon given at Coral Gables Congregational United Church of Christ for the Theologian in Residence series, Coral Gables, FL, January 24, 2010.

———. *A New Christianity for a New World: Why Traditional Faith Is Dying and How a New Faith Is Being Born.* San Francisco: HarperSanFrancisco, 2001.

Storrar, William F., and Andrew R. Morton, editors. *Public Theology for the Twenty-First Century: Essays in Honor of Duncan B. Forrester.* London: T. & T. Clark, 2004.

Sugirtharajah, R. S., ed. *Voices from the Margin: Interpreting the Bible in the Third World.* Maryknoll, NY: Orbis, 2006.

Sweeney, Jon M. *Almost Catholic: An Appreciation of the History, Practice, and Mystery of Ancient Faith.* San Francisco: Jossey-Bass, 2008.

Swimme, Brian, and Thomas Berry. *The Universe Story: From the Primordial Flaring Forth to the Ecozoic Era.* San Francisco: HarperSanFrancisco, 1992.

Swinton, John, and Harriet Mowat. *Practical Theology and Qualitative Research.* London: SCM, 2006.

Tanner, Katherine. "Trinity." In *The Blackwell Companion to Political Theology,* edited by Peter Scott and William T. Cavanaugh, 319–32. Malden, MA: Blackwell, 2004.

Tashakkori, Abbas, and Charles Teddlie. *Handbook of Mixed Methods in Social and Behavioral Research.* Thousand Oak, CA: Sage, 2003.

Taylor, Mark. "Tracking Spirit: Theology as Cultual Critique in America." In *Changing Conversations: Religious Reflection and Cultural Analysis,* edited by Dwight N. Hopkins and Sheila Greeve Davaney, 123–44. New York: Routledge, 1996.

The Holy Bible. New Revised Standard Edition. New York: American Bible Society, 1989.

Thiselton, Anthony C. *The Hermeneutics of Doctrine.* Grand Rapids: Eerdmans, 2007.

Tickle, Phyllis. *The Great Emergence: How Christianity Is Changing and Why.* Grand Rapids: Baker, 2008.

Tilley, Terrence W. *Inventing Catholic Tradition.* Maryknoll, NY: Orbis, 2000.

Tracy, David. *The Analogical Imagination: Christian Theology and the Culture of Pluralism.* New York: Crossroad, 1981.

———. "Approaching the Christian Understanding of God." In *Systematic Theology: Roman Catholic Perspectives,* edited by Francis Schüssler Fiorenza and John P. Galvin, 1:131–48. Minneapolis: Fortress, 1991.

———. *Blessed Rage for Order: The New Pluralism in Theology.* San Francisco: Harper & Row, 1988.

———. *Plurality and Ambiguity.* San Francisco: Harper & Row, 1987.

Tummolini, Luca, et al. "From Mirror Neurons to Joint Actions." *Cognitive Systems Research* 7 (2006) 101–12.

United States Census Bureau. *USA Quick Facts.* 2008. Online: http://quickfacts.census.gov/qfd/states/00000.html.

United States Conference of Catholic Bishops. *Asian and Pacific Presence: Harmony in Faith.* 2001. Online: http://www.usccb.org/issues-and-action/cultural-diversity/asian-pacific-islander/asian-and-pacific-presence-harmony-in-faith.cfm.

———. "The Catholic Church in America: Meeting Real Needs in Your Neighborhood." 2006. Online: http://www.nccbuscc.org/comm/cip.shtml#toc2.

———. *The Official Catholic Directory: Anno Domini 2006.* New Providence, NJ: P. J. Kenedy, 2006.

———. *Our Hearts Were Burning within Us: A Pastoral Plan for Adult Faith Formation in the United States.* Online: http://old.usccb.org/education/ourhearts.htm.

Vanhoozer, Kevin J. *Dictionary for Theological Interpretation of the Bible.* Grand Rapids: Baker, 2005.

Van Huyssteen, J. Wentzel. "Human Origins and Religious Awareness: In Search of Human Uniqueness." *Spiral: A Publication of the Metanexus Institute.* May 3, 2007. Online: http://www.metanexus.net/magazine/tabid/68/id/9929/Default.aspx.

Veling, Terry A. *Living In the Margins: Intentional Communities and the Art of Interpretation.* New York: Crossroad, 1996.

———. *Practical Theology: On Earth as It Is in Heaven.* Maryknoll, NY: Orbis, 2005.

Ven, J. A. van der. *Practical Theology: An Empirical Approach.* Leuven: Peeters, 1998.

———. *Ecclesiology in Context.* Grand Rapids: Eerdmans, 1996.

Viau, Marcel. *Practical Theology: A New Approach.* Translated by Robert Hurley and Chantal Tanguay. Leiden: Brill, 1999.

Voas, David, and Alasdair Crockett. "Religion in Britain: Neither Believing Nor Belonging." *Sociology* 39 (2005) 11–28.

Volf, Miroslav, and Dorothy C. Bass, editors. *Practicing Theology: Beliefs and Practices in Christian Life.* Grand Rapids: Eerdmans, 2001.

Walsh, Andrew, and Mark Silk, editors. *Religion and Public Life in New England: Steady Habits, Changing Slowly.* Walnut Creek, CA: AltaMira, 2004.

Weaver, Jay. "From I-Hermeneutics to We-Hermeneutics: Native Americans and the Post-Colonial." *Semeia* 75 (1996) 153–76.

West, Gerald O. *Biblical Hermeneutics of Liberation.* 2nd ed. Maryknoll, NY: Orbis, 1995.

Westhelle, Vítor. "The Church's Crucible: Koinonia and Cultural Transcendence." *Currents in Theology and Mission* 31:3 (2004) 211–18.

Whitehead, James D., and Evelyn Eaton Whitehead. *Method in Ministry: Theological Reflection and Christian Ministry.* Rev. ed. Kansas City: Sheed & Ward, 1995.

Willis, Robert J. "Crisis in American Catholicism." Online: http://rjjwillis.wordpress.com.catholocism-must-adapt/.

Willows, David, and John Swinton, editors. *Spiritual Dimensions of Pastoral Care.* London: J. Kingsley, 2000.

Wilson, Charles Reagan, and Mark Silk, editors. *Religion and Public Life in the South: In the Evangelical Mode.* Walnut Creek, CA: AltaMira, 2005.

Woodard, James, and Stephen Pattison, editors. *The Blackwell Reader in Pastoral and Practical Theology.* Malden, MA: Blackwell, 2000.

World Council of Churches. "Koinonia and Justice, Peace and the Integrity of Creation." *Ecumenical Chronicle* 45:2 (1993) 226–36.

Yong, Amos. *The Spirit Poured Out on All Flesh: Pentecostalism and the Possibility of Global Theology.* Grand Rapids: Baker Academic, 2005.

Bibliography

Zandra, Wagoner. "A Pragmatic Feminist Ethic of Conflict." *American Journal of Theology and Philosophy* 24 (2003) 64–82.

Zappen, James P. *The Rebirth of Dialogue: Bakhtin, Socrates, and the Rhetorical Tradition.* Albany: State University of New York Press, 2004.